Jewish-Christian Dialogue
Drawing Honey from the Rock

Jewish-Christian Dialogue
Drawing Honey from the Rock

Alan L. Berger & David Patterson

with David P. Gushee, John T. Pawlikowski, &
John K. Roth

PARAGON HOUSE
ST. PAUL, MINNESOTA

First Edition 2008

Published in the United States by
Paragon House
1925 Oakcrest Avenue
St. Paul, MN 55113

Library of Congress Cataloging-in-Publication Data

Berger, Alan L., 1939-
  Jewish-Christian dialogue : drawing honey from the rock / by Alan L.
Berger & David Patterson ; with David P. Gushee, John T. Pawlikowski, &
John
K. Roth.
      p. cm.
  Includes bibliographical references and index.
  Summary: "Constructively addresses the hard challenges of
Christian-Jewish
cooperation in a global post-Holocaust world"--Provided by publisher.
  ISBN 978-1-55778-856-6 (pbk. : alk. paper)
  1. Judaism--Relations--Christianity. 2. Christianity and other
religions--Judaism. 3. Holocaust (Jewish theology) 4. Holocaust (Christian
theology) I. Patterson, David, 1948- II. Gushee, David P., 1962- III.
Pawlikowski, John. IV. Roth, John K. V. Title.
  BM535.B465 2008
  296.3'96--dc22
                              2008013051

The paper used in this publication meets the minimum requirements of
American National Standard for Information Sciences—Permanence of
Paper for Printed Library Materials, ANSIZ39.48-1984.

Manufactured in the United States of America
10 9 8 7 6 5 4 3 2 1

For current information about all releases from Paragon House,
visit the web site at http://www.paragonhouse.com

To the memory of Alan's mother-in-law Rozalia Benau, Auschwitz survivor, with the hope that all who read this book will summon the courage to wrestle with the questions raised here, and to the memory of Bud Seretean, who was devoted to the meaning of *Am Yisrael Chai*.

ACKNOWLEDGMENTS

The authors are pleased to acknowledge Bornblum Judaic Studies of the University of Memphis and the Friends of the Raddock Family Eminent Scholar Chair in Holocaust Studies at Florida Atlantic University as well as the FAU Foundation for their support in providing the index for the volume. We are also grateful for the editorial wisdom of Ms. Rosemary Yokoi of Paragon House Publishers. In addition, a word of appreciation is owed to Bernard and May Smith for their careful reading of an earlier draft.

Contents

listening. That absence of dialogue culminated in the radically "imposed absence" called Auschwitz. Only in the aftermath of Auschwitz—and with the subsequent rebirth of the Jewish state—has there been any attempt at a genuine Jewish-Christian dialogue. Can this history be a Torah from which we extract any learning? Can the attempts at a Jewish-Christian dialogue add any depth to our prayers? Can it lead to an increase in deeds of loving-kindness in the world? The future of Jewish-Christian dialogue rests on how we respond to these questions. And the questions are more intractable than a rock. For in the post-Holocaust era, we seek to draw honey from something even more impenetrable than the rock of a barren wilderness. In the post-Holocaust era we are faced with drawing honey from the ashes of the Jewish dead.

And yet from those ashes there has emerged an ember of hope: For the first time in history, Jews and Christians are speaking to one another, with the aim not just of getting along but of actually understanding each other. This all-but-miraculous phenomenon has occurred in the aftermath of the murder of more than 6 million Jews in the heart of Christendom. The Shoah plunged both traditions into crisis. Locked into an intimacy that exists only between victim and perpetrator, Jews and Christians seek to retrieve the light of their traditions from the Kingdom of Night through a dialogue with one another. But that dialogue is itself in a state of crisis. Indeed, it is in danger of dying before it has truly begun.

The faltering attempts at this dialogue have understandably consisted of half measures and false starts. After all, a few years cannot shift the momentum of two millennia. If we add the post-Holocaust tensions within Christianity and Judaism to the historical hostility between Christians and Jews, we marvel at the little progress that has in fact been made. Indeed, it is unprecedented. Few can fathom, for example, the earthshaking ramifications of Pope John Paul II's visit to the Jewish state of Israel. Nevertheless, dialogue cannot live without movement, and the movement within the institutional level of Jewish-Christian dialogue has all but come to a standstill. And while there is far more activity on the academic and scholarly levels of the dialogue, we note sadly the failure of the scholars' efforts to

PREFACE

He led him to suck honey from the rock
And oil from the stone of flint.

—Deuteronomy 32:13

These lines from the Book of Deuteronomy refer to ways in which God sustained Israel as the Jewish people made their way through the wilderness and into the Holy Land in the time of Moses. The honey from the rock is a sustenance and a sweetness in a realm that seems to be devoid of sustenance and sweetness. In Jewish tradition honey is also associated with Torah, which is a divine teaching that enters into a realm where, it seems, there can be nothing divine. Thus, when a child reaches the age of five and officially begins his Torah study, in some Jewish circles it is a custom to hold a celebration. The little one is seated before a *Chumash*, the Five Books of Moses, with the volume opened to the Book of Leviticus. Why Leviticus? Because Leviticus deals with matters of purity, and a child's soul is pure. Next a drop of honey is ceremoniously placed upon the first word, *Vayikra*, "And He called out." The child puts his finger to the honey and then to his lips, so that he may associate his learning and the divine calling with sweetness. The true sweetness, however, comes from the intractable text—the honey comes from the rock—only with persistent study, prayer, and deeds of loving- kindness.

For nearly two thousand years Jews and Christians have wandered in a wilderness all but empty of any sustenance or sweetness. It has been a wilderness empty of dialogue empty of teaching and understanding, empty of learning an yield results in popular culture, as evidenced in the vast popularity of Mel Gibson's patently antisemitic film *The Passion of the Christ*. Because the dialogue may be foundering on the rock of historical baggage and theological miscommunication, this book is an attempt on the part of two Jewish scholars to draw some trace of honey from that rock. And that can be done only if we bring some life and depth to a genuine post-Holocaust dialogue between Christians and Jews.

In an effort to take the next step in the process, we have stated some of the fundamental issues at hand and have retraced some of the historical aspects of Jewish-Christian tensions, which, we believe, have not been thoroughly articulated. Because these issues are especially charged in their post-Holocaust contexts, we have kept those contexts before us throughout the volume. Indeed, those are the contexts that have both occasioned the budding dialogue between Christians and Jews and continue to threaten it. The stake in this endeavor far exceeds the theological inquiries and the philosophical ruminations of a few scholars: They affect not only the relation between the followers of Judaism and Christianity, but also the future of the two traditions. Our approach to responding to these questions, then, is both theoretical and applied. On the theoretical side, we examine historical, philosophical, and theological matters that may enhance or further endanger the Jewish-Christian dialogue. On the applied side, we present an example of dialogue in action, with Jewish scholars Alan Berger and David Patterson in dialogue with Christian scholars John Pawlikowski, John Roth, and David Gushee, to whom the authors are deeply grateful for their courage, their insight, and their devotion to humanity. It is with a great sense of respect, trust, and admiration for these Christian scholars that we bring to the table some very difficult questions for all of us.

Thus we set out to draw the honey of human relation from the rock of alienation. While Jews and Christians may not hold as much in common as is often assumed, there is, nevertheless, important common ground between the two and therefore some hope for a genuine dialogue to emerge. Both traditions, for example, embrace the view that divine revelation is at work in the unfolding of history. Both regard their traditions as an instance of sacred history, as the intersection of time and eternity. Both teach that salvation lies in human relation. Both count the Torah among their Scriptures, where it is written, "It is not good for the human being to be alone" (Genesis 2:18). Humans are created not as animals but as "speaking beings" (see, for example, Maimonides' *Moreh Nevuchim* 1:51), so we realize our humanity by *speaking* to one another—not just offering each other the candy-coated script of propriety, but putting to one another the questions that spur us on in our quest to attest to the inherent, absolute sanctity of every human being. That is where we Jews and Christians may oppose the hate-filled, Nazi-like genocidal worldviews that still waft over the globe in various forms.

Yes, this book is written from an admittedly Jewish perspective; although we do not presume to speak for all Jews in our "Jewish perspective," it is not an arbitrary perspective but one that is based on centuries of the texts and teachings, of the testimony and tradition, that have defined Jews and Judaism—and that have provoked Christians and Christianity—over the centuries. We would like to see a subsequent volume written by Christians offering a Christian perspective on similar issues surrounding Jewish-Christian dialogue in post-Holocaust contexts. Perhaps in the dialogical encounter that follows there may emerge a trace of the eternal in time, as we struggle to fetch from a very dark time the light of loving relation, if not the light of deeper understanding. There lies the honey that we would draw forth from the rock.

Alan L. Berger
David Patterson

Introduction

Jews and Christians are bound by an intimacy unprecedented in the history of religions; Jesus, Mary, Paul, and the first apostles were Jewish. Theologically, Christianity needs Judaism. But the relationship between the two religions is fundamentally asymmetrical, both demographically and theologically. There are approximately 1.2 billion Catholics/Christians worldwide. Jews, on the other hand, number some 14 million. John Roth succinctly states the theological imbalance: "Nothing in Jewish life logically or theologically entails Christian existence. Christian life, however, does depend essentially on Jewish life. Christianity makes no sense, it would not even exist, if the world contained no Jewish history."[1] Given this intimate connection, one might assume that dialogue between the two religions would come naturally. The opposite, however, is the case.

Authentic Jewish-Christian dialogue is a new historical phenomenon whose birth is directly related to the horror and shame of the Holocaust. Auschwitz marked a turning point. From the ashes of the death camps there emerged an ember of hope. The murder of 6 million Jews in the heart of Christian Europe precipitated a theological crisis for both traditions. For Jews, adherence to the Covenant provided no protection from gas chambers and crematoria; regardless of belief or disbelief in the Covenant, birth itself was a death sentence. Jews felt abandoned by God and humanity. The survivor Alexander Donat writes, "The very bases of our faith had crumbled: the

1

Polish fatherland whose children we had always considered ourselves; two thousand years of Christianity, silent in the face of Nazism; our own lie-ridden civilization. We were alone, stripped of all we had held sacred."[2] For Christians, devotion to Jesus as the Christ who taught an ethic of love failed to prevent them from becoming murderers, as planners, implementers, and passively as bystanders to the *Endlösung*, the "final solution" of the Jewish question. There were very few righteous who viewed themselves as their brother's keeper. Franklin H. Littell states that the Holocaust, "more than anything else that has happened since the fourth century,… has called into question the integrity of the Christian people and confronted them with an acute identity crisis."[3]

Following the Shoah, Christians and Jews seek to rescue the light of their traditions from the darkness of the Kingdom of Night through dialogue, fraternal study of the Bible, joint action for social justice, and mutual respect. But the dialogue itself is under assault from a variety of sources both within and outside the two great faiths. Cultural, historical, ritual, and theological issues are barriers to dialogue even as the two communities seek to explore more deeply what binds them together. However, the unarticulated question remains—in David Patterson's searing words—is Christianity a branch or a breach of Judaism? What can Christians and Jews learn from each other? How can dialogue be taken to a deeper level?

SOME FUNDAMENTAL ISSUES

Contemporary Jewish-Christian dialogue is occurring at a tumultuous historical moment. Six decades after Auschwitz, we live in an age marked by the ugly resurgence of anti-semitism in Europe and its reinforcement in Muslim lands. Moreover, religious fanaticism puts the lives of all people at risk: gas chambers and ovens *then*, suicide bombers and nuclear weapons *now*. Globally linked, we may also be globally doomed. Our anxiety is palpable. Crucial questions arise about the role of the "night side" of religion in aiding extremism, the increasingly polarizing culture wars, and the coarsening of language dealing with other human beings. Hovering

over the fractious contemporary landscape is the ominous shadow of the Shoah.

One aim of our study is to explore how much of the contemporary crisis that threatens Jewish-Christian dialogue stems from fundamental misunderstandings on the part of both Christians and Jews concerning the linguistic, historical, and theological issues that separate the two faith communities. It may well be that Christians and Jews are *divided by a common language*; the notion of the Messiah is a good example of how Christians and Jews employ the same term but understand it very differently. For many Christians the term refers to a *personal savior*, the Son of God who redeemed the world by his death and resurrection and whose return is awaited. For Jews the Messiah may be associated either with an anticipated *national savior* or with a *historical era*. Moreover, both traditions seek theological meaning in historical events, but their readings of this meaning dramatically differ. The Church Fathers interpreted the exile of the Jews from the Promised Land and the Roman destruction of the Jerusalem Temple as punishment for the crime of deicide. The rabbis, for their part, declared that *sinat hinam* (causeless hatred) was the reason for exile.

The Christian cross is perhaps an even better example of how the same word signifies two entirely different historical experiences and worldviews. For Christians the cross symbolizes the passion and resurrection of Jesus. Moreover, the Christ event is nothing less than incarnational. It is the symbol of hope and redemption, and the advent of the Christ signifies the incarnation of the divine. In the words of the groundbreaking 1965 document *Nostra Aetate,* note four, "the cross of Christ [is] the sign of God's universal love." But the cross in Jewish historical remembrance was frequently employed as a sword at the point of which Jews were humiliated, exiled, or murdered. It carried the connotation of Jews as a deicide people. The Crusades, for example (see below), were led by people carrying a cross. Elie Wiesel in *A Beggar in Jerusalem* portrays the tragedy of the cross in Jewish history. He imagines a dialogue between Shlomo, a madman, and Jesus (Yehoshua). "You think you are suffering for my sake and for my brothers', yet we are the ones who will be made to suffer for you, because of you," says Shlomo. He continues, "I painted a picture of the future which made him see the innumerable victims persecuted and crushed under the sign of his law."[4]

A second aim of this study resides in the current context of the predicament in Jewish-Christian dialogue. After Auschwitz, interfaith issues assumed a particular urgency. While the Holocaust was not monocausal—the ocean of hatred was fed by rivers of religious, antireligious, economic, demographic, bureaucratic, technological, and modernizing elements—Christianity was the necessary if not sufficient cause for National Socialism's program of annihilating the Jewish people. In Roth's words, "The Holocaust remains unthinkable apart from the anti-Jewish practices of the Christian traditions and 'church roads' that had gained so much authority and dominance in the world."[5] We note that this dominance is also present in the secular world. The British National Association of Teachers in Further and Higher Education has proposed an academic boycott of Israeli scholars and institutions. In the United States, Lawrence Sommers, former president of Harvard University, expressed considerable concern over the stench of antisemitism that emanated from the call for Harvard to divest its holdings in companies doing business with Israel. This is not to say that the state of Israel is beyond criticism. It is, however, the case that Israel, alone among the nations of the world—in a contemporary perversion of the Book of Numbers 23:9: "Lo, a people dwelling alone, and not reckoning itself among the nations"—is being singled out as the archvillain of history, held to standards to which its enemies are not accountable. The process of theological self-critique in certain Christian circles initiated by *Nostra Aetate*, and the adjustment in Jewish thinking about the possibility of authentic interfaith dialogue, has yielded both acceptance and resistance in the two faith communities.

In large measure the Shoah was the outcome of the very misconceptions that continue to plague Jewish-Christian dialogue. The extermination of the Jewish people was planned and implemented by those claiming to be Christian. The "logic of destruction" owed its ideological roots both to the history of Christianity's teaching of contempt and to the theological differences between Christianity and Judaism. While Christianity needed Judaism, this need was expressed in supersessionary terms. "Christian theology," write Susannah Heschel and Sander Gilman, "colonized Judaism theologically, appropriating its scriptures (now called the Old Testament) and drawing on its central religious ideas (a messiah, redemption, election, covenant) to explain and justify its own claims regarding Jesus as the Christ anticipated by the prophets."[6] Although recent scholarship suggests that the two communities did not separate until as late as the fifth century CE, the Heschel/Gilman observation stands largely intact, especially as it reflects the teachings of the Church Fathers and the subsequent rise of theological triumphalism inaugurated by the Constantinian Church. Paradoxically, Judaism was both necessary to and rejected by Christianity.

A third aim of our study is to explore the meaning of dialogue itself. Until the middle of the twentieth century there was little or no authentic theological discussion between Christians and Jews, if we mean by that term a reciprocal respect and a desire to learn from each other. Rather, there was disputation, the goal of which was to convert Jews while simultaneously revealing the fallacy of Jewish belief. Polemical in nature, such disputation was the practical outcome of theological absolutism, which characterized the history of the pre-Auschwitz Catholic Church. Built on the twin pillars of supersession and triumphalism, the Church believed it was in sole possession of the truth. Consequently, it sought first to convert then expel or burn at the stake those who refused to embrace this truth. The Holocaust revealed in a horrifying manner the outcome of absolutism, whether political or theological. One goal of the contemporary dialogue is to replace theological absolutism with a healthy theological self-critique.

What, then, constitutes authentic dialogue? Probably most would agree with Jacob Neusner's three criteria: "Each party proposes to take seriously the position of the other; each party concedes the integrity of the other; and each party accepts responsibility for the outcome of the discussion: that is, remains open to the possibility of conceding the legitimacy of the other's viewpoint."[7] We add another criterion: The expectations of the dialogue partners need greater articulation, especially concerning antisemitism and the state of Israel. Following the

Holocaust, in a world where antisemitism is still flourishing and the existence of the state of Israel is continually threatened, Jewish existence itself is a primary concern. The poisonous anti-semitic outbursts of Iranian president Mahmoud Ahmadinejad, who bellows his determination to wipe Israel off the map and sponsors a Holocaust denial conference, reinforce this concern. While the Vatican has *diplomatic* ties to Israel and views the Jewish state as a *political entity*, it is unclear as to whether the Church understands the intimate *existential* and *religious* association of Israel and Jewish identity.

The goal for Christian partners in the dialogue should be to interrogate their sacred texts and contextualize those passages that preach hatred of or demonize the Jews, such as the infamous blood curse of Matthew 27:24, which led to the deicide charge, as well as John 5:39–47 and 8:44–47, passages that liken Jews to the devil; then there is the anonymous letter to the Hebrews, which is defined by its theological supersession and triumphalism. Further, Christian dialogue partners can learn to abandon negative stereotypes while seeking to understand Judaism in its own terms. A primary lesson for Christians to learn is that the Jewish rejection of the messiahship of Jesus is an affirmation of Judaism. They can also affirm the dissonance between Christianity and antisemitism by renouncing supersessionism and rejecting efforts to missionize among the Jewish people.

The followers of Judaism, for their part, participate in the dialogue for two basic reasons. On the one hand, they can help their Christian partners better understand Judaism, its religion, history, customs, and rituals. Jews in the dialogue can also help sensitize their partners to the basic precariousness of Jewish existence in a world where antisemitism continues to be a threat both in religious and in secular realms. Second, Jews can learn much about Christianity by engaging in fraternal study of the Christian Scripture. It is a basic fact that there is an entrenched suspicion of Christian outreach in the Jewish community. This suspicion, justifiable in the face of two thousand years of the Christian "teaching of contempt" for Jews and Judaism, can be lessened by dialogue. Furthermore, Jews can learn a great deal about their *own* tradition. For example, the research of Jon D.

Levenson reveals the important role played by resurrection in early Judaism and how it can be seen as linking early Judaism and Christianity.[8] But this is a new historical experience between the two communities. Not every Christian is an enemy; some are good friends. If there had been more such friends during the Shoah, both Jews and Christians would have been better off. This is not to minimize the real differences between the two faiths. It is, however, true that genuine dialogue, as Neusner points out, is preferable to parallel monologues.

WHAT DIALOGUE CAN ACHIEVE

Dialogue holds great promise not only for interreligious understanding, but for global tranquility as well. Catholic theologian Hans Küng sagely observes that "there will be no peace among nations without peace among the religions but there will be no peace among the religions without dialogue between the religions, but there can be no dialogue between the religions without each religion engaging in a fundamental reexamination of its basic assumptions."[9] Küng's position establishes the goal, and the conditions, of an authentic dialogue. Attaining this goal, which requires theological self-critique, is both worthwhile and difficult. At the very least, Jewish-Christian dialogue has important things to say about the relationship between church and state, the role of religion in the public square, biblical studies, social justice issues, and the Middle East. Such dialogue, at its best, can help shed light on theological issues that for too long have been manipulated to wreak havoc on the other. It can contribute to the vital post-Auschwitz task of what the Jewish tradition terms *tikkun olam* (mending, repair, or restoration of the world), inasmuch as this is possible after Auschwitz.

To take an example of one form of Jewish-Christian dialogue, the dialogue between Catholics and Jews appears to have embarked on a new post-Auschwitz course. Fresh theological winds first seemed to blow in 1947 with Christian and Jewish meetings in Seelisberg, Switzerland (see chapter 2). In 1962, Pope John XXIII convened Vatican II, one of the most important religious events of the twentieth century, initiating as it did a process of sweeping reform in the Catholic Church. One major outcome of Vatican II was the declaration *Nostra Aetate (In Our Time)*, which set forth the Church's post-Holocaust position on ecumenism. Doubtless its most important statement from the point of view of Catholic-Jewish dialogue was note four on Judaism, which augured nothing less than a paradigm shift in the Church's theology of Judaism. However flawed (see chapter 5), *Nostra Aetate* opened the door for a fundamental rethinking of Catholic-Jewish relations.

A series of implementing documents issued by the Vatican further clarified the Church's post-Holocaust theology of the Jewish people. Moreover, the late twentieth century witnessed two remarkable interfaith documents. On the Catholic side, the Vatican document *We Remember: A Reflection on the Shoah* (1998) was a call to remembrance and an apology. Two years later, in response to an overall positive development in Catholic-Jewish relations, *Dabru Emet*, a Jewish declaration of interfaith principles, appeared. These statements (discussed in chapter 5) could not have come about prior to Auschwitz. On the other hand, and despite goodwill and hopeful intentions, these documents refrain from fully and honestly confronting fundamental issues such as the relationship between the Church's responsibility for hateful teachings about Judaism and their role in the Shoah, the meaning of repentance, the nature of the deity, and the two traditions' understanding of words such as *forgiveness*, *memory*, and *repentance*, all of which signify ongoing wounds.

BARRIERS TO DIALOGUE

To the extent that religious fundamentalism is increasing, the task of Catholic-Jewish dialogue is made both more necessary and more perilous. Dialogue is impossible with those who are convinced that God is on their side alone and that their adversaries are evil. Murdering in the name of God is characteristic of fanaticism and is by no means a new phenomenon. We of course think here of the Islamist terrorist attacks of September 11, 2001, and other acts of terrorism since that time. We also recall, however, the Crusades, which marked an ominous turning point in Catholic-Jewish relations. Crusaders marched under the sign of the Christian cross. Ostensibly seeking to defeat the Muslim "infidels" in Jerusalem, the Christian warriors murdered Jewish "infidels," slaughtering entire Jewish communities such as those at Mainz, Speyer, and Worms on the way to Jerusalem. The killing was done in the name of Christ.

We also are mindful of the *spiritual* destruction and triumphalism implied in the contemporary "great awakening" of American fundamentalist religious fervor. A defining element of this movement is the emergence of a new, antimodernist, de facto coalition between certain evangelical groups and conservative Catholics. Members of this coalition embrace theological absolutism and reject dialogue with those whom they brand either un- or anti-Christian. Rabbi A. James Rudin writes of American Christocrats who believe that divine law supersedes human law, including the American Constitution; only the Christocrats, Rudin observes, can "determine precisely what God desires for the United States."[10]

The wall of separation between church and state famously declared by Thomas Jefferson is facing the battering ram of conservative Christianity. Religion in this reading refers not to pluralism, but rather to an intolerant Christian orthodoxy. Kevin Phillips writes of an "evangelical, fundamentalist, and Pentecostal counterreformation" in response to "secular advocates" who, beginning in the 1960s, were "determined to push Christianity out of the public square."[11] The case of evangelizing cadets at the United States Air Force Academy at Colorado Springs illustrates this "counterreformation." Officials at the academy have condoned a policy that is religiously insensitive. Rudin reports that some of the Jewish cadets have been called "Christ killers."[12] Under pressure from James Dobson's conservative group, Focus on the Family, Congress has written a set of guidelines for the academy's handling of religious freedom that are, at best, ambiguous. As of this writing, we note that the situation remains volatile and that those who are not evangelicals or fundamentalist Catholics continue to be harassed. Both Rudin and Phillips point to an enormous obstacle to any attempt at meaningful dialogue: the rise of a fundamentalist Christianity that maintains biblical inerrancy and a fascination with the apocalypse.

Among mainstream Christian denominations, too, barriers to dialogue remain in place. Roth notes that the "post-Holocaust reform of the Christian tradition is far from finished and continues to be necessary."[13] While Christians do have "post-Holocaust theologies that denounce anti-Judaism and that identify antisemitism as a sin," Christians "must recognize that such outlooks are... new to our tradition."[14] Further, the sweeping reforms engendered by *Nostra Aetate* are for many a dim memory. There are powerful contemporary counter-trends at work, especially within the popular culture. We think of Mel Gibson's film *The Passion of the Christ,* whose theological worldview is both pre– and anti–Vatican II. As we shall see in what follows, the enthusiastic reception of this film reveals that the fault lines between Christianity and Judaism are deep and abiding. That reception, too, has its Holocaust contexts.

CHRISTIAN ANTISEMITISM AS A NECESSARY CONDITION FOR THE HOLOCAUST

One can understand the significance of the contemporary, post-Holocaust dialogue only by reference to the preceding two millennia of Christian Judeophobia. We do not intend to recapitulate the entire story here; there are excellent and extensive bibliographies on the topic, and we address it directly in chapter 4. It is, however, important to note the following: Although Christianity never officially called for the extermination of Jews, the Church Fathers—*saints* one and all—did not hesitate to heap scorn upon the Jewish people. John Chrysostom, 347–407 C.E., preaching in Antioch, describes the Jews as enemies of God, and uses the word *deicide.* Ambrose, 340–397 C.E., bishop of Milan, preached a sermon comparing the richness of the Church to the poverty of the synagogue. Further, it was no crime, according to Ambrose, to burn a synagogue. At its best the Christian position was one of ambiguity. Augustine, 354–430 C.E., bishop of Hippo, for instance, proclaimed Jews a witness people to the truth of the Hebrew Scriptures, which Christians read as the promise fulfilled with the coming of Jesus of Nazareth. Further, the Jews in exile bore witness to divine judgment against them as a deicide people.

Judeophobia became inextricably bound to civil law in the fourth century, when Constantine legalized Christianity and Theodosius made it the official religion of the Roman Empire. While it is true that anti-Judaism was present in the pre-Christian, Greco-Roman world, it is only with the advent of Christianity that, as Robert Wistrich notes, a wholly new theological and *metaphysical* dimension appeared in antisemitism.[15] Further, Wistrich emphasizes the fact that during the centuries following the Crusades, "new and even more irrational myths were added [to the negative stereotype of Jews as a 'nation of Christ-killers, and infidels in league with the Devil'], that of the Jew as a ritual murderer, desecrator of the Host wafer, an agent of Antichrist, usurer, sorcerer and vampire."[16]

Jules Isaac in *The Teaching of Contempt* underscores the fact that traditional Catholic triumphalism relied on a theology of supersession, which in turn rested on three demonstrably false pillars: the dispersion of the Jewish people was God's punishment for the crucifixion, the alleged degenerate state of Judaism at the time of Jesus, and the guilt of the Jewish people for the crime of deicide. Isaac's study did much to reveal the deep flaws in Catholic teaching about Jews and Judaism. The fact that antisemitism persisted, and found expression even after the erosion of Catholicism as a religious tradition, attests to the abiding power of Jew hatred.[17]

Littell notes that cultural antisemitism found expression in the "language and images and instincts" over centuries of "Christendom."[18] Defining itself against the "Jewish other," Christianity made anti-Judaism compatible with Christian faith and practice. The denigration of Jews and Judaism can be seen not only in the writings of theologians, but in the visual arts as well. One did not have to be literate to see, and comprehend the meaning of, classic medieval depictions of *Ecclesia* versus *Synagoga*. Although there are various versions of this struggle, constant themes include the synagogue blindfolded. Blind to the truth and defeated by the Church, the synagogue is cast to the ground. *Ecclesia* is, on the other hand, portrayed as triumphant, casting her eyes heavenward and clearly favored by God.

The identification of Jews with the devil, a leitmotif of the medieval period, drew both on Christian teachings such as the

Gospel of John and popular folkloristic beliefs. The best-known portrayal of this equation is represented in Michelangelo's magnificent *Moses* in the Church of San Pietro in Vincoli, Rome. Based on a faulty translation of the Hebrew word *keren* as "horns" rather than "rays" (of light) springing from the head of Moses, the great artist literally set in stone the "fact" that Jews are in league with the devil. Consequently, repetition of this equation occurred both in Church sermons and in the "public square." This is but one of many examples in Christendom of what the sociologist and survivor Nechama Tec, writing of her experience as a hidden child in Poland, terms "diffuse cultural antisemitism." To be sure, the image of the Jews was not based on portrayals of the devil; rather, what became the image of the devil—a creature with horns, a tail, and hoofed feet—was based on earlier artistic portrayals of the Jews.

Of course, cultural antisemitism has its political manifestations. Political antisemitism, writes Littell, is an "ideological weapon" employed by "modern despotisms and totalitarian movements and regimes."[19] In this regard there appears a straight line from antiquity—for example, Pharaoh and Haman, the villain of the Purim story who, although he may never have existed, advocated a genocide of the Jews—to the Church Fathers and Martin Luther, through Tsar Nicholas II, on to Hitler and Stalin, and most recently the aforementioned Iranian president. Each of these genocidal figures, whether actual or potential, stands as a warning; humanity faces a choice between dialogue and destruction. Totalitarian regimes cannot abide the presence of Jews who are the cipher for a counter-cultural movement against easy pieties and what Littell terms culture religion. Contemporary Jewish-Christian dialogue in America is shadowed both by theological and by cultural dimensions of antisemitism.

The Crisis in Jewish-Christian Relations Manifest in Popular Culture

The unhappy legacy of these phenomena came out in the controversy over Mel Gibson's film *The Passion of the Christ* and in Michael Radford's film version of Shakespeare's play *The*

Merchant of Venice. Each of these films—having great cultural impact, especially in Gibson's case—employs a fundamentally flawed and fatal Christian teaching about Jews and Judaism that has reverberated throughout the centuries. Gibson's film, the most widely viewed Passion play in history, revives the ancient canard of Jews as deicide people. We note the toxic nature of the Passion play historically. Hitler attended the infamous Oberammergau Passion play and praised it as a great tool for fighting the Jews. Gibson, a conservative Catholic, rejects the teachings of the second Vatican Council and believes that Pope Pius XII was the last legitimate occupant of the throne of Peter. Moreover, the filmmaker is contemptuous of scholarly biblical and historical research, not to mention his misrepresentation of the Gospel itself.[20] *The Passion of the Christ* is both a broadside against the reforms established by Vatican II and a key factor in the contemporary culture war. Roth puts the matter succinctly: "Gibson's film has much more in common with pre-Holocaust Christian animosity toward Jews than it does with post-Holocaust reconciliation between Christianity and Judaism."[21]

Gibson's film reopens old theological wounds in a spectacular, gruesome, and unrelenting manner. While we will not recapitulate the many critiques of the film, we do wish to point to three salient features: its embrace of antisemitism, its false claims to historical accuracy, and its focus on the medieval ideal of atonement theology. Further, reaction to *The Passion*, both at the popular level and in certain official quarters, is worrisome. Widespread enthusiasm for Gibson's film among evangelicals and conservative Catholics, who hailed it as a great teaching tool, raises grave concerns about the nature of post-Holocaust Christian pedagogy on Jews and Judaism.[22] No less a concern is the official response by the bishop's film office which, despite the film's violation of every one of the official guidelines contained in the 1988 document "Criteria for the Evaluation of Dramatization of the Passion," described the film as one of the best of the year and saw no antisemitic elements. In the light of John Pawlikowski's observation that "Gibson's reseeding of Christian consciousness with the traditional antisemitic imagery must be identified for what it is—a basic violation of post-Holocaust morality," we wonder why the bishops ignored their own guidelines.[23]

Gibson's film appears at a fraught moment in the post-Shoah dialogue. Rancor and controversy separate the two faith communities concerning a variety of issues: the convent and crosses at Auschwitz; the canonization of Edith Stein, a Jewish woman who became a Carmelite nun but who was murdered because of her Jewish birth; the dispute over access to the wartime record of Pope Pius XII; and the revelations about the murder of Jews by their Polish neighbors in Jedwabne during the Holocaust. Concerning the post-Holocaust context of the film and its significance for this book, we note that James Carroll contends that the film's aim is to "remove the Holocaust as a defining point of moral reference." Moreover, it is not only displacement of the Shoah as the central reference point of the failure of both Catholic Christianity and Western civilization that the film hopes to achieve. Carroll contends that the film's antisemitic message is, "You want to see what real suffering looks like, check out the flayed Christ. And, by the way, look who caused his misery."[24] Perpetuating antisemitic stereotypes, to which Gibson wrongly imputes divine sanction, imperils efforts at dialogical honesty.

Further, Gibson relies heavily upon an extrabiblical source: the "eyewitness" accounts of a German Augustinian nun, Anne Catherine Emmerich (1774–1824), who in the book *The Dolorous Passion of our Lord Jesus Christ*, published by Clemons Brentano nine years after her death, claims to have been present at Jesus' crucifixion. Emmerich's alleged account provides Gibson with his androgynous devil, the emphasis on Jesus' scourging, an indecisive Pontius Pilate, and the compulsion to blame Jews for deicide. The extent of his reliance on Emmerich prompted John Dominic Crossan to observe of the film credits: "If accuracy or even courtesy were followed, the opening credit should read 'A Mel Gibson Film,' followed by 'Based on the Book by Anne Catherine Emmerich.'"[25] We wonder why the Vatican insisted on sending mixed signals by beatifying Emmerich in October 2004.

Despite official statements that the case for her beatification rests on her virtues and not on what she has written, this act will likely be taken as signaling Vatican approval of Emmerich's views. While the Church is free to beatify anyone it chooses, beatification signals to most people that the person's life, thought, and deeds are exemplary. The Church is clearly sending a message to the faithful. At the very least, the timing reveals a lack of sensitivity to the real accomplishments of inter-faith dialogue over the past forty years. Given the combustible mix of culture, religion, and politics in the contemporary set-ting, this act is likely to increase the latent cloud of suspicion hanging over contemporary interfaith dialogue.

Gibson's film plays a significant role in the contemporary culture war. Widespread public acceptance of the film and its enthusiastic endorsement as an evangelistic tool by many clergy underscores what Mary C. Boys terms a perception of "a Christianity under siege from a 'godless' culture."[26] This is the context for Gibson's response to the report of an inter-faith scholars committee that received an advance copy of the film. The scholars, Catholic and Jewish, were appointed by Dr. Eugene Fisher, emeritus director of the secretariat for Catholic-Jewish Relations of the United States Conference of Catholic Bishops. Working independently, the scholars underscored the script's deficiencies, chief among them being: complete dis-regard for evidence of scientific historical scholarship on the Gospels, uncritical acceptance of Anne Catherine Emmerich's bogus version of the crucifixion, and linguistic issues—the Gospels are in Greek but the actors spoke Aramaic and Latin. All the scholars cited the film's inflammatory portrayal of Jews as bearing great potential for antisemitism. Although minor revisions were made in the final script, Gibson's production company Icon threatened to sue the committee members and sought to defame the scholars involved.

The Passion of the Christ relentlessly exposes the post-Holocaust discrepancies between Christians and Jews in how they view the world. Many in the Christian community would agree with the assessment of William Donahue, who, while lacking scholarly credentials, is president of the conservative Catholic League for Religious and Civil Rights. He described the film in an open letter to the Jewish community as "mag-nificent beyond words" and derided those who believe the dei-cide charge is "demented."[27] Most in the Jewish community, on the other hand, would agree with the observation of Richard L. Rubenstein, who "saw Jesus' sufferings, presented graphically on the screen, as foreshadowing all agonies my people had endured because of the deicide accusation and the 'inability' to share in the 'good news' of Christ's promise of salvation. Deicide," continues Rubenstein, "places *unbelieving* Jews squarely in the camp of Satan, as does Gibson's film."[28] Mary Boys correctly observes that responses to the Gibson film reveal an instance of Christians and Jews "talking past each other."[29]

The film raises significant moral and pedagogical questions about post-Holocaust Christianity. Pawlikowski underscores the fact that "Christians have a moral obligation in the post-Holocaust era to wipe out any remaining vestiges of this cancer [antisemitism] embedded in the institutional church"; he speaks of the need for "spiritual chemotherapy."[30] Gibson's film, however, is a carrier of traditional antisemitism, which "moves us in the other direction." "Clearly, institutional Christianity," notes Pawlikowski, "generally failed its membership in not making clear the return to classical Christian antisemitic themes in the film."[31] In other words, it is a relapse. In terms of education, we note with alarm that the DVD version of Gibson's film was released in September 2004; a study guide to the film, published by Zondervan, displays the same erroneous and antihistorical view of first-century religious life in ancient Israel. Utterly lacking any theological sophistication, the guide is manipulative, as it pushes readers into being on the side of the "good" Jesus as opposed to the "sinful" Jews.

We also recall that Gibson's arrest for drunken driving in the summer of 2006 revealed the filmmaker as harboring antisemitic attitudes. Stopped by a police officer for erratic driving, he launched into a tirade against [expletive deleted] Jews, adding that Jews are responsible for wars raging around the world. He ended his verbal screed by asking the arresting officer, "Are you a Jew?" There is a Hebrew saying, *nichnas yayin yatzah sod*, that translates as "in goes the wine, out comes the truth." At the very least we hope and pray that this incident will both highlight Gibson's antisemitism and reduce the religious and cultural impact of his film.

As Jews, we must refrain from commenting on what Christians should believe. Pawlikowski and other Christian scholars, however, note that Gibson's Jesus plays no salvific role. The central Christian message equating Jesus with love and compassion is nowhere to be found. Further, the film barely hints at the resurrection. Many Christian scholars wonder what kind of God would require such intense violence and suffering—of his own son or any of his other children—in order to send a message to humanity. Far from promoting a religious life lived with faith and compassion, Gibson's film stresses the importance of unbearable agony (atonement theology). Suffering rather than compassion defines his representation of Jesus. We wonder whether the director wished to oppose other artistic images of Jesus as homosexual *(Corpus Christi)*, Jesus as rock star *(Jesus Christ, Superstar)*, or Jesus as heterosexual *(The Last Temptation of Christ)*. We also believe that far more work needs to be done in order to sensitize the Christian dialogical partner to the core history, and continuing presence of, antisemitism in Christianity.

In this context we note the appearance of a far different passion play: *Sister Rose's Passion* (2005). It is the story of Sister Rose Thering, a Dominican nun who fifty years ago wrote her doctoral dissertation exposing the systemic presence of hateful language toward and widespread negative stereotyping of Jews, such as the blood libel and the deicide charge, in Catholic educational material. Sister Rose's work exercised a powerful and positive influence on Cardinal Bea, whose Secretariat for Christian Unity drafted *Nostra Aetate*. Rose Thering continued to work throughout her life (she died in May 2006 at age eighty-five) to educate congregations to embrace the Church's new theology of Judaism, and to fight antisemitism within the Church. Although the film by Oren Jacoby won in the 2005 Best Documentary Short category, it needs far greater attention and should be used extensively in educating for Catholic-Jewish dialogue.[32]

Michael Radford's *The Merchant of Venice*, on the other hand, perpetuates the image of the Jew as bloodthirsty usurer. Shylock is portrayed, true to the Bard's text, as being more interested in law than mercy. Nevertheless, James Shapiro argues, the "current wave of interest in Shylock could be a kind of reaction" to Gibson's film.[33] While this is a possibility, it strikes us that Alan Rosen is more on the mark in writing, "Shakespeare, following in the footsteps of Christian theology, aligns law with the hard-hearted Jew and mercy with the softhearted Christian."[34] Consequently, the play—and its cinematic representation—conflates the medieval British notion of the infamous blood libel accusation and the Pauline false dichotomy between the law (which allegedly kills) and the spirit (which allegedly gives life).

Shakespeare probably knew no Jews; very few lived in London at the time. Rather, as Shapiro notes, "ideas about the Jews that emerged in Shakespeare's lifetime continued to influence notions of Jewish identity"—indeed, the play "had come to embody English conceptions of Jewish racial and national difference."[35] Yet, next to the trial of Jesus, that of Shylock has had enormous influence in Western culture. The play emphasizes three major themes in Christian antisemitism. First, there is the image of the Jew as usurer, greedily preying on the misfortune of others and as religiously unassimilable "other." Second, there is the matter of Shylock's infamous demand for the "pound of flesh." This representation of Jews not only violates *halakhah* (Jewish law), but it feeds into the subterranean yet explosive Christian libel that Jews murder Christian children in order to use their blood for ritual purposes. It is no accident that the first such accusation occurred in Norwich (in 1144). Finally, the conversion of the Jews, a fervent hope among English Protestant millenarians, while tinged with ambiguity, was an important dimension of the public perception of the play.

We believe that the Jewish-Christian dialogue requires both a short- and long-term assessment. Somewhat ironically, we think that the short-term prospects may be brighter. The uproar caused by the Gibson film, among other phenomena, will be a stimulus for more intense discussion on a variety of topics, some of which we have enumerated; many people, for example, are reflecting on the role of religion in their own life and rereading or, in some cases, reading for the first time sacred texts. Further, ecumenical study groups have formed to discuss issues such as Gospel accounts versus history, the socioreligious world of ancient Israel, and relations between Judaism and the nascent Christian community in the first two centuries of the Common Era.

Long term, however, the dialogical prospects appear less optimistic. Rabbi Ricardo DiSegni, chief rabbi of Rome, comments that the enthusiasm with which Gibson's film was greeted leaves a sad impression in the Jewish world that "when confronted with strong mystical experiences and huge interests of a pastoral nature, but also other types, the problem of the correct relationship with the Jews seems to be the last thing to worry the church, which then thinks that a generic reference to the official documents (contradicted by the facts) is sufficient to patch up the damage."[36] We wonder whether the Gibson film will, after the publicity following his antisemitic outburst noted above dies down, become a new "gospel" for the upcoming generation, energizing those who feel put upon by "godless secularists" to fight back. Moreover, the weak and contradictory response of Catholic officialdom is a worrying sign; might it signify that this dialogue is not on the theological front burner? Or that Catholics and Jews are "talking past each other"?

But these works have implications that point beyond themselves. The implications not only expose the fault lines between Christianity and Judaism broadly conceived; they reveal the intramural differences between liberals and conservatives among Christians and Jews. Liberals in each tradition have more in common with each other than they do with conservatives in their own faith. The vastly different reactions of Christians and Jews to Gibson's film, as well as the cultural acceptance of Shylock's character as viewed through Shakespeare's borrowing from Christian theology, underscore the misconceptions about how the two faith communities think about the relationships between God and humanity, between human and human, and between Christians and Jews.

Furthermore, the two traditions live in a global village, the majority of whose inhabitants are neither Christian nor Jewish. What is the universal relevance of interfaith dialogue? Can this dialogue serve in a paradigmatic way to inspire a search for and commitment to morality, peace, justice, and tranquility? Can it do so while simultaneously affirming distinctive theological differences on issues such as covenant, the integrity of the other, the nature of the deity, and the role of various religions in God's plan for salvation? The answers to these queries will measure the success of the dialogue. If the dialogue succeeds, it will—in the sense of Hans Küng's description—have gone a considerable distance toward achieving a *tikkun* of the world to the extent that this is possible after the rupture caused by the Holocaust. Consequently, Jewish-Christian dialogue has universal potential. In a time of great cultural, political, and religious upheaval and the ascendancy of an intolerant orthodoxy, dialogue models the possibility of constructively engaging the other.

We seek to pursue this task by articulating the unarticulated dilemmas and by pursuing the historical and theological issues separating Christians and Jews. Our premise is twofold: Christians and Jews should not fear the differences between them, and dialogue requires difference. Rabbi Jonathan Sacks observes that if faith is what makes us human, then those who do not share my faith are less than fully human. From this absolutist position, great human catastrophe—typically perpetrated in the name of God—"flowed the Crusades, the Inquisitions, the Jihads, the pogroms, the blood of human sacrifice through the ages. From it—substituting race for faith—ultimately came the Holocaust."[37] Like Noah, we have survived the Flood. Unlike our biblical predecessor, however, the Rainbow still eludes us.

Post-Holocaust Contexts

When we speak of post-Holocaust contexts for the next step in Jewish-Christian dialogue, two main points must be kept in mind. First, as already stated, the extermination of the Jewish people was, in part, the outcome of centuries of Christian anti-semitism. Occurring as it did in the heart of Christendom, the Holocaust was generally perpetrated by baptized Christians. While it is true that the tenets of Nazi ideology were contrary to Christian teaching, the Nazis' contempt for the Jews was largely in agreement with Christian teaching. Nor were there any Christian excommunications of Nazi murderers. Had the majority of Christians and Christian institutions voiced an objection to the slaughter of the Jews, then Christians could claim that the Holocaust was un-Christian. The majority of Christians and Christian institutions, however, either actively participated in the mass murder of European Jewry or silently stood by as it took place. They did so not from a lack of conviction but precisely *from* the conviction that the New Covenant had long since superseded the Old. Therefore the Jews were either damned or superfluous or both.[38]

From a perennial Christian standpoint, the Jews are at best a stiff-necked people who reject the evidence of redemption attained in the Christ; at worst they are satanically evil, since only one who is evil would say no to self-evident salvation. Hence the medieval myth that Jews are the minions of the devil. In the time of the Holocaust, with the ruthless Nazis all around, the Jews simply were not worth the risks involved in making rescue attempts. Some may object that an effort on the part of Christian individuals to save the Jews would have been useless, given the overwhelming power of the Third Reich. The example of the righteous among the nations, those Christians who did save Jewish lives, is the best response to that objection. Others have claimed that if Christian institutions had taken a stand, the Nazi wrath heaped upon the Jews would have been even worse. Already stretched by hard facts, however, the imagination is hard pressed to envision how it could have been worse. More than that, like any religious tradition, Christianity is defined by testimony, not by utility. And the Christian testimony on behalf of Jewish life—indeed, on behalf of the few Christians who had the courage to risk their lives for the Jews—was all too scant.

The second point that must be kept in mind when dealing with the post-Holocaust contexts for Jewish-Christian dialogue is the *post-* in post-Holocaust. Because we live in the shadows of Auschwitz, cultural and political forces at work in the world have unprecedented implications for how we understand the Jewish presence in the world. As in the time of the Third Reich, in the postmodern world, antisemitism has become respectable. European academics openly and without embarrassment call for the boycott of Israeli scholars and universities. Thus in 2002, Miriam Shlesinger of Bar Ilan University and Gideon Toury of Tel-Aviv University were dismissed from the editorial board of the British journal *The Translator* solely because they were from Israel. Intellectuals in American universities, from Columbia to San Jose State, either stand by in their postmodern muteness as Jewish people are attacked, or they assail the Jewish state—the Jewish *haven*—under the ruse of academic freedom. Institutions of "higher learning" host conferences for overtly Jew-hating organizations, such as the ones held by the Palestine Solidarity Movement at Berkeley, Ohio State, Michigan, Rutgers, and Duke. As for the intellectual distinction between anti-Zionism and antisemitism, in *post*-Holocaust contexts it is sheer sophistry. One does not critique the Jewish state by beating up Chasidim in Brussels or by burning Jewish libraries in Saskatchewan.

Most of us who pursue a Jewish-Christian dialogue come from this academic world. And when we see antisemitism running rampant in that world, we must remember that the Holocaust was conceived and perpetrated not by lunatics and brutes, but by doctors and lawyers, philosophers and scientists, theologians and engineers—in short, by the most highly educated people on the planet. Eight of the fourteen men who met at the Wannsee Conference on January 20, 1942, to discuss the logistics of the final solution had doctorate degrees, as did three of the four commanders of the *Einsatzgruppen*, the killing units that followed the *Wehrmacht* eastward. These points cannot be forgotten in the scholars' pursuit of a Jewish-Christian dialogue in post-Holocaust contexts; that endeavor requires an awareness of an ongoing Jew hatred as well as a contempt for Christianity among certain left-wing, postmodern intellectuals. After all, the father of postmodernism, Martin Heidegger, was an unrepentant, card-carrying Nazi.

In the post-Holocaust era very few academics have questioned the intellectual traditions that contributed to the event; most would be shocked at the suggestion that the giants of German philosophy, art, and literature could in any way be linked to the likes of Hitler, Heydrich, and Himmler. Therefore we speak of the *scandal* of Heidegger, and not just of the logical consistency in Heidegger's being a Nazi, an allegiance that the philosopher himself saw as an expression of his philosophy.[39] Much more effort to mend the world after Auschwitz has come from those who have recognized the antisemitism in their religious traditions. And so we find a number of Christians who have had the integrity to rethink certain aspects of Christian tradition in the post-Holocaust era.

We have already noted Pope John XXIII and the Second Vatican Council. Catholic scholars who have been among the courageous voices in their tradition are Harry James Cargas, who referred to himself not as a Roman Catholic but as a post-Auschwitz Catholic, Johann-Baptist Metz, and John Pawlikowski. More recently young Catholic theologians such as Didier Pollefeyt and Jürgen Manemann (a student of Metz's) have adopted the radical position that for the Jews, the Covenant of Torah is sufficient for redemption and that Jesus is necessary for the salvation only of the Gentile nations. Among the Protestants, in *Long Night's Journey into Day* Alice L. and A. Roy Eckardt argued that the redemption attained through resurrection was suspended at Auschwitz. Franklin Littell maintains that, in Christian terms, antisemitism must now be regarded not merely as the sin of racism, bigotry, prejudice, and the like. No, says Littell, antisemitism is blasphemy, the "sin against the Holy Spirit,"[40] which, according to the Gospel, *cannot be forgiven* (Matthew 12:31). John Roth and David Gushee have been equally admirable in their fearless reexamination of ancient teachings in the light of modern history. These thinkers have recognized that antisemitism lies not in a "fear of the other" or some other form of xenophobia; it is not a case of seeking out scapegoats or of racism run amok. Rather, it has metaphysical dimensions with very real, very physical consequences. It is *blasphemy*.

The post-Holocaust awakening shared by these courageous Christians is this: While Judaism endures without—*and in spite of*—Christianity, Christianity cannot endure without Judaism. They realize, in other words, that if Judaism is undone with the advent of Christianity, then Christianity is done for. If allowed to continue, the charge of deicide, the teaching of contempt, the myth of supersession, and other elements of Christian antisemitism threaten *Christianity itself* with extinction. In the post-Holocaust period, then, one difficulty that arises for Christians is this: If God died at Auschwitz, as some maintain, it was not the God of Abraham, but rather the God of Paul and the apostles. While Jewish teaching did not prevent the Jews from being murdered, Christian teaching did not prevent the Christians from becoming murderers. And that is a far more serious issue. It poses for Christianity a problem of credibility, and credence is the cornerstone of Christianity.

Here one wonders whether there might be something to an ancient Jewish teaching concerning the Messiah. According to the teaching, Moshiach ben Yosef—Messiah, Son of Joseph—will be murdered by the Edomites, whom the Jews identify with the Romans; for that crime a curse will fall upon the souls of his murderers. Ever since the establishment of the Church in Rome, Edom has signified Christendom. If Christianity became the official religion of Rome; if antisemitism is a defining feature of Christianity; if it was a necessary precondition for the annihilation of the Jews, the Chosen of God; and if it is the sin against the Holy Spirit, as Littell maintains—then the question facing the Christians is this: Could the curse upon Edom be Christianity itself? If Christianity defines itself as the New Covenant that overtakes the old—if Christians see themselves as a people newly chosen under a new dispensation—then Christianity *has* to be anti-Judaic: Might that antisemitism be the curse upon Christendom for the murder of Messiah, Son of Joseph?

The rise of antisemitism in popular, intellectual, and religious cultures throughout the world exacerbates the question. Why? Because while some Christians have faced the grim necessity of bravely confronting Christian theology in the post-Holocaust world, most proceed as if the Holocaust had never happened. Millions of Christians are blind to the rising tide of violence aimed at the Jews and deaf to the antisemitic diatribes that resound throughout the Muslim world. Nor do most Christians find any particular difficulty with the Holocaust. It was a horror, yes; it was an atrocity on a massive scale, yes. But it had nothing to do with "true Christianity." And so Christian congregations sleepwalk through history right into the movie theaters to be deeply moved by a truly powerful film such as *The Passion of the Christ*. They think the issue between Muslims and Jews in the Middle East is merely a political matter about sharing land; or they suppose it is just an ethnic or cultural or religious conflict that goes back for centuries; or they believe we are in the "last days," when the Jews will be returned to the land and either embrace Jesus or be damned. In any case, sixty years of post-Holocaust Christians' rethinking of their tradition have not undone nearly two thousand years of Christian teaching—which is not surprising. As in any tradition, along with their teaching, the Christians have inherited the categories of thought that belong to the tradition. And those categories have had definitive ties to antisemitism.

Prior to the Holocaust one might have been able to read the Christian claim that Judaism is at an end without necessarily reading into it the injunction to get rid of the Jews. Prior to the Holocaust the sincere Gibsonian assertion "I love the Jews" might have been construed to mean "I would love to save the Jews by converting them to Christianity" without the implication of complicity in the Nazi project of rendering the world *Judenrein*, that is, cleansed of the Jews. But no more. The Nazis had no intention of taking similar actions against other peoples; they had no concept of *Slavenrein*, *Zigeunenrein*, *Kommunistenrein*, *Homosexuellenrein*, or any other sort of *–rein*. It was the Jew alone who *contaminated* the earth; it was the Jew alone who had to be exterminated at all costs. In view of this single word, *Judenrein*—a Nazi word that has transformed history—any Christian project for the conversion of the Jews, even in the "last days," bears exterminationist implications. Therefore the Christian proselytizing of the Jews can no longer be viewed in benign terms: Any Christian who believes the world would be a better place if the Jews were to convert to Christianity plays into the hands of the murderers of the Jews.

As time puts Auschwitz at a greater distance from us, it seems that more and more, when Christians speak and when they do not speak, Jews encounter traces of a centuries-old, anti-Judaic outlook that remains deeply ingrained in much of Christian consciousness. Christians may insist that they "had nothing to do with it," yet the Nazis were able to promote their agenda by quoting Christian sages, from Saint John Chrysostom to Martin Luther, without any editing. Here we have another major difference between Christianity and Judaism with regard to the problems they confront in the post-Holocaust era. While thinkers such as Emil Fackenheim urge Jews to seek a *tikkun*, or a mending, of tradition by returning to it[41]—that is, by returning to the teachings of their Scriptures and their sages—the Christians are faced not with mending but with abandoning many of the teachings of their sages and saints in order to save Christianity itself. And the craze over productions like Gibson's film demonstrates just how difficult that is.

There are other symptoms of a serious disconnect that come from Christian institutions and scholarly organizations, and not just from filmmakers and popular culture. The Russian Orthodox Church continues to print *The Protocols of the Elders of Zion*, the Church's antisemitic forgery that dates from the time of Nicholas II and claims to expose the plot of international Jewry to take over the world; in 1997 the Russian Church asked for an investigation to determine whether the tsar's family was in fact the victim of a worldwide Jewish conspiracy. In the world of academia, in 2002 a scholar submitted a proposal to present a paper at the Conference on the Future of Christianity in the West, held at the University of Otago, New Zealand, in December 2002. The paper's thesis was that, if Christianity is to have a future in the West, then it must develop a much deeper connection to Judaism; without Judaism, the paper maintained, Christianity had no future. Indeed, European Christendom had annihilated its Jews only to witness its own collapse. Rather than open the floor to such an argument, however, the conference organizers rejected the proposal for the reason that the thesis was absurd. It is the Jews who need the Christians, the evaluators insisted, not the Christians who need the Jews, for without the Christians there would be no Jewish state and no protection from a world hostile to the Jews.

While the modern intellectual tradition has been hostile toward Jews and Judaism, as indicated earlier, the antisemitism that grew with the growth of Christianity has found new hybrids in the post-Holocaust world. If post-Holocaust Christianity is to free itself from its traditional antisemitic outlook, then its followers must at least object to Jew hatred wherever it occurs. The post-Holocaust period has seen an increasing hostility toward the Jews, not only among the intelligentsia, but more violently and more brutally in the Muslim world. And Christian leaders have been involved in some of the Muslim assaults on the Jews, both by their words and by their silence.

They were involved, for example, in the incident that took place at the Church of the Nativity in Bethlehem in April–May 2002. Never was there a more dramatic opportunity for Christendom to show the world a face cleansed of Jew hatred than when Palestinian terrorists occupied the church built on the reputed site of the Savior's birth. The church was first exploited and then desecrated by the terrorists hiding behind its sanctity. From the squalid condition in which the gunmen left the church—with broken relics, desecrated shrines, and feces all over the floor—it was altogether evident that they had no respect for the holiness of the Christian site. But they knew that the Israelis would respect that holiness; in fact, they were counting on it. And, sure enough, the Israelis made every effort to protect the site, when they could have easily taken the church and the murderers hiding inside. When the standoff came to an end, what was the Catholic comment? Accusations leveled at the Jews by Michel Sabbah, the Latin patriarch in Jerusalem. Not a word about the murderers who intentionally vandalized the church. No, the Jews were the evil ones.[42]

Sabbah's invectives paralleled the Vatican's silence over another incident, one that happened a year earlier. When the pope was in Syria on May 5, 2001, Bashar al-Assad greeted him by declaring that the Jews are out to kill the principles of religion "with the same mentality with which they betrayed Jesus Christ." This statement to the pope came just weeks after Assad proclaimed the Israelis to be more racist than the Nazis. On both occasions the pope said nothing.[43] Nor is Assad the only Muslim to incite Christian hatred toward the Jews by invoking the deicide charge; Bassam Abu Sharif, former adviser to Yasser Arafat, often used the same ploy, even though the Koran denies that the crucifixion ever took place (see *Sura* 4:157). To be sure, with their hatred of the Jews stronger than their belief in the Koran, many Muslims were quick to exploit *The Passion of the Christ* by using it to fuel an openly exterminationist discourse vis-à-vis the Jews.

The Jew hatred that stokes religious fervor also shows itself among Muslims in the academic world. Scholars such as the Saudi intellectuals Dr. Umymah Ahmed al-Jalahima and Dr. Muhammad bin Saad al-Shweyir frequently proclaim the truth of the blood libel, which they learned from the Christians, with the variation that the Jews make not just the Passover matzah but also Purim pastries from the blood of children.[44] And *The Protocols of the Elders of Zion* is gospel truth, as it were, in the Muslim world. Article 32 of the Covenant of Hamas invokes *The Protocols* as "the best proof" of their cause. A television drama based on the *Protocols* titled *A Rider without a Horse* is routinely aired throughout the Arab lands during Ramadan, and selections from the antisemitic forgery appear in the *al-Shuhada* guidebook published by the Political Indoctrination Apparatus of the Palestinian Border Guard. The Muslim nations, in fact, are the world's leading publishers and distributors of *The Protocols*, just as they lead the world in the publication and distribution of Hitler's *Mein Kampf*. If the Christians were interested in a dialogue with the Jews, then their leaders and their institutions would respond to such horrors. And surely in the post-Holocaust period, the Christians would resoundingly respond to the Holocaust denial that runs throughout the Muslim world.

Indeed, the prevailing view among the Arab Muslims, including their intellectuals and political leaders, is that the Holocaust is nothing but a hoax perpetrated by the Jews to solicit sympathy for the Jewish state, as witnessed by Ahmadinejad's latest Holocaust denial fiasco in December 2006. Long before the Ahmadinejad debacle, on July 14, 1998, Egyptian politician Hasan Rajab published an article in the daily *Al-Akhbar*, in which he maintained that the Holocaust is yet another Jewish lie. On May 13, 2001, the Union of Jordanian Writers met in Amman for a conference on the theme that "the Holocaust never happened." Among the scholars who routinely deny that the Shoah ever happened and yet glorify Hitler's feats of murder is Dr. Issam Sisalem of the Islamic University in Gaza. His colleague, the Palestinian leader Dr. Mahmoud Abbas (Abu Mazen), upon whom the world was quick to pin its hopes for peace between Israel and the Palestinians, defended the Holocaust denial thesis in his doctoral dissertation. Other notable Holocaust deniers include Dr. Rifat Sayyed Ahmad of the Jaffa Research Center in Cairo, Syrian columnist Mohammad Daoud, and Palestinian sheikh Ibrahim Mahdi, the mufti of Jerusalem. One is not surprised, then, to find that in 2005 very few Muslim nations joined more than one hundred other members of the United Nations to support the observance of the sixtieth anniversary of the end of Auschwitz. And so the Jews begin to wonder: Will the Christians continue to stand silently by, knowing what they know now, and simply wait to see where this rising Jew hatred will lead?

Chief among the post-Holocaust contexts for the pursuit of the next step in the Jewish-Christian dialogue, then, is a resurgence of the same hatred of the Jews that led to the murder of millions then and that threatens the lives of millions now. Will there be enough Christians to mitigate that threat? When, where, and how firmly will the Christians stand with the Jews now? What will they be willing to risk by speaking out on behalf of the Jews, making themselves vulnerable not only to Muslim but also to Christian outrage? And what price will they pay if they remain silent—again?

Areas Addressed in This Volume

In order to demonstrate that there are serious difficulties in Jewish-Christian dialogue, chapter 2, "The Symptoms of a Malady," begins by outlining a brief history of the post-Holocaust Jewish-Christian dialogue, with all its wonders and all its pitfalls. Given our history, there is, to be sure, something that approaches the miraculous in the sheer phenomenon of Jews and Christians speaking to one another, even if that interchange is problematic (how could it be otherwise?). But a next step in the dialogue cannot be taken without an awareness of its history and of its problems. Those problems stem, in part, not only from the history of Jewish-Christian encounter but also from the theological difficulties that each tradition faces in the aftermath of Auschwitz. Chapter 2, then, addresses the Holocaust's threat to each tradition, so that both parties might have a clearer vision of how the Holocaust troubles each of them. Upon considering the threat to each tradition, one realizes that the two traditions may be more different than alike and that what we take for a dialogical relation between even well-meaning parties might be an illusion.

Because both traditions are rooted in their own views of history, chapter 3, "Historical Considerations from a Jewish Perspective," delves into matters of history relevant to the theologies under consideration. Its primary aim is to determine how and why the two traditions became two separate and distinct traditions. First, we present a portrait of the Jewish Jesus, so that this crucial figure might be better understood both from Jewish and Christian perspectives. Because Jesus had to be torn from Judaism in order to determine a new and distinct religion, chapter 3 goes on to explore the tension between history and parable, particularly with regard to the extrahistorical aims of the Gospels and the Pauline texts. Like most scriptural texts of most religious traditions, the purpose of the Gospels and the rest of the Christian canon is not so much to present a historical account of events as to establish the truth of a certain theological claim. The aim, in other words, is to convince the reader to adopt a certain *belief* with regard to his or her salvation. How and why that belief proceeds from an anti-Judaic to an antisemitic position, as well as the differences between the two, is explained in the final portion of chapter 3.

Having made this transition from history to theology, chapter 4, "Theological Issues," begins by examining the fundamental differences between traditional Christian and traditional Jewish thinking about God, humanity, the world, and Messiah. Here we demonstrate that Christianity is not a branch of Judaism—it is a breach of Judaism. Jews and Christians, it is argued, do not pray to the same God, except perhaps on some mystical level that transcends prayer, thought, and all theology. The God to whom Jews pray, for instance, is not triune, cannot become incarnate in any human being, and does not offer up His son in sacrifice for the sins of the world. Nor does the human being, according to the Jewish view, inherit the burden of Adam's sin, and the Messiah is not the son of God. In what sense, then, do Jews and Christians pray to the *same God*? With the advent of Christianity, the new thinking about God and humanity, indeed, required a "New Testament," which was necessarily at odds with some Jewish teaching on God and humanity. Defining itself in terms of that opposition, the new Christian teaching was first anti-Judaic and then antisemitic. Thus it is precisely the Jews—and not the Hindus or the Buddhists—with whom the Christians are at odds in the effort to define themselves.

But this is just where a new difficulty arises: Can the Christians deny the chosenness of the Jewish people and the Covenant of Abraham without also denying the truth of Christianity? If not, then is the teaching of contempt contrary to the biblical teaching that the Jews are the beloved of God? In other words, if Christians adopt the Hebrew Scriptures—as they must, in order to justify their teachings concerning the Messiah—can they teach contempt for the Jews without also teaching contempt for God? Raising these questions, chapter 4 considers whether antisemitism is indeed "the sin against the Holy Spirit," inasmuch as it amounts to a denial of scriptural teachings on God's relation to the Jews. In its effort to overturn the teaching of contempt, the myth of supersession, and the deicide charge, Vatican II suggests that the Catholic Church has some intimation of the blasphemy of antisemitism. Nevertheless, it remains only an intimation: While at Vatican II the Church *finally* declared antisemitism to be a sin, it has not gone so far as to say it is blasphemous and therefore might merit something like excommunication. Thus chapter 4 ends with a look at some of the theological and political divisions within the Church itself.

What all of this means for interfaith dialogue is the topic of chapter 5, "Can There Be a Jewish-Christian Dialogue after Auschwitz?" The chapter begins by addressing the challenges for such a dialogue in the post-Holocaust era. How frank can we be, for example, without bringing the dialogue to an end before it gets started? What can each tradition learn from the other? And what are the agendas at work in the dialogue? Having identified these challenges, we consider next some of the attempts to bridge the chasm that has separated the two traditions, particularly the documents *We Remember: A Reflection on the Shoah* and *Dabru Emet*. Bringing out the problematic aspects of these documents, we attempt to advance the interests of this interfaith dialogue by saying out loud some things that Christians and Jews have been afraid to say to each other. For example: Can a Christian look upon a Jew without counting him among the damned for his explicit denial of Jesus? Can a Jew accept a Christian's embrace of the passion of the Christ, which is essential to Christianity, without seeing in that embrace a tacit rejection of Jews and Judaism? Can we build a dialogue based on the differences, as well as on similarities, between the two traditions? Indeed, how does a tradition that emphasizes the content of belief enter into a dialogue with a tradition that emphasizes commanded actions?

Because interfaith dialogue is never a mere theoretical matter but rather concerns a concrete reality, chapter 6 presents an example of "Dialogue in Action." It consists of an actual dialogue held between the two Jewish authors of this volume and three of the world's most prominent Christian thinkers: John Pawlikowski (Catholic), John Roth (Protestant), and David Gushee (Evangelical). With the issues raised in the book before us, we address the matter of self-critical reflection, the role of sacred texts and traditions, the dangers of absolute claims, and other concerns. One aim of this example of dialogue in action is to determine the nature of the tension between human responsibility and covenantal allegiance. At what point, in other words, is the doctrine more important than the dialogue, or the dialogue more important than the doctrine? If a Jewish-Christian dialogue is truly possible, the parameters that would make it so have yet to be articulated. And if we cannot determine some of those parameters, then there can be no next step in Jewish-Christian dialogue.

Finally, in our Conclusion we discuss what we have learned from the foregoing investigation and from its implications for post-Holocaust Jewish-Christian relations. This discussion includes a consideration of the current state of Jewish-Christian dialogue and how it can develop into an authentic dialogue. Among the sensitive issues addressed here is the growing antisemitism in the world and ways in which the two communities have come together—or have failed to come together—to respond to it. Among certain academic intellectuals on the extreme left and right and Arab Muslim fundamentalists, both Christianity and Judaism have been the object of sheer contempt and terrorist attacks. One of the questions for the future, then, is this: How can Jews and Christians work as partners to respond not only to antisemitism, but also to the terrorism than threatens both communities. Here it becomes clear that in this book we are not dealing with mere abstractions, but with material matters that have very real social, cultural, and political implications. In our post-Holocaust and now post–9/11 world, it is not too much to say that the future of both traditions is at stake in this interchange.

Two

THE SYMPTOMS OF A MALADY

To address the issue of post-Shoah Jewish-Christian dialogue requires acknowledgment of the unhappy fact that for the preceding nineteen hundred years there has been no dialogue worthy of the name. Rather, there were disputations, which, during the first three centuries of the Common Era, and based on the Gospels, were marked, as Edward Flannery observes, by "the refutation and debasement of Judaism" and "a certain Judeophobia" on the part of the Church.[1] Literary works such as Justin Martyr's second-century *Dialogue with Trypho,* although maintaining a "high level of courteousness and fairness," also articulated for the first time the "ominous theme" that Jewish historical misfortunes were divine punishments for having caused the death of Christ. Medieval disputations coerced Jewish rabbis and scholars into participating in public theological discussion, the outcome of which was predetermined; frequently such "discussions" ended by burning copies of the Talmud. The Holocaust proved the truth of Heinrich Heine's aphorism that one begins by burning books and ends by burning people. In the post-Holocaust era—for the first time in history—some serious attempts have been made to address what Heine recognized as the symptoms of a serious malady.

A BRIEF HISTORY OF POST-HOLOCAUST
JEWISH-CHRISTIAN DIALOGUE

In the aftermath of the Shoah, there began to emerge a recognition that, in the words of Franklin H. Littell, "in a season of betrayal and faithlessness the vast majority of the martyrs for the Lord of History were Jews."[2] Some Christians—those few who had been on the front lines in opposing Nazism and helping Jews—understood the need for a *chesbon hanefesh* (reckoning of the soul). This recognition originated on the part of individual Christian theologians and thinkers—those in the forefront of fighting antisemitism—rather than from Church leaders. Thus early on in the postwar years, leading Catholic figures such as Jacques Maritain, Gertrude Luckner, Johannes Willebrands, Cardinal Augustin Bea, Edward Flannery, and Sister Rose Thering, and, on the Protestant side, A. Roy and Alice Eckardt, Franklin H. Littell, Hubert G. Locke, and the indomitable James Parkes began the painful work of confronting the history and result of the Christian teaching of contempt that thoroughly prepared the way for the Holocaust.[3] These thinkers also addressed issues of biblical interpretation and the Church's relationship to modernity. With the passage of time, a new generation of scholars such as Harry James Cargas, Eugene Fisher, John Pawlikowski, Paul Van Buren, and John K. Roth joined in this essential task.

Christian churches were, however, much slower in recognizing what Littell terms Christianity's "massive credibility crisis" in light of Auschwitz. Indeed, he writes of Christianity's being "conditioned to flee from history." "Enlightened Christians," he maintains, "have long preferred a spiritualized 'Judaism' to having to deal with the Jewish people."[4] In large measure, post-Holocaust dialogue can be seen as an attempt on the part of some Christian churches to reenter history and deal with contemporary Jewish people rather than biblical Israel. Yet these attempts are neither consistent nor unambiguous. For instance, the Stuttgart Declaration of Guilt by the Confessing Church (1945) never mentioned the Holocaust. Three years later the German Evangelical Conference at Darmstadt attested that the Holocaust was a "divine visitation" and a

"call to the Jews to cease their rejection and ongoing crucifixion of Christ." Rabbi Irving Greenberg inquires, "May one
morally be a Christian after this?"[5]

Examining key post-Holocaust proclamations of Christian
churches reveals a twofold phenomenon. On the one hand,
there is a welcome proliferation of creedal statements confessing contrition and rejecting antisemitism. The teaching of contempt has been officially discredited, replaced doctrinally with
the teaching of respect for Judaism and the Jewish people. Further, a host of interfaith organizations has been established on
international, national, and local levels. We think here of groups
such as the International Council of Christians and Jews, the
International Catholic-Jewish Liaison Committee, the International Jewish Committee on Interreligious Consultations, and
the Consultation on the Church and the Jewish People.

On the national level there has been much dialogue between
Christian groups such as the United States Conference of Catholic Bishops, the Presbyterians, Baptists and Lutherans on the one
side, and Jewish groups such as the American Jewish Committee and the Anti-Defamation League, each of whom has established an office for interreligious affairs. Many Jewish thinkers
have also been involved in the dialogue process. Scholars and
theologians such as David Berger and Michael Wyschogrod are
noteworthy examples. Additionally, there has been much interfaith activity on the state and local levels.

Scholarly and academic conferences are held on the topic.
The Annual Scholars' Conference on the Church Struggle and
the Holocaust, established by Franklin Littell and Hubert Locke
in 1970, is the pioneer American conference in this field. International interfaith conferences are held in Jerusalem, Rome,
and elsewhere. Several international conferences were held in
2005 dealing with the fortieth anniversary of *Nostra Aetate*. The
number of interfaith dialogue and study groups is also growing. As noted in Chapter 1, a scholars committee composed of
both Christians and Jews examined an advance script of *The
Passion of the Christ* and, working independently, came to the
same conclusion about its flawed history and overt antisemitism. Further, there are significant interchanges on an interper-
sonal level between Christians and Jews.

One of the earliest post-Holocaust Christian-Jewish dialogues occurred in Seelisberg, Switzerland. There a conference was convened in 1947 by the International Council of Christians and Jews (ICCJ), an organization that was founded the preceding year as the "younger brother" of the American National Council of Christians and Jews. The ICCJ was committed to combating antisemitism and prejudice. The Christian delegates to Seelisberg included Willebrands and Luckner. Willebrands worked with the Apeldoorn circle in the Netherlands rescuing Jews during the Holocaust. Luckner, one of the few German Catholic wartime resisters of Nazism, was arrested and spent two years at Ravensbrück concentration camp. She also carried on an extensive dialogue with the venerable Rabbi Leo Baeck during and after the Shoah. With guidance from their Jewish colleagues, the Christian representatives began confronting the implications of the Shoah for Christianity. Jules Isaac, the celebrated French scholar, worked with Maritain, Luckner, and Karl Thieme, in helping formulate the Seelisberg theses.

Seelisberg is noteworthy for its condemnation of antisemitism, which the delegates rightly noted played an important role in leading to the Holocaust, and its indictment of Christians who have "failed to be true to the teaching of Jesus on the mercy of God and love of one's neighbor." The delegates issued a ten-point statement, four of which emphasized positive dimensions of the perceived relationship between Jews and Christians:

1. One God speaks to both faith communities through the Old and New Testaments.

2. Jesus was born of a Jewish mother.

3. The first disciples, apostles, and martyrs were Jewish.

4. And both faith communities are commanded to love God and neighbour [sic].

Six statements were negative admonitions to their fellow Christians:

1. Do not misrepresent Judaism for the purpose of extolling Christianity.

2. Do not use the word "Jew" as enemy of Jesus.

3. Do not present the killing of Jesus as being the fault of all Jews.

4. Do not refer to scriptural curses against the Jews.

5. Refrain from teaching that the Jewish people are reprobate.

6. Do not deny that the first members of the Church were Jews.

The Seelisberg declaration had a great impact on the signers of the declaration. Moreover, it demonstrated that Christians and Jews could speak to each other openly about the pathology of antisemitism. However, it had little or no discernable wide-spread impact on ecclesial institutions or on Western or Eastern Christianity as a whole. But its early confrontation with the Church's sordid history of the teaching of contempt set the stage for much of what was to come regarding official Church statements about antisemitism. It was, however, lacking in any attempt to articulate either a Christian theology of Judaism or a statement against mission to the Jewish people.

One year after Seelisberg, the first assembly of the Protestant World Council of Churches (WCC) in Amsterdam produced "The Christian Approach to the Jews," which declared that people should look with "penitent eyes" in regard to the extermination of 6 million Jews. The WCC document emphasized three points:

1. God has bound Jews and Christians in solidarity linking their destinies.

2. The churches contributed to antisemitism in the secular world by teaching that the Jews were the sole enemies of Christ.

3.   Antisemitism is a sin.

However, the declaration upheld the normative Protestant tradition of missions to the Jews and failed to specifically
address the deicide issue. The third WCC meeting, held in New
Delhi (1961), reiterated the earlier call to fight antisemitism,
which was declared a sin against God and man. Repeating the
Seelisberg formulation, the 1961 resolution stated that it was
the sins of all humanity that occasioned the death of Christ.

On the Catholic side, the Second Vatican Council's 1965
promulgation of *Nostra Aetate* dealt with Catholicism's relations
with non-Christian religions. Note four specifically treats Judaism. This note reversed the Church's bimillennial sanctioning
of antisemitism, opening the door for a self-critique on the part
of the Church. Subsequent Vatican documents such as the 1974
"Guidelines and Suggestions for Implementing the Conciliar
Declaration *Nostra Aetate* (no. 4)," and the 1985 "Notes on the Correct Way to Present the Jews in Preaching and Catechesis in the
Roman Catholic Church," pushed this door further ajar and held
out the possibility of a Catholic-Jewish dialogue based on recognition of the historical and theological legitimacy of Judaism and
the Jewish people. The history behind *Nostra Aetate* is as important as the declaration itself as it reveals the potential—which has
yet to be fully realized—for Catholic-Jewish dialogue.

"Two old men, both of whose lives had been touched by the
Holocaust," writes Michael Phayer, "provided the immediate
spark that generated *Nostra Aetate*."[6] Pope John XXIII and Jules
Isaac had personal experience of the Shoah. As Angelo Ron-
calli, the future pope had been stationed in Istanbul during the
war and helped rescue Jews. Jules Isaac, a French historian who
spent the war years in hiding and who lost all his family, save
a young son who had fled to England, in the Holocaust, wrote
Jesus and Israel, a book he hoped would extirpate the Christian
roots of antisemitism. Further, Isaac assumed a leadership role
in the French interfaith organization l'Amitié Judéo-Chrétienne.
At the time of their 1960 meeting, it was likely that neither man
envisioned *Nostra Aetate*'s ultimate impact.

Pope John XXIII, unlike Pope Pius XII, whom Isaac had met
eleven years earlier, took Isaac's proposal seriously. The pope

himself was committed to achieving an *aggiornamento* (updating) of the way of the Church in the world. He sent Isaac to speak with Cardinal Bea, whom the pope had designated head of the newly formed Secretariat on Religious Relations with the Jews. Specifically concerning Catholic-Jewish dialogue, the Second Vatican Council received important input from three Jewish agencies: the American Jewish Committee, the World Jewish Congress, and the International B'nai B'rith. The latter two submitted a statement on antisemitism, while the committee was concerned in addition with helping reform Catholic educational and liturgical understandings of and references to Jews and Judaism.

The input of three important Jewish thinkers also played a decisive role in the council's deliberations. Isaac has already been mentioned. Abraham Joshua Heschel, a theologian and the scion of an Eastern European Chasidic dynasty, was invited by the American Jewish Committee to help in discussions with the Vatican. Heschel and Cardinal Bea had several meetings in Rome, and the American theologian hosted a dinner for Bea when the cardinal came to New York. Joseph Lichten of the Anti-Defamation League supplied each of the council delegates with a copy of the contemporary Charles Glock and Rodney Stark study that revealed a deep current of antisemitism among American Catholics.

Heschel pushed for three goals: (1)"to reject and condemn those who assert that the Jews as a people are responsible for the crucifixion," (2) to "acknowledge the integrity and permanent preciousness of Jews and Judaism," and (3) "to eliminate abuses and derogatory stereotypes" by promoting scholarship and combating religious prejudice.[7] Pope John XXIII did not live to see the council's final declaration that was approved under the leadership of Pope Paul VI, who lacked his predecessor's deep-seated commitment to improving relations with the Jews. In fact, Paul VI preached a Passion Sunday sermon in 1965 that unambiguously accused Jews of deicide.

The language of *Nostra Aetate*'s final declaration was compromised, disappointing many in the Jewish world and some Catholic thinkers as well. For example, early drafts were much stronger in condemning antisemitism and deicide. Concerning the former, the final statement uses the word *decries* rather than the much stronger *condemns*, which appeared in earlier drafts. Regarding the deicide issue, the draft statement read, "May Christians never present the Jewish people as one rejected, cursed or guilty of deicide." The approved text read, "Although the Church is the new people of God, the Jews should not be presented as repudiated or cursed by God, as if such views followed from the Holy Scriptures." (An assessment of *Nostra Aetate* and the Second Vatican Council is presented in chapter 4.)

"Memory and Reconciliation: The Church and the Faults of the Past" (MR) is the last, post-1965, twentieth-century Vatican document dealing with how the Church understands memory and history as it pursues an uncompromised Catholic-Jewish dialogue. Published in December 1999 by the International Theological Commission, MR speaks of "purifying" memory. This means "eliminating from personal and collective conscience all forms of resentment or violence left by the inheritance of the past. The memory of division and opposition is purified and substituted by reconciled memory, to which everyone in the Church is invited to be open and become educated." The temptation here, however, is to avoid *working through* the past in an honest and open way.

If purifying memory is simply a theological version of "letting bygones be bygones," MR presents a twofold danger. First, the Church's role in fostering hatred is left unexamined. Second, without directly confronting the past, it becomes more difficult to combat hatred in the future. As James Carroll observes, "If the Catholic Church as the 'Bride of Christ' is entirely sinless and the crimes committed in the name of the Church—Crusades, Inquisition, etc.—were the acts of 'sinful children' of the Church but never 'the Church as such,' it is furthering (the) deadly refusal to examine the way in which religion as such can prompt inhuman behavior."[8] The willingness to engage in sincere theological self-critique is one necessary ingredient for authentic dialogue.

We contrast the attitude toward memory in the 1999 document with that of Elie Wiesel, who writes, "If we stop remembering, we stop being."[9] Memory in the Wieselian sense is ontological. It is inclusive rather than compartmentalized. Further, there are a variety of memories. Edward Linenthal distinguishes among four types of memory: burdensome, treacherous, murderous, and hopeful.[10] The memory of Church-sanctioned antisemitism is deeply painful and burdensome. It has also prepared the way for unparalleled genocide. This memory needs to be confronted rather than distorted, effaced, or trivialized. One of the tensions in Catholic-Jewish dialogue remains the Jewish insistence on speaking about history, which carries with it theological meaning, while the Catholic position emphasizes theology, which frequently either ignores or relies upon supersessionary history.

This brief history reveals both the beginnings of a momentous change in Catholic-Jewish dialogue as well as the persistence of a fundamental conflict between liberalizing and conservative tendencies within the Church. This tension can be seen in papal and other official pronouncements that contradict each other such as *We Remember: A Reflection on the Shoah* and *Dominus Ieus*. Further, conflicting theological positions may occur even within a single document, as is the case with *We Remember* (see chapter 5). The positive elements include the following: The Church has undertaken a theological self-critique, issuing guidelines that overturn the teaching of contempt; Christians and Jews are speaking to each other on the basis of parity; and disagreements on certain issues have been acknowledged without disrupting the dialogue. On the other side of the ledger, key theological questions such as the meaning of election, the relationship between rival truth claims, and the delicate nature of trust between the two faith communities await further serious reflection.

Of course, this history of post-Holocaust Jewish-Christian dialogue unfolds in the contexts of certain ways in which the Holocaust has threatened the Jewish and Christian traditions. Let us now consider those contexts.

THE HOLOCAUST'S THREAT TO JEWISH TRADITION

Throughout their multimillennial history, and even now, Jews have asserted in their prayers, "I place my trust in Your kindness; my heart shall rejoice in Your deliverance" (Psalms 144:15). And they have asserted that, with their devoted adherence to the Covenant, God will assure them a secure place in the land "as long as the heavens are above the earth" (Deuteronomy 11:21). But the Holocaust has shown that there are times when the heavens are no longer above the earth. There are times when the sky is transformed into a cemetery and the earth becomes an abyss. It is written that, as the Romans tortured the great sage Rabbi Ishmael ben Elisha for his persistence in teaching Torah, he screamed so horribly the angels cried out, "Is this the reward for the saint's devotion to Your Torah!?" God answered, "If Rabbi Ishmael should scream just once more, I shall return heaven and earth to chaos and void!" And the sage fell silent (see *Otzar Midrashim, Esrei Harugi, Malakhot* 6). But those tortured in the Shoah have not fallen silent: Their screams cry out from the pages of thousands of diaries and memoirs, from the ashen earth itself. Has the world, then, been returned to chaos and void? Perhaps. For in the wake of the Holocaust, Jewish tradition has collided with an unprecedented overturning of creation. Briefly stated, the Holocaust's threat to Jewish tradition is this: Centuries of devotion to the sacred tradition were not enough to prevent the Jews from being murdered by the millions.

In his commentary on the Torah, the thirteenth-century sage Nachmanides makes the following prophecy: "The children of Esau [Christians] will not formulate a decree against us designed to obliterate our name entirely, but they will do evil to some of us in their countries."[11] Unfortunately the Ramban was mistaken: Although he knew all about the Crusaders' slaughter of the Jews, he had no conception of the Shoah that would befall his people seven hundred years later. Indeed, how could he? The Shoah was a devastation unparalleled in its scope and singular in its implications. It cut a wound into the body of all of Israel. The *Midrash Chinukh* says that if the blood of a single human life is shed, the victim's blood raises an outcry that reverberates throughout the universe.[12] What, then, must be the outcry of a sea of blood? The cry, indeed, is deafening. If we cannot hear it, it is because it is unceasing, a dissonance that has drowned out the music of the spheres.

The blood poured out in the murder of European Jewry continues to surge in the blood of every Jew—indeed, of all humanity. Each soul, said the Baal Shem Tov, founder of eighteenth-century Chasidism, is "a limb of the Shekhinah," which is the Divine Presence in this world, so that "a sorrow caused to one affects all."[13] As Yitzhak Katznelson asserts in his *Vittel Diary*, "It is against the great Beth Hamedrash [the dwelling place of the Shekhinah], the spirit and soul of East European Jewry, that the nations have set this Horror."[14] This attack upon the spirit and soul of Israel lies in the calculated destruction of Jewish cemeteries and synagogues, of Jewish texts and sacred artifacts, of Jewish homes and families—all of which was planned according to the Jewish calendar of holy days. And all of which came to an assault on the Holy One Himself.

The Nazis targeted the Jews not because they prospered during an economic depression; otherwise it would have been enough to impoverish them. Nor was it because they were an easy scapegoat for social problems; otherwise it would have been enough to rid only Germany of its Jews. No, it was because the Jewish presence in the world signifies a testimony that is fundamentally at odds with Nazi thinking. In a word, the Nazis were not antisemites because they were racists; rather, they were racists because they were antisemites. For in order to determine a racist position on humanity, one must first undermine the Jewish position, which teaches that every human being is of the same "race," descended as we are from a single human being. In the Nazi worldview, the Jews were not an economic or political or social problem, but a cosmic, *ontological* evil that had to be eradicated. The Nazis fought the Jews because, according to their infamous ideologist Alfred Rosenberg, the Aryan race "has been poisoned by Judaism," and not merely by Jewish blood, since the –ism is *in* the blood.[15] Therefore, insisted Rosenberg, all Jews are prone to think Talmudically, "whether they are atheistic Bourse-speculators, religious fanatics, or Talmudic Jews of the cloth."[16] The Holocaust, then, is not reducible to a case of genocide, but is a singular case of deicide.

Since, from a Jewish standpoint, God is the ground of tradition, this assault on the God of Abraham poses a singular threat to the thinking that has characterized Jewish tradition for centuries. Steven Katz divides the various Jewish responses to this threat into nine categories, according to the thesis that guides each one:

1. The Holocaust is essentially the same as all other Jewish tragedies (for example, Eliezer Berkovits, *Faith after the Holocaust*).

2. The Holocaust is a punishment for the Jewish sin of complicity in the project of modernity (for example, Bernard Maza, *With Fury Poured Out*).

3. Israel is the suffering servant who was afflicted for the sins of humanity (for example, Ignaz Maybaum, *The Face of God after Auschwitz*).

4. The Holocaust is a modern *Akedah*, a binding of Isaac, and is a test of our faltering faith (for example, Irving Greenberg, "Cloud of Smoke, Pillar of Fire").

5. The Holocaust is a temporary eclipse of God (for example Martin Buber, *Eclipse of God*).

6. The Holocaust means that God and His Covenant with the Jewish people are dead (for example, Richard Rubenstein, *After Auschwitz*).

7. God chooses to be powerless for the sake of human freedom, and the Holocaust is the price paid for that freedom (for example Hans Jonas, *Mortality and Morality*).

8. The Holocaust is a moment of revelation and a call for Jewish survival (for example, Emil Fackenheim, *God's Presence in History*).

9. The Holocaust is an inscrutable mystery and eludes all thought (for example Elie Wiesel, *One Generation After*).[17]

As one can see, the Jewish thinkers' attempts to respond to the Holocaust's threat to Jewish tradition have ranged from being overwhelmed by the threat to ignoring it. Most, however, have attempted to rescue from the ashes at least some remnant of the tradition that the Nazis set out to destroy through the extermination of the Jews. Indeed, if Jewish-Christian dialogue is to have a future, then both traditions must have a future. Those who abandon the Jewish tradition have nothing to dialogue about, at least not in the contexts of *interfaith* dialogue. Therefore the real threat of the Holocaust to Jewish tradition comes not only from the Nazis, who set out to obliterate it, but also from Jewish thinkers who play into their hands by totally rejecting it.

Among the best known of Jewish thinkers who respond to the threat to Jewish tradition by abandoning the tradition is Richard L. Rubenstein. In his most famous work, *After Auschwitz: Radical Theology and Contemporary Judaism* (1966), Rubenstein insists that in no sense is the Torah from God and that Jewish religious life possesses no "superordinate validation."[18] In other words, the Jews are not chosen, and there is no Covenant. From Rubenstein's perspective, the religious adherence to Jewish tradition has no more than a therapeutic value. Basing the future of the Jews on an accidental "peoplehood"[19] and a pagan "return to the cosmic rhythm of natural existence,"[20] Rubenstein's response to the Holocaust's threat to Jewish tradition amounts to an abrogation of the defining essence of Jews and Judaism. To be sure, he maintains that ultimately there is no future for the Jewish people and no meaning in human life. Contrary to all Jewish teaching, Rubenstein maintains that "there is only one Messiah who redeems us from the irony, the travail, and the limitations of human existence. Surely he will come. He is the Angel of Death. Death is the true Messiah and the land of the dead the place of God's true Kingdom."[21] No view could be more contrary to Jewish tradition. While Rubenstein softened his position in the second edition of this work, titled *After Auschwitz: History, Theology, and Contemporary Judaism* (1992),[22] he remains the Jewish thinker perhaps best known for a radical theology that seriously challenges traditional Jewish thinking about chosenness, Covenant, Torah, and other key categories in Jewish thought.

This is not to say that those who follow a more traditional path of Judaism see no threat to Jewish tradition. Among the

Orthodox rabbis known for their responses to the Shoah, for example, are Irving Greenberg and Eliezer Berkovits. One of Greenberg's most frequently cited statements on the Holocaust is: "No statement, theological or otherwise, should be made that would not be credible in the presence of the burning children."[23] This remark is from his essay "Cloud of Smoke, Pillar of Fire," the title of which invokes ways in which the Shoah has threatened Jewish tradition. It refers to the smoke and fire of the Divine Presence as it guided the Israelites through the wilderness. The smoke and the fire, however, have now taken on quite a different presence: They are the smoke and the fire that rose from the pits where Jewish children were burned alive. Contrary to watching over us, the smoke and the fire haunt us. What once signified the presence of God now signifies His eclipse. The ashes that have rained down from the cloud of smoke and the pillar of fire now cover the earth—that is where the eclipse of God takes place: not in the heavens but on the earth.

But what *can* be said in the presence of burning children? Dare one speak at all? Dare one remain silent? Sara Nomberg-Przytyk offers a hint of what might be said in her remembrance of a children's transport that arrived one night in Auschwitz: "Suddenly, the stillness was broken by the screaming of children,… a scream repeated a thousand times in a single word, 'Mama,' a scream that increased in intensity every second, enveloping the whole camp. Our lips parted without our being conscious of what we were doing, and a scream of despair tore out of our throats…. At the end everything was enveloped in death and silence."[24] Has Jewish tradition, then, been reduced to a scream of despair that tears itself from our throats? Shall it now be enveloped in death and silence? That seems to be Greenberg's view. But apart from appealing to our emotions, which is perhaps needful, being silenced by the burning children does not take us any closer to a mending of Jewish tradition or to a dialogical relation with our Christian neighbors.

It does, however, raise serious questions about the covenantal relation between God and the Jews after the Holocaust, as Greenberg understands all too well. Here we come to what Greenberg calls a "voluntary covenant." During the Holocaust, he maintains, the Covenant's "authority was broken, but the

Jewish people, released from its obligations, chose voluntarily to take it on again."[25] A possible difficulty with this idea is that if the Covenant is voluntary—if we are free to choose *not* to enter into the Covenant—then we are also free not to reaffirm life through acts of love and life-giving kindness, the very actions that Greenberg urges us to undertake. True, Greenberg insists that "after the Holocaust one *must* challenge the absolute claims of a secular culture that created the matrix out of which such a catastrophe could grow."[26] And he is absolutely right. But how can this *must* be voluntary for a Jew? For if we are not bound, as Jews, by the Covenant, then we are not bound by the commandments, from the prohibition against pork to the prohibition against murder. Without the Covenant that chooses us *prior* to any choices we make, we have no real obligation, and our choices have no ultimate meaning. Here, too, the post-Holocaust dilemma facing the Jewish theologian is very problematic.

One Orthodox Jewish thinker who responds to the Holocaust's threat to Jewish tradition by striving with God is Eliezer Berkovits; to be sure, he insists that in Judaism faith demands that we question God in the aftermath of such a catastrophe.[27] And, invoking Isaiah 42:15,[28] he is aware of a very important tension that characterizes Jewish thinking about God and humanity: "That man may be, God must absent Himself; that man may not perish in the tragic absurdity of his own making, God must remain present."[29] Therefore, Berkovits rightly understands, Jewish tradition is not characterized by settling matters with the fixed formulas and ready answers of theodicy; as Shmuel ben Nachman teaches in the Talmud, "whoever holds that someone is suffering due to his sins is in error" (*Shabbat* 5a). The aim, rather, is to maintain the tension of a strife of the spirit through an adherence to Torah, Talmud, and Covenant. Without that adherence we lose the very categories that create the tension. For without that adherence we lose both the grounds and the meaning of any objection to evil; indeed, we lose the very notion of evil. Therefore even in evil—"at the very doors of the gas chambers," as Berkovits points out[30]—we encounter God.

Among the most profound of the Jewish thinkers to respond to the threat of the Holocaust to Jewish tradition is one of the most neglected in these contexts: It is Emmanuel Lévinas. Like Rubenstein, Lévinas rejects theodicy. Unlike Rubenstein, who takes being to be something neutral and meaningless and rejects the Torah, Lévinas holds that "being has meaning. The meaning of being, the meaning of creation, is to realize the Torah.... To refuse the Torah is to bring being back to nothingness."[31] Thus Lévinas sees arising from the Holocaust not just the injunction to survive as Jews but also the demand for an ethical absolute, which derives not from the landscape of being but from what is "otherwise than being," from the "exigency of holiness"[32]—in a word, from the Torah that is the basis of Jewish tradition. "To renounce after Auschwitz," he writes, "the God absent from Auschwitz—no longer to assure the continuation of Israel— would amount to finishing the criminal enterprise of National Socialism, which aimed at the annihilation of Israel and the for- getting of the ethical message of the Bible, which Judaism bears, and whose multi-millennial history is concretely prolonged by Israel's existence as a people."[33] And by *Judaism*, Lévinas under- stands the Judaism of Torah and Talmud, as evidenced by his studies of the Talmud.

Of all the Jewish thinkers, the one who sees perhaps most profoundly the Holocaust's threat to Jewish tradition is Emil Fackenheim. He puts it this way: Under the Third Reich, Jews were murdered not because they abandoned Torah, but because their grandparents adhered to it.[34] The newness of the threat, however, does not necessarily demand that we abandon Torah, Talmud, and Covenant—just the opposite: It demands that we take our Jewish thinking and our Judaism to even deeper lev- els. In contrast to Berkovits, Fackenheim recognizes the defin- ing singularity of the Nazis' assault against the God of Israel and His Chosen. When the Crusaders slaughtered the Jews, a Christian could object to the slaughter and remain a Christian; a Christian could say "We are going too far" and remain within the teachings of Christianity. With a Nazi, however, there was no "going too far"; indeed, when it came to murdering Jews, a Nazi could not go far enough. Out to eliminate the divine prohi- bition against murder through the murder of God Himself, the Nazis had no limiting principle, no divine injunction, to curtail their actions. What the Nazis perpetrated against the Jews, then, was not unimaginable—it was everything imaginable. For the imagination was the only limit to their actions. Thus in undertaking an assault on the Infinite One, their evil approached the infinite: It was as infinite as the imagination.

Unlike most other Jewish thinkers, Fackenheim finds in the aftermath of Auschwitz not a divine silence, but a divine commandment, what he calls the 614th Commandment, namely that Jews must survive *as Jews*, so as to refuse the Nazis a posthumous victory.[35] The point of the 614th Commandment is Jewish survival, not for its own sake but for the sake of the "millennial testimony" of Jewish tradition, a chief component of which is the divine prohibition against murder. If the Jews and Jewish tradition should be lost, the prohibition would be lost. If the Holocaust represents a singularity in human history, as Fackenheim maintains, it is not only because of the exterminationist policy of a modern state, the development of technology for purposes of mass murder, the criminalization of Jewish being, and so on. More than that, its singularity lies in its metaphysical dimensions as an instance of divine revelation in the midst of a human assault on the Holy One.

How do the Nazis undertake that assault? By making murder a defining principle of their worldview, so as to undo the divine image itself. To be sure, one move requires the other. Here too we see a threat to Jewish tradition, in the horrifying realization that perhaps the image and likeness of the Holy One within the human can be destroyed. With an insight that eludes others, Fackenheim sees that "the murder camp was not an accidental by-product of the Nazi empire. It was its pure essence. The divine image *can* be destroyed. No more threatening proof to this effect can be found than the so-called *Muselmann* in the Nazi death camp.... The *Muselmänner* are a new way of human being in history, the living dead."[36] And: "The Nazi state had no higher aim than to murder souls while bodies were still alive. The *Muselmann* was its most characteristic, most original product. He is a *novum* in human history."[37] Demonstrating the connections between the Nazi assault on God and the Nazi undoing of the human image, Fackenheim opens up implications of the event and its threat to Jewish tradition that no other thinker has breached.

The threat that the Holocaust poses for Jewish tradition is real, but within that tradition the Jews have a tradition of argument that they can turn to; indeed, the argument, the outrage, can be maintained only from within the tradition. Only if we can cry out to God, "*Hinneni*—Here I am!" can we then cry out, "*Ayekah!?*—Where are You?" and thus turn the first question put to the first man back on God Himself (see Genesis 3:9). But it is more than a question. *Ayekah* has the same root as *Eikhah*, the opening word in the Book of Lamentations. It is a cry of anguish meaning "How?" as if to say, "How could You!?" There lies the threat—and the challenge—for Jewish tradition: how to raise a cry to God from within the tradition, without losing the tradition. For if we lose the tradition, we lose the divine prohibition against murder, as the murdered Jews of the Shoah sink into the anonymous morass of history's suffering humanity.

THE HOLOCAUST'S THREAT TO CHRISTIAN TRADITION

The Holocaust's threat to Christian tradition is rather different from the threat to Jewish tradition—and more difficult for those Christians who have the courage to confront it. With Job, the Jew cries out, "Though He slay me, yet will I defend my ways to His face" (Job 13:15). Even though God may abandon him, the Jew who clings to the Covenant retains a hold on his soul. But in the matter of the Holocaust, the pious Christian has a very difficult task in defending his ways to God's face. Even though God may not have abandoned him, the Christian clings to the New Covenant, only to feel his soul slipping through his fingers. Briefly stated, the Holocaust's threat to Christian tradition is this: Centuries of devotion to the sacred tradition were not enough to prevent the Christians from murdering millions of Jews. In fact, precisely that devotion prepared the soil that would become a mass grave for European Jewry.

While the Nazis did indeed exploit Christian teachings to suit their own ends—they could quote Martin Luther, for example, without editing—they drew their ideology more directly from certain strains of German philosophy and Teutonic lore than from Christian theology. For German and Western European thinking over the last three hundred years has been largely a process of thinking God out of the picture, a process that served the aspirations of the Master Race quite well. Yes, the SS had *Gott Mit Uns*—"God With Us"—embossed on their belt buckles, but that is just the point: Instead of asking, "Are we with God?" they assert that God is with them in an appropriation of God that makes them independent of God. Among the philosophical positions that played into the Nazis' ideological hands, then, was the Kantian identification of freedom with autonomy, where autonomy was defined in terms of being self-legislating, and not subject to anything so heteronomous as a divine commandment.[38] Subsequently, Fackenheim points out, "divinity vanishes in the process of internalization, to be replaced by a humanity potentially infinite in its modern 'freedom.'"[39] Because it is infinite, the "modern freedom" eliminates the Infinite One, so that human beings may do whatever they have the will to do. Indeed, they are justified by will alone.

Thus at the June 1939 meeting of the National Socialist Association of University Lecturers, its head Walter Schultze declared before the assembly, "What the great thinkers of German Idealism dreamed of, and what was ultimately the kernel of their longing for liberty, finally comes alive, assumes reality.... Never has the German idea of freedom been conceived with greater life and greater vigor than in our day."[40] A leading intellectual in Nazi Germany, Schultze saw clearly the link between the German philosophical tradition and National Socialism. In any case, for their ideological stance, the Nazis found as much justification in their intellectual tradition as in the Christian tradition.

In the Christian tradition, they found all too easily not only a social and cultural ground but, more important, a *theological* justification for the final solution to the "Jewish question." Where mainstream Christian teaching came to the Nazis' aid was not so much in the formulation of their ideology as in the implementation of their program of extermination. There they had all-too-eager Christian accomplices, without whom the Nazis could never have attained their end. Most Christians, particularly in Eastern Europe, viewed the Jews in the same way the Nazis viewed the Jews: as a cosmic evil that preys on all of humanity. And so they joined in the mass murder, not only as members of the German killing units but often on their own, uninstigated by the Nazis, as in the case of the massacres at Jedwabne, Poland, [41] and Viliampole, Lithuania.[42] Nor was it merely the uneducated Christian masses that betrayed their own teachings. From the complicity of Father Josef Tiso to the silence of Pius XII, the Christian leadership often proved to be as culpable as the Christian following. Even Dietrich Bonhoeffer, who was executed for his courageous rebellion against Hitler, insisted that an end to the suffering of the Jews, who "nailed the redeemer of the world to the cross," would come only with "the conversion of Israel."[43]

The tree is known by its fruit, as a Jew once said (Matthew 12:33), and the Christian tree has produced fruit deadly to the Jews. Whether by conversion or by extermination, the Christian aim—*in keeping with Christian tradition*—has been the elimination of the Jews. Indeed, the Holocaust has made all the more conspicuous the Christians' history of murdering Jews by the tens of thousands *precisely in the name of Christianity*, from the Crusades to the Chmielnicki massacres, from the Inquisition to the pogroms. "It is not the Jewish people that has become incredible," Littell states the Holocaust's threat to Christian tradition, "it is Christianity and those who call themselves 'Christians.'"[44] Scholars already speak of Europe's entry into "the post-Christian" era: Having purged itself of the Jews, European Christendom lost its Christianity. One wonders whether European Christendom could have sustained itself without the Jews there for the Christians to hate: The Jews are the ones the Christians are *not*, the ones the Christians displace. Most Christians would agree that Christianity could not have emerged without Judaism. But its relation to Judaism has always been a negative one: Judaism is the religion that Christianity has surpassed. The question for Christians in this connection is this: can Christianity define itself in other than supersessionist terms vis-à-vis the Jews and Judaism?

While there were brave Christians who, on their own, undertook a struggle against the Nazis, there was no *church* struggle against the Nazis, unless one might deem the Jehovah's Witnesses a church. Even there, however, the struggle was more in opposition to Nazi idolatry than in support of Jewish victims. Franklin Littell, Hubert Locke, and other Christian scholars have

spoken eloquently about the Holocaust and the church struggle. But they do not refer to the church's struggle *against* the
perpetrators of the Holocaust; rather, they refer to the struggle
within a church that was complicit in the Holocaust. If Europe
has indeed entered a post-Christian period, as theologians such
as Didier Pollefeyt and Jürgen Manemann claim, it would seem
that the church lost the struggle against itself, for itself. Any
Christian who can fathom this prospect will understand a question that Harry James Cargas raises, in fear and trembling: "The
Holocaust is, in my judgment, the greatest tragedy for Christians since the crucifixion. In the first instance, Jesus died; in
the latter, Christianity may be said to have died. In the case of
Christ, the Christians believe in a resurrection. Will there be,
can there be, a resurrection for Christianity?"[45] What Cargas
does not ask—what Jews might want to ask but are afraid to
ask—is this: *Should* Christianity be resurrected? We, as Jews,
have seen two thousand years of Christianity—do we really
want to see more?

There's the rub. Jewish thinkers such as Berkovits, Fackenheim, and Lévinas can insist, without shame, that a Jewish
future rests upon a Jewish return to the texts and the teachings
of the sacred tradition, if for no other reason than to maintain
the argument with God. In the post-Holocaust era a Jew can say,
"Let us learn again from Rabbi Akiva and the Rambam, from
Nachmanides and the Baal Shem Tov," without being accused
of turning his or her back on the 6 million. We can make a case
for a *Kiddush Hashem*, for a "sanctification of the name," on the
part of those who were murdered, in the light of Alfred Rosenberg's assertion that they must be eliminated for their propen-
sity to or practice of Judaism,[46] despite Fackenheim's claim that
in the Shoah martyrdom itself was murdered.[47] To say no to the
sages and relegate them to oblivion, in fact, would be playing
into the Nazis' hands. Even Richard Rubenstein finds room for
the beauty and depth of the tradition in midrashic teachings
and Chasidic tales.

For the Christians, the situation is different. Whereas, for
the Jews, the Holocaust's threat to tradition might call for a
renewal of tradition, for the Christians the threat calls for a
rejection of Christianity's traditionally negative teachings on the

Jews—which, as we shall see in chapter 4, may well be a *defining* element of Christian doctrine, at least as it has been articulated over the centuries. A Christian has greater difficulty trying to seek a resurrection or a renewal of Christianity by returning to the Gospel of John, the writings of the Church Fathers, papal bulls, or the teachings of Martin Luther. How, in the light of the Holocaust, are Christians to return to Scriptures such as this one: "In speaking of a new covenant he [Jeremiah in Jeremiah 31:31] treats the first as obsolete, and what is becoming obsolete and growing old is ready to vanish away" (Hebrews 8:13)? To embrace once more their sages and saints might, at least to some extent, amount to playing into the hands of the Nazis. And yet the teachings of those sages and saints constitute the *sacred* tradition; is the sacred tradition, then, not so sacred after all? If not, where does that leave Christianity? The Holocaust's threat to the Christian tradition, then, is this: The Holocaust may call for such a radical revision of the tradition that a resurrected Christianity may no longer be able to recognize itself as Christian. For if it is to be reborn, Christianity must lose one of the defining features of its sacred tradition: triumphalism.

Christian triumphalism is not the triumphalism of a people that has survived centuries of murderous persecution. It is not the triumphalism of a people who cries, "*Am Yisrael chai!—*The people of Israel live!*" despite* centuries of slaughter. Such a cry—the cry of the Jews—pertains not to a redemption won for the next world, but to the flesh-and-blood life of a people, sinner and saint alike, that continues its struggle to dwell in this world. When, however, a Christian invokes, with Paul, "our Savior Christ Jesus, who abolished death and brought life and immortality to light through the Gospel" (2 Timothy 1:10), he is suggesting the triumph of a truth for the next world, through a belief in the Savior who has defeated death and vanquished sin—a belief that seems to allow no room for Jews and Judaism.

To be sure, it is precisely the Jews and Judaism that have been defeated in this triumph. For the triumph over death is a triumph over the flesh, and the Jews are Jews "according to the flesh" (see Romans 9:5). Since "it is not the children of the flesh who are the children of God" (Romans 9:8), the Jews have been displaced as the children of God. Thus, as Mel Gibson rightly understood, the flesh had to be flayed from the Jew Jesus, so that the victory over the mortal flesh might be attained in the resurrection. The graphic scenes of the flaying of the Jew—of the bloody removal of the flesh from the Jew—are not part of the Gibsonian reputation for indulging in violence for the sake of violence. No, they are part of the triumphal announcement that the Christians have won. Can Christianity remain Christian without this victory over the mortal flesh? Stated differently: Can Christianity remain Christian without the doctrine of the resurrection? For here, as a triumph over the mortality of the flesh, the resurrection itself appears to sow the seeds of hatred of the Jews.

Alice L. Eckardt and A. Roy Eckardt had the insight to see this implication of traditional triumphalism in Christianity. With regard to the Holocaust's threat to that triumphalism, they outline three basic categories of the Christian response to the threat:

1. The Holocaust poses no threat to Christian tradition; indeed, only when Jews embrace Christ will there be an end to antisemitism and a reconciliation between Christians and Jews (for example, Friedrich Gruenagel, *Die Judenfrage*). Here unapologetic Christian triumphalism remains intact.

2. The Holocaust poses a partial threat, but not a serious one, since Christian tradition already has in place the categories for dealing with it (for example, Jürgen Moltmann, *The Crucified God*). Here we have triumphalism with guilt feelings.

3. If the Holocaust threatens Christian tradition, it is because Christians have not attained a liberation from the tradition, a liberation that would release them from their triumphalism over the Jews; what the Holocaust demands, therefore, is a "total revolution" of Christian tradition (for example, Johann-Baptist Metz, *The Emergent Church*). Here we have the complete abandonment of triumphalism.[48]

But, it must be asked, what exactly is the nature of the "total revolution" that would completely abandon triumphalism? Can any tradition undergo a "total revolution" without becoming something else?

As for the Eckardts themselves, they take the radical position that, in view of the Holocaust, Christian tradition, particularly in its triumphalist mode, is undone. "No past event, however holy, or divine," they insist, "can ever redeem the terror of the present" that the Holocaust represents.[49] Therefore, they maintain, the resurrection has not taken place; it is relegated to a future yet to be attained.[50] Such a move poses both a threat and an opportunity for Christian tradition by returning Christianity to *time*. With the resurrection and the ascension, time comes to a halt, inasmuch as the one thing needful—redemption—has been accomplished. Therefore nothing that has happened since the resurrection is of any ultimate importance. History becomes a matter not of laboring for a redemption that the Messiah has *yet* to bring, but of simply marking time until the "end." That is to say, the Christian has had nothing to *work* for, just something to *believe* in. The Eckardts, however, turn this around, as if to say, contrary to the cry from the cross, "It is *not* finished!"

But is this not heresy, at least from the standpoint of Christian tradition? If so, is a Christian, then, to remain a Christian by becoming a heretic? What can that mean? Recall Paul's teaching that if Christ is not risen, then the Christian's faith is in vain (see 1 Corinthians 15:14). What, then, is to become of faith? What can be higher than faith? Observance of Torah? Has the Christian *as Christian* not been "liberated" precisely from Torah (see Galatians 3:24–25)? If both Paul and the Eckardts are right, however, then Christianity must be grounded in something other than faith as the basis for the tradition. To be sure, the Eckardts seem to suggest that the Christian's faith *is* in vain and that there must be a tireless *laboring* for the resurrection, even though the one to be resurrected may tarry.

Here the Christians might learn something positive from the Jews, as Littell suggests.[51] For many Protestant Christians, there is no specific set of laws, outside of a moral code, that they must observe every day in order to claim that they are *practicing* Christians or that they are *working* for the coming of the Messiah.

A Jew, on the other hand, must wash his hands, give charity, study Scripture, put on tallit and tefillin, pray at certain times, watch what he eats, wear certain clothes, and observe an array of laws pertaining to the Sabbath and other occasions in order to claim to be a practicing Jew. For a practicing Jew, faith alone is not enough; it is not even primary, as the cry of the Israelites at Mount Sinai indicates: "[First] we will *do*, and [then] we will *hear*" (Exodus 24:7). After the Holocaust, faith can no longer be enough for a practicing Christian. James asserts that "faith without deeds is dead" (James 2:17), but a Christian has no *specific, divinely commanded* deed that he or she must perform on a daily basis to keep that faith alive, other than to treat one's neighbor with kindness—which, if observed, may well be enough. But is it enough to define the Christian as a Christian, that is, as someone following a tradition distinct from others? History seems to have shown that a Christian who cannot say, in concrete terms, how his daily actions set him apart from non-Christians may either fall deaf to the supplications of others or fall prey to the exhortations of Nazis. Here, contrary to Paul (for example, Romans 3:28), the Holocaust puts the Christian tradition in a position of having to justify itself *not* by faith alone.

A practicing Jew, moreover, has a profound sense of peoplehood and understands salvation not in personal terms but in communal terms; here too, Littell maintains, the Christians can learn something from the Jews.[52] As when Moses declared to God that if He should wipe out the Israelites, then He should erase Moses' own name from the Torah (see Exodus 32:32), the Jewish attitude is "Either we all shall enter the Kingdom, or no one will enter." One sees this stance in the Jewish concern for what befalls Jews, no matter where they may be in the world; the Jewish press and websites are full of information about attacks on Jews throughout Eastern and Western Europe, Muslim diatribes against the Jews, and the plight of the Israelis. Subsequently, Jewish federations and community centers throughout the world raise funds for Jews throughout the world. To be sure, wherever there are Jews there are Jewish community centers that stand very much apart from "denominational" affiliations; as it is written, "The people of Israel are compared to a lamb. What is the nature of the lamb? If it is hurt in one limb, all its limbs feel the pain" (*Mekilta de-Rabbi Ishmael, Bachodesh* 2). The Christians have nothing comparable with respect to the notion of *peoplehood* couched in this teaching—and that might be a threat to Christian tradition in the post-Holocaust era. Whether we set out to bring the Messiah or to bring the resurrection, surely it must be a communal affair.

For the Jews, moreover, the community of salvation includes "all the nations of the earth," for whose sake God enters into the Covenant with Abraham (Genesis 12:3) and for whose sake sacrifices were brought to the Temple during Sukkot—not so that the nations should convert to Judaism but so that the peoples of the world may treat each other with loving-kindness (see *Sukkah* 55b). But where in any Christian eschatology is there room for salvation for a humanity that remains outside of Christianity? Such a sense of Christian peoplehood and human salvation is generally absent among Christians. While the Vatican and regional churches have cried out against the Muslim attacks on Christians in Indonesia and the Philippines, among many Christians one hears little uproar, for example, over the Muslim assault on Christians in Kosovo, Nigeria, Central Asia, Ethiopia, and the Sudan, not to mention the West Bank. And certainly among Christians there is no teaching concerning salvation for those who are not adherents of Christianity. After the Holocaust, Christians can no longer understand salvation in strictly personal terms or in terms reserved only for Christians. After the Holocaust—and in the interest of Jewish-Christian dialogue—Christians may want to reexamine the teaching from Jesus saying, "I am the Way, the Truth, and the Life; no man comes unto the Father except through me" (14:6). But what does that mean for traditional Christian doctrine?

One can see that, in terms of the threat to their respective traditions, the post-Holocaust contexts for Jewish-Christian dialogue are complicated indeed. In order for that dialogue to have a future, Jews and Christians must have at least a rudimentary understanding of (1) their own traditions, (2) each other's tradition, and (3) the Holocaust's distinctive threat to both traditions. As it stands, all three areas are woefully lacking. In any case, what the foregoing has demonstrated is this: Neither party in the Jewish-Christian dialogue can proceed from a stance of business as usual. Both must come to terms with a serious threat to their respective traditions. But that is no easy matter either for the Jew or for the Christian. Still in its infancy, the dialogical relation between Jews and Christians may be more of an illusion than a reality.

THE ILLUSION OF RELATION

Any assessment of post-Holocaust Catholic-Jewish relations needs to distinguish between human relations on the one hand and theological inquiry on the other. Thus, one may correctly point to numerous improvements in the dialogical atmosphere, although these steps themselves reveal the ambiguity involved in dialogue on the lay level. For instance, there is a vast array of proclamations, pulpit exchanges, and fraternal interfaith gatherings. And, if truth be told, these meetings are far preferable to the hostility that marked earlier Catholic-Jewish relations. Perhaps if the Jewish people had had more friends during the Holocaust, the Nazi "yield" of Jewish victims would have been far less. Rabbi Leon Klenicki correctly observes that "dialogue involves more than 'tea and sympathy.'"[53]

The illusion that (almost) all is well between the two faith communities is nurtured by paradox. On the academic level, it is important to note the establishment of chairs of Jewish studies at several Catholic universities in America: for example, Notre Dame, the University of Scranton, and Georgetown University. Further, there are Jewish-Christian dialogue centers at various institutions of higher learning that help foster critical inquiry and scholarly participation in dialogue. We think here of the Center for Christian-Jewish Learning at Boston College, the Cardinal Bernardin Center at Catholic Theological Union, and the Sister Rose Thering Center at Seton Hall University, among others. Additionally, there are centers outside of university settings, such as the Graymoor Ecumenical & Interreligious Institute, the Tannenbaum Center for Interreligious Understanding, and the Institute for Jewish-Christian Understanding in Baltimore, under whose auspices *Dabru Emet* was issued (see chapter 5). These are places of serious study of the problems and possibilities attendant on Catholic-Jewish dialogue, places that seek to advance the discussion past the tea and sympathy stage.

Intellectuals who are associated with universities, Christian-Jewish centers, and Christian and Jewish agencies have given much time, thought, and effort to elevate the level of dialogue while addressing fundamental issues. These efforts have proven fruitful even when disagreement exists. As pointed out earlier, an interfaith scholars group rightly raised alarms over the script of the Mel Gibson film, noting its premodern and pre-Vatican II fundamentalism. Yet, even on this level there are issues that seem continually to challenge protestations of change.

Consider the panel discussion "Should Catholics Seek to Convert Jews (If Jews Are in True Covenant with God)?" based on *Reflections on Covenant and Mission* and sponsored by Boston College's Center for Christian-Jewish Learning and Theology Department (February 9, 2005). Seeking to convert Jews is incompatible with the Church's post–Vatican II profession of love and respect for Judaism, as well as its assertion that God's covenant with the Jewish people has not been abrogated. We wonder why this topic is even on the dialogical table forty years after *Nostra Aetate*. Further, what does this say about how Vatican pronouncements are viewed, accepted, rejected, or modified at the parish level?[54]

Earlier, the episodes of the Carmelite convent and the crosses planted at Auschwitz revealed in a dramatic and fundamental manner the theological flash points between Catholicism and Judaism. The convent, established at Auschwitz-Birkenau in 1984 in order that the nuns might pray for both the murdered and the murderers, demonstrated the difference in Christian and Jewish understanding of prayer while causing an enormous rift in Catholic-Jewish and Polish-Israel relations. David Patterson writes insightfully that for Christianity prayer is an *asking for*, and implies a retreat from the human community. Prayer in Judaism, however, is an encounter that is for the "redemption of the community." Prayer in Judaism eventuates in *mitzvot* (*commanded* deeds) performed in the world on behalf of humanity. The silence of the cloister's walls, however, is—from the standpoint of the victims—"the silence of indifference."[55]

The convent controversy was resolved only after a long period of diplomatic and political negotiations. Efforts at alleviating the tensions were led on the Catholic side by intellectuals such as Father Stanislaw Musial, S.J., and Cardinals Jean Marie Lustiger and Albert Decoutray of France. The Jewish partners included Rabbi René-Samuel Sirat, Markus Pardes, Professor Ady Steg, and Tulia Zevi. The International Jewish Committee on Interreligious Consultations, an umbrella group of various Jewish agencies and synagogue movements, was also involved in attempts to resolve the convent crisis. In the course of negotiations, ugly antisemitic epithets were uttered by the Polish primate, Cardinal Józef Glemp, and broadcasts on Radio Marja, the nationalistic radio station in Poland.

The crosses at Auschwitz were removed by decree of the Polish government after consultations with the Church. Unlike the Carmelite convent, however, Jewish representation was neither invited nor sought; rather, Polish Jewish leaders were informed of the decision. In neither instance were theological issues confronted. For example, the convent was moved from the perimeter of Auschwitz-Birkenau and an interfaith center was erected, but the different purposes of prayer were not addressed. The large cross, erected at a Catholic prayer center on the perimeter of Auschwitz-Birkenau and misidentified as the papal cross, is to be hidden behind a row of tall trees. Hiding is covering up rather than confronting the radically different Catholic and Jewish historical memories of the cross. The Church is still conflicted between premodern and modern worldviews concerning its history of supersession in relation to Judaism and to the face of the other.[56]

On the lay level, frequently the dialogue assumes the dimension of ecumenical cheerleading. This model is especially appropriate in the American context, where the myth of the Judeo-Christian tradition—as the late Arthur A. Cohen described it—prevails. According to Cohen, this myth rests on "a shallow rhetoric in which distinctions are fudged, diversities reconciled, differences overwhelmed by sloppy and sentimental approaches to falling in love after centuries of misunderstanding and estrangements."[57] Further, it advances the American ideals of religious pluralism and human relations, which tend to obfuscate the difference between social amity and dialogue over differences.

Alan Berger had the experience of attending an address by the president of an important American Catholic university. The event was held in south Florida in 2005. The audience was primarily composed of Catholic seminary students and Jewish communal leaders. The president outlined all the positive steps in Catholic-Jewish relations taken by Pope John Paul II: visiting the synagogue in Rome, diplomatic recognition of Israel, his visit to the Jewish state, and to Yad Vashem, and placing a note of apology in the Western Wall. Each of these actions is ecumenically and symbolically powerful. A local rabbi, long active in pulpit exchange with a Catholic priest, stood and told the audience how much he had learned about Judaism from teaching Catholic students. A Jewish communal leader then expressed the gratitude of the American Jewish Committee to the Vatican. Yet when Berger asked about the origin of the teaching of contempt, the president said that post–Vatican II Catholicism was interested in change. One Jewish member of the audience wondered why the questioner had "spoiled" the mood of the day.

In Europe as well the issue revolves around what is meant by dialogue. In May 2001, in the context of the inaugural March of Remembrance and Hope—an international gathering of nearly three hundred university students, the overwhelming majority of whom were non-Jews, who had come on a pilgrimage to Auschwitz-Birkenau and Majdanek—a meeting was held at the Center for Christian-Jewish Dialogue in Lublin, Poland. The topic was "Christian-Jewish Relations in the Twenty-first Century." The Archbishop of Lublin, Joseph Zycinski, and Alan Berger were the speakers. Archbishop Zycinski, echoing the greeting of Pope John XXIII to a delegation of visiting Jewish leaders, began by stating, "I am Joseph, your brother." The archbishop then told a tale of two young Jewish boys who had been hidden by Christians during the Shoah. The Jewish boys subsequently converted and became priests. Archbishop Zycinski's comments left the audience wondering if this is the model outcome of Jewish-Christian dialogue.

Various European countries have proclaimed a "Day of Judaism." Ostensibly this is an occasion for educating the population about the history and culture of the Jewish people and to emphasize the Jewish origin of Christianity. The idea originated with nuns in the Our Lady of Sion (Notre-Dame of Sion, or NDS) order. Italy was the first country to have such a day. Poland also marks the occasion. However, the events of this day typically are by and for the intellectuals. Moreover, the extent of involvement of the populace is dependant on the attitude of local parish priests, some of whom do not accept the Church's new ecumenical teachings. The rise of antisemitic statements and actions in Europe coupled with the lack of official response on the part of the Church hierarchy are not encouraging signs.

On the local level many communities have signed interfaith agreements. The one in Rochester, New York, is illustrative. The Jewish-Catholic agreement of that city, signed in 1996, specifies five points of common concern:

1. Education, where churches and synagogues open their doors to children of the other faith.

2. Priests and rabbis meet regularly, but largely refrain from discussing theological matters.

3. Joint statements are issued calling for social justice.

4. The directors of Catholic and Jewish social agencies meet.

5. The executive director of the Jewish Federation and the bishop of Rochester (or their appointees) meet regularly.

We obviously have no quarrel with the desire to feed the hungry, shelter the homeless, and clothe the naked. Social justice, issues of war and peace, and a clean environment are all necessary and desirable goals for human beings sharing an increasingly overcrowded planet. David Patterson contends, in fact, that by putting the *mitzvah* at the center, "the question guiding Jewish-Christian dialogue is not 'How can we serve one another?' but rather 'How can we help each other serve those whom God's love commands us to serve?'—to serve by feeding, clothing, sheltering, comforting, and healing bodies" (rather than souls).[58] Moreover, even contentious matters such as abortion, stem cell research, and school vouchers have demonstrated that Catholic-Jewish dialogue can be, on one level, maintained and prove educational. But mature dialogue needs to grapple with fundamental theological differences such as the nature of God, the meaning of prayer, the issue of evil, and the continuing presence of antisemitism. Further, the centrality of Israel is an issue that, despite the Vatican's political recognition of the Jewish state, continues to be a lightning rod for misunderstanding in the dialogue.

The move for divestment on the part of mainline Protestant churches such as the Presbyterian Church and the United Church of Christ (UCC) illustrates both a lack of awareness of Israel's significance for Judaism, as well as for Christianity, and the continued influence of deicide imagery. We wonder why the Protestant churches single out Israel for censure and say nothing about Muslim pogroms against Christians in the West Bank. While no state is above criticism for its various policy decisions, there is a profound difference between criticism motivated by love—the motive of the Hebrew prophets—and criticism based either on ignorance or on antisemitic stereotypes.

Naim Ateek, former canon of St. George's Cathedral in Jerusalem, and now president of the Sabeel Center, a Palestinian Christian group, is a case in point that illustrates how easily antisemites can distort legitimate issues. In remarks to a recent UCC General Synod meeting, Ateek compared Israeli officials to Herod, who sought to kill the baby Jesus. He also claimed that Israeli officials are "crucifying" the Palestinians.[59] In 2001 this same individual likened Israeli occupation to the "stone placed on the entrance to Jesus' tomb."[60] Historically, this type of language has been used to incite violence against Jews. That an antisemite such as Ateek uses such incendiary and false language is deplorable and unacceptable. That liberal Protestant churches accept this hate speech bears powerful witness to the power of deicide imagery despite myriad Christian proclamations absolving the Jewish people from this canard. The rhetoric of contempt needs to be challenged. Christian churches should not again be silent. Speaking out against and rejecting antisemitism *in deed* is infinitely more significant than the issuance of proclamations.

The Sabeel "theology" is a twenty-first-century restatement of the old Christian replacement theology. Rabbi Eugene Korn, former Jewish affairs director of the now defunct American Jewish Congress, attests that the Palestinian group reinterprets God's covenant with the Jewish people as "a metaphor for God protecting and helping the weak. In biblical times, this meant the Jews. Now—according to Ateek and his ilk—it refers to the Palestinians."[61] This blatant stealing of the Jewish narrative—some call it "storycide"—is a familiar theme of Christian antisemitism, now utilized in the service of attempting to delegitimize the Jewish state. Many Jewish leaders of the antidivestment struggle view the 2001 conference on racism and xenophobia held in Durban, South Africa, under United Nations auspices as legitimizing the divestment movement. The conference was in reality a forum for antisemitism and attacks on Israel, complete with copies of *The Protocols of the Elders of Zion* made available to participants.

We have noted the asymmetry between Christianity and Judaism both in terms of demography and theology. Here we need to state an additional, psychological, consideration. Richard Rubenstein pointed out long ago a fundamental difference between Christians and Jews concerning the Holocaust. "Every Jew," observes Rubenstein, "says of the Shoah, 'It happened to us.' For non-Jews, the Shoah is something that happened to another people."[62] This is an inescapable, even if unarticulated, datum of Jewish identity, an identity for which one paid with one's life no matter their embrace or rejection of the tradition. One lesson for mature dialogue emerges from this observation. A dialogue worthy of the name must acknowledge the reality of this asymmetry while simultaneously seeking to honestly grapple with its contemporary implications. These implications are at least fourfold:

1. There is the need for a clear articulation of the centrality of Israel for Judaism. This means an acknowledgment of Jewish rootedness in history, which, in turn,

necessitates understanding that if Israel had existed during the Holocaust, millions of Jewish lives would have been saved rather than murdered.

2. There is the degree of trust that the Jewish partners can legitimately bring to dialogue. In this case it is helpful to recall that Paul Ricouer spoke of a "hermeneutic of suspicion" as being appropriate for the postmodern world.

3. There is the issue of the continuing scourge of antisemitism and its attendant charge of deicide. Pope John Paul II declared antisemitism "sinful" yet it is far from being eradicated and requires conscientious and continuous effort to combat.

4. There is the ever present temptation of supersession on the part of the Church as it grapples with the role of Jesus and the ongoing validity of the Jewish covenant.

The dialogue at this historical moment must navigate between suspicion and trust in the face of official promulgations whose messages are contradictory. Respect and love for Judaism cannot be reconciled with the attestations of *Dominus Ieus*, even though most view this document authored by Cardinal Joseph Ratzinger before he became Pope Benedict XVI as directed against Asian non-Christian religions. Nor can respect for the Jewish tradition be fostered by discussions on the desirability or necessity of evangelizing the Jews. Forty years, a biblical generation, of post-Auschwitz dialogue may be viewed as a preliminary step for both partners. Progress has been made, but much more needs to be accomplished. Any such accomplishments will, however, need to seriously grapple with differences more than with similarities. For it is the differences that define us and that will ultimately determine how far the dialogue can advance while the partners seek a deeper understanding of their own beliefs, as well as an understanding of the plausibility of the belief system of the other.

THREE

HISTORICAL CONSIDERATIONS FROM A JEWISH PERSPECTIVE

If Jewish-Christian dialogue is to take a next step, then each party must understand more clearly how the other perceives the historical contexts for the dialogue. Such an understanding should enable each to see where there other is "coming from" with regard to the premise and the perspective that shape the discourse of both. Here we shall consider ways in which some Jews might view some of the Christian historical contexts that may elude Christian thinking. To be sure, for reasons outlined below, Jews may be in a better position to explore certain historical contexts of Christianity than many Christians are, simply because Christians are so deeply embedded in the internal structures of their own tradition. This point, of course, cuts both ways: The position of an outsider may help anyone operating within a tradition to attain a broader view of that tradition. Therefore it is possible that a Christian view of the historical contexts of Judaism might also prove helpful to the Jews. In any case, it is in the spirit of attaining a better understanding of one another that we now proceed.

First of all, history is central to the ways in which Jews view anything. When encountering any tradition, including our own, we ask: What is the story of that tradition? In the Book of Deuteronomy, in fact, the Torah relates the history of its own unfolding, so that the *history* of Torah is part of the *revelation* of Torah. The Torah includes its own history because the Torah is about meaning in life, and meaning is rooted in time. To have a sense of meaning is to have a sense of direction, and to have a sense of direction is to move toward a horizon that we have *yet* to attain. Thus storytelling, at least with regard to sacred tradition, is as much about the future as it is about the past. Why does Moses relate to the Israelites the history of Torah? So that they may bear that history and that memory into the land where they will dwell *in the future*. History, then, narrates a past that has *already* transpired for the sake of a future that is *yet to be* decided. The historical consciousness of the Jewish people is a consciousness of the future: Jewishly speaking, history is a memory of the future, precisely because it is a memory of the Covenant of Torah. To enter into the Covenant of Torah is to engage a task that is forever before us.

André Neher argues that "the history of mankind *receives its meaning* by the intimacy of God and Israel."[1] Therefore "the human situation in history begins with the covenant."[2] The Covenant of Torah finds its fulfillment in a future redemption attained through Torah. Thus understood, history is made of a certain anticipation of a messianic time; it is made of a certain mode of *waiting*, which is a *doing* that paves the way for the Messiah. Constituted not by spirit but by a strife of the spirit, the Jewish concern with history is much more than a chronological sequence of reported facts: It is a history of the interaction, of the wrestling, between God and humanity, as that interaction unfolds in human affairs. Hence the name *Israel*, which means: "one who strives with God." Viewed Jewishly, "history is the encounter of the eternal and the temporal," as Abraham Joshua Heschel states it. "Just as the Word is a veil for revelation and a sign for prayer, so history may form a vessel for God's action in the world and provides the material out of which man's doing in time is fashioned."[3] History, then, is a major thread in the fabric of Jewish thought, words, and deeds, all of which make up the material of God's *levushim*, of God's clothing. From a Jewish standpoint—and later from a Christian standpoint—history is *sacred* history. Which means: history is a manifestation of the divine.

A glance at the holy calendar will illustrate this point. Passover is a remembrance of the Jewish people's emergence from Egypt, Shavuot is a remembrance of the revelation of Torah to the Jewish people, Chanukah is a remembrance of the rededication of the Temple that had been desecrated by the Greeks, and Purim is a remembrance of the deliverance of the Jewish people from extermination in Persia. The Ninth of Av is a remembrance of various catastrophes in Jewish history, from the destruction of the First Temple in 586 BCE to the destruction of the Second Temple in 70 CE to the expulsion of the Jews from Spain in 1492; the Fast of Gedaliah is a remembrance of the assassination of Gedaliah ben Achikam, the last of the "righteous ones" in the time of Nebuchadnezzar; and Lag BaOmer is a remembrance of the death of the great sage Shimon bar Yochai, as well as the day when a plague was lifted from Rabbi Akiva's disciples. Thus, like the Jewish Scriptures, the Jewish liturgy is steeped in memory and spans centuries of concrete events in the multimillennial life of the Jewish people. And, from the standpoint of Jewish history, the liturgy makes every Jew contemporary with these events, as well as with a future redemption. On the holy day we are contemporaneous with all time.

Thus understood in terms of a memory of the future, the Jewish concern for history is a concern for the redemption *yet* to be attained with the advent of the Messiah. Because Jews view that redemption as yet to be attained, Jews remain deeply situated in time, and time is understood in human terms. The holy calendar, for instance, measures time not from the first day of creation but from the sixth day, from the moment of the creation of the first human being. Jewishly speaking, time unfolds within human relationship, and in a relationship there is always something *yet* to be said, to be determined, to be accomplished. Living in a relationship with God, where that relationship rests primarily on deeds and not on faith, a human being must *change*, and time is made of that change. The Hebrew word for "year," *shanah*, in fact, has the same root as the verb "to change," *lishnot*. And the issue begins with Adam. It begins with the need for redemption.

Christian doctrine, by contrast, invokes the Second Adam, with whom time begins and ends through the offering up of his blood, which has *already* attained redemption for us all. With that *already*, history is consummated. Thus the Christian calendar dates from a new time, the time of *Anno Domini*, the Year of Our Lord. Which, historically speaking, is nontime, insignificant time, empty time, since his kingdom is no longer of this time and space, "not of this world," as it is written (John 18:36). In the Christian Scriptures, liturgies, and holy day observances, therefore, history plays a more minor role, at least any history that takes place after the advent of the Messiah. And understandably so: From a Christian standpoint, time may begin but history surely ends with the coming of the Messiah. Between now and the last days, we do not live time—we mark time. For the drama of redemption is over, as declared from the cross: "It is finished" (John 19:30).

For a Christian, then, the interest lies much more in the story of "our Lord" than in the history of a people. In fact, there is no Christian "people," that is, no Christian "nation" with a common tie to anything as concrete as a common land, a common language, or a common ancestry. No college or university has a course on the history of the "Christian people," but many have courses on the history of the Jewish people. From a Christian viewpoint, any time that unfolds after the resurrection, what Heschel calls "man's doing in time," is superfluous; when Jesus vanquished sin and death, time itself was conquered and all that is needful to redemption was accomplished. Jews, on the other hand, await and work for the coming of a Messiah whose kingdom is very much of this world; deeply situated in time, Jews take history to be a defining dimension of religious life. And so a Jew may raise questions and bring to the Jewish-Christian dialogue considerations that perhaps are not so central to Christian consciousness.

A Jew, for example, cannot forget that his or her ancestor Jesus was a religious Jew of the Second Temple period. A Jew will ask, "How did he live? Who were his teachers? And what does his teaching have to do with Torah?" In the past, Christians have generally deemed such questions to be irrelevant: The important thing is to believe in him, so that you may have everlasting life, as stated in John 3:16. When a Jew reads the Christian Scriptures, he or she is not interested in attaining faith or arriving at a belief—not because they are not Jewish but because life is attained through the observance of Torah, not through a belief in the Redeemer. Therefore a Jew seeks the tension between revelation and history, between divine commandments and human events, between what is taught and how we live.

From the tension between the tale intended to inspire belief and the narrative of historical events, there emerged in the history of Christianity the development of Christian myth[4] and the formulation of Christian doctrine. Because the creed—that is, the content of belief—is emphasized more in Christianity than it is in Judaism, the latter had no specific statement of its principles of faith until the twelfth century, when Maimonides listed the Thirteen Principles of Faith in Judaism. This development, which happened more than two thousand years after the advent of Judaism, came only when historical circumstance made it necessary: Maimonides listed the Thirteen Principles in the light of Christian and Muslim efforts to forcibly proselytize Jews, as a kind of countercreed. With regard to the Christian creed, Jews understand that, inasmuch as Christianity takes itself to *supersede* Judaism, it *has to oppose* Judaism; the question remains, however, as to whether there is a difference between Christianity's theological anti-Judaism and its historical antisemitism.

In this chapter we shall consider these historical matters that form a vast background to Jewish-Christian dialogue. We shall briefly explore the Jewish life and the Jewish teachings of Jesus as well as the tensions between history and myth. From that tension the Christian doctrine is born; the question we shall examine is whether or not that doctrine has to be anti-Judaic, if not antisemitic. The perspective presented here is admittedly Jewish. It is likely that Christians will have a different perspective. In any case, our hope is that this Jewish perspective will add depth to the Jewish-Christian dialogue. Indeed, the differences in perspectives are essential to this dialogue that seeks a next step.

THE JEWISH JESUS

A certain convert from Christianity to Judaism once had to address some concerns from his family regarding his conversion, even though his family was quite supportive of his decision to become a Jew. In the course of his discussions with his parents, one day his mother said to him, "I know you are converting to Judaism. But you still believe in Jesus, don't you?"

Wanting to honor his mother and at the same time honor the truth, he answered, "Well, I've simply decided to follow the religion that Jesus followed."

And his mother replied, "Oh, I think that's wonderful!"

The historical Jesus is shrouded in mystery. But one thing is fairly clear: Jesus of Nazareth, the one whom the Christians deem the "Christ," was a practicing, observant, religious Jew. While most Christians are on some level aware of this fact, it seldom occurs to them that they do not follow the religion that the defining figure of Christianity followed; indeed, throughout their history they have deprecated his religion and murdered his coreligionists. Zoroaster was in some sense a Zoroastrian, Confucius a Confucian, Lao-tzu a Taoist, the Buddha a Buddhist, Muhammad a Muslim, and Moses a Jew. There are, of course, certain nuances among these and other founding figures of various religions with regard to their connections to the traditions they established. But most of them were in some sense adherents of the religion associated with them. Not so with Jesus and Christianity: In no sense was he a Christian.

While Judaism and Christianity are quite different in their understanding of God, humanity, and Messiah (as will be shown in the next chapter), Jews have a tie with the flesh-and-blood person of the Christian Messiah that Christians do not have. Jews know Jesus "from within," in the words of Martin Buber, "in the impulses and stirrings of his Jewish being, in a way that remains inaccessible to the peoples submissive to him [that is, to the Christians]."[5] Having some notion of "the impulses and stirrings of his Jewish being," Jews know perhaps more intimately the anguish that Jesus must have felt in a Hellenized, Romanized world hostile toward Jews and Judaism. He knew the stories of how Jews turned from Torah to follow Greek and

Roman ways, of how they traded God for power, prayer for fashion, and loving-kindness for self-interest. This conflict in the Jewish world, in fact, dated from the time of Antiochus Epiphanes, whose attempts to force Greek ways upon the Jews led to the Hasmonean revolt against the Greek Seleucid rule in 165 BCE When the Hasmoneans fell from power with the entry of the Romans into Jerusalem in 37 BCE, the old animosity between Greek and Hebrew thinking arose once more. After all, with regard to their cultural and philosophical outlook, the Romans were themselves fundamentally Greek.

Generally speaking, religiously observant Jews have some sense of how deeply devoted to Torah Jesus must have been, and they comprehend more thoroughly than most Christians the Hebrew and Aramaic languages that shaped the Nazarene's thinking. They know about his *mezuzah* and his *tzitzit*, his *tallit* and his *tefillin*, his immersions involving the *mikveh* and *tevilat kelim*, his adherence to *kashrut* and the *menuchah* of *Shabbat*, his concern for *muksah* and *shatnetz*, for *terumot* and *maaserot*, his devotion to *brit milah* and *pidyon haben*, his preparations for Pesach and Sukkot, his observance of Shavuot and Yom Kippur, his awareness of the meaning of the Temple and the high priests' departure from that meaning—everything that defined Jesus as a Jew who knew all too well the history of the threat of Greek and Roman oppression to the Jewish way of life from Antiochus to Pompey. The Jews see him as one who tried to return Jews to Judaism and who, like many others, was murdered by the Romans. They know him as the one called Yehoshua, the son of Yosef and Miriam, who was circumcised on the eighth day of his tragic life and who studied Torah, the prophets, and the writings. Just as a proselytizing Christian might approach a Jew and ask, "Do you know Jesus?" so might the Jew reply, "Do *you* know Jesus?"

To remove from Jesus these dimensions of his religious life is to remove what was essential to who he was. As for any devout adherent of any religion, his religion *was* his life. Can a Christian—or anyone else, for that matter—have any sense of who Jesus was and ignore the Jewish Jesus? After all, what Christian or any other person would say, "Yes, so-and-so knows me very well," if so-and-so knew nothing of his or her religion? Can anyone imagine the Lubavitcher Rebbe saying, "Yes, so-and-so knows me very well, but he does not know I am a Chasidic Jew"? To the extent that Christians know little or nothing of the life he lived, the language he spoke, the teachers he had, the texts he studied, or the religion he followed *as a Jew*, in what sense can they be said to know Jesus at all? Many Christians would say, "I know Jesus as my Redeemer, the Son of God, who was crucified and rose from the dead to conquer sin and death for my sake. And that is all I need to know." But was Jesus not also a flesh-and-blood human being who followed a certain way—a *Jewish* way—of concrete, everyday life? Can anyone who wants to have a relation with him ignore that? If Judaism is Christianity's "elder brother,"[6] the elder may have something to teach the younger in this regard, beginning with how the younger may recognize the elder.

In recent years an increasing number of Christians have become increasingly sensitive to this matter. Partly due to the development of a fledgling Jewish-Christian dialogue, some Christians have sought to know Jesus "from within," as a Jew. In the area of scholarship, the interest in the Jewish Jesus can be seen in numerous works, many of which have come from Christian authors.[7] Realizing more profoundly that Jesus was a Jew circumcised according to the commandments of Torah (see Luke 2:21), Christians hold Passover Seders to acquire a better sense of what the Last Supper might have been like, at least on a liturgical level. There are even some who try to live as Jesus lived, that is, as an observant Jew, following the commandments of Torah, observing the holy calendar, and using Hebrew words, phrases, and even prayers. Much of this Jewish observance among Christians, however, comes from Jews who have converted to Christianity, such as those who belong to Brit Hadashah congregations.[8] In unprecedented numbers Christian students enroll in Jewish studies courses to learn more about who the Jews are and who Jesus was; they learn Hebrew to better understand what the Scriptures so important to Jesus really said, and they travel to Israel, the Jewish state, to see where the Jewish Jesus actually walked. Instead of setting out to convert Jews to Christianity, more and more churches are inviting Jews to come teach them about Judaism. For both Christians and

Jews, knowing something more about the Jewish Jesus might enhance Jewish-Christian dialogue.

Searching for the Jewish Jesus actually requires very little detective work. In fact, we need look no further than the Gospels. Living in the first century CE, Jesus was very likely a disciple of the Pharisees of the House of Hillel and lived in such a way as to emulate Hillel's Pharisaic teachings. If the words ascribed to Him in the Gospels were His words, then a reading of the Gospels suggests that Jesus received from his teachers the Oral Torah, which includes Mishnah, Midrash, and Kabbalah. The teachings transmitted through the mishnaic tradition were elaborated upon in the Gemara, so that here too, in the Gemara or Talmud, one finds a great deal of resonance with many of the teachings attributed to Jesus. When Jesus upbraids the Pharisees as hypocrites (Matthew 23), for example, it is not because they were living as Pharisees—just the opposite: It is because in truth they were *not* living as Pharisees, that is, they were not living according to the Pharisaic teachings that they preached. That is what it means to be a hypocrite. To be sure, the teachings of Jesus were in large part Pharisaic teachings.

In keeping with the Pharisees, for example, he taught, "Whoever relaxes one of the least of the commandments and teaches men so, shall be called least in the kingdom of heaven; but he who does them and teaches them shall be called great in the kingdom of heaven" (Matthew 5:19).[9] Jesus' insistence upon teaching and observing even the least of the commandments of Torah—an insistence that was soon lost among the Christians— is very similar to what we receive from the oral tradition: "One who studies Torah in order to teach is given the means to study and to teach; and one who studies in order to practice is given the means to study and to teach, to observe and to practice" (*Mishnah Avot* 4:6). Although uncharacteristic of Christianity, the observant Jew Jesus emphasizes the meticulous adherence to all the commandments of Torah. Contrary to Paul, who was among the first to de-Judaize Jesus and his teachings, in this verse from the Gospel of Matthew it appears that the Jew from Nazareth has opened our eyes to the blessings of the law, rather than "redeemed us from the curse of the Law" (Galatians 3:13). For it is precisely the Law—the Torah, which is the "Tree of

Life" (see, for example, Proverbs 3:18)—that sanctifies life, and, as Matthew 5:19 suggests, Jesus almost certainly shared this view. He surely knew this teaching.

Regarding life's sanctity, just as Jesus taught that "the Sabbath was made for man, not man for the Sabbath" (Mark 2:27), so the Oral Torah teaches that "man shall live by the laws of the Sabbath, not die by them" (*Yoma* 85b). Just as Jesus taught that "a man's life does not consist in the abundance of his possessions" (Luke 12:15), so the Oral Torah teaches that "blessing is not found in something weighed, nor in something measured, nor in something counted, but in something hidden from the eye" (*Bava Metzia* 42a). When reading Jesus' teaching that the kingdom of God is made of the likes of little children (Luke 18:16), a Jew cannot help but recall the midrashic teaching that only where there are children is there holiness (see *Eichah Rabbah* 1:6:33). And when reading the story of the accused adulteress and Jesus' admonition, "Let him among you who is without sin cast the first stone" (John 8:7), a Jew cannot help but recall the admonition from the Oral Torah, according to which only one who is pure can accuse a woman of adultery (see *Kiddushin* 27b).

Throughout the Gospels there are many other examples of how the reported teachings of Jesus are in keeping with the teachings of the Oral Torah. For our purposes, however, let us consider just a few teachings from the Sermon on the Mount (Matthew 5:1–7:27) and their parallel teachings in the Oral Torah:

1. "Blessed are those who mourn, for they shall be comforted" (5:4), and "God counts tears shed for a worthy man and stores them in His treasure house" (*Shabbat* 105b).

2. "Blessed are the meek, for they shall inherit the earth" (5:5), and "Those who have a humble spirit and a meek soul are among the disciples of our forefather Abraham" (*Mishnah Avot* 5:22).

3. "Blessed are the peacemakers, for they shall be called children of God" (5:9), and "Hillel says: Be among the

disciples of Aaron, loving peace and pursuing peace, loving people." (*Mishnah Avot* 1:12).

4.   "Let your light shine through before men, that they may see your good works and give glory to your Father who is in heaven" (5:16), and "I place in you a lamp, therefore you are commanded to light the lamp and let it shine" (*Shabbat* 32a).

5.   "You have heard it said, You shall not commit adultery. But I say to you that every one who looks at a woman lustfully has already committed adultery with her in his heart" (5:27–28), and "Resh Lakish said: Do not suppose that only he who has committed the crime with his body is called an adulterer. If he commits adultery with his eyes he is also called an adulterer" (*Vayikra Rabbah* 23:12).

6.   "Let what you say be simply Yes or No; anything more than this comes from evil" (5:37), and "Rabbi Chuna said in the name of Rabbi Samuel ben Isaac: The *yes* of the righteous is *yes*, and their *no* is *no*" (*Ruth Rabbah* 7:6).

7.   "Love your enemies" (5:44), and "Shmuel HaKattan says: When your enemy falls be not glad" (*Mishnah Avot* 4:24). And: "If a passerby finds his friend needs help to unload a fallen animal, and his enemy needs help to load an animal, his first obligation is to his enemy, in order to subdue his own evil inclination" (*Bava Metzia* 32b).

8.   "When you give alms, do not let your left hand know what your right hand is doing, so that your alms may be in secret" (6:3–4), and "The highest form of charity is in secret" (*Bava Batra* 10a–b).

9.   "Do not lay up for yourselves treasures on earth, where moth and worm consume and where thieves

break in and steal" (6:19), and "Hillel used to say: The more flesh, the more worms; the more possessions, the more worry" (*Mishnah Avot* 2:8).

10. "With the judgment you pronounce you will be judged, and the measure you give will be the measure you get" (7:2), and "He who judges his neighbor in a scale of merit is himself judged favorably" (*Shabbat* 129b). And: "In the measure with which a man measures, it is meted out to him" (*Mishnah Sotah* 1:7).

11. "Whatever you wish that men do to you, do so to them; for this is the law and the prophets" (7:12), and "Said Hillel, What is hateful to you, do not do to your neighbor. This is the whole Torah" (*Shabbat* 31a).

12. "Those who hear these teachings and do them are wise; those who do not do them are not wise" (see 7:24–27), and "If your good deeds exceed your wisdom, your wisdom will endure; if your wisdom exceeds your good deed, your wisdom will not endure" (*Mishnah Avot* 3:11).

There is more. In Matthew 18:20, it is written, "Where two or three are gathered in my name, there I am in the midst of them"; compare this to the passage in the Talmud, where the sages state, "If two are sitting and studying the Torah together, the Divine Presence is with them" (*Berakhot* 6a)—and studying Torah entails living Torah. In Mark 12:42–43 we have the story of the widow's mite, teaching that a poor woman who gives less than a rich man in fact gives more; compare this to the passage in the Midrash, where we are told, "God views the poor man's gift as if he had given his life" (*Midrash HaGadol* 2:1). And in Luke 12:3 it is written, "What you have whispered in the dark will be heard in the light"; compare this to "Do not speak what cannot be heard, for in the end it will be heard" (*Mishnah Avot* 2:5). These are but a few illustrations of the Jewish essence of the Nazarene's teachings.

Neither Jews nor Christians should find it so incredible that in the first century CE the Jew Jesus, who learned from Jewish teachers, might have taught these Jewish lessons to his Jewish followers. Like many Jewish teachers who over the centuries have sought to revitalize Judaism, it seems that Jesus urged Jews to embrace their Judaism on a deeper, more intense level, to return to their teachings and their traditions—to make a movement of *teshuvah*—rather than abandon the Covenant of Torah in favor of a new covenant. Knowing very well the Torah's teaching that "you shall not add to the word that I have commanded you, nor shall you take away from it" (Deuteronomy 4:2), the notion of a New Covenant or New Testament would very likely have been unintelligible, if not utterly unacceptable, to Jesus, as it would have been to any religious Jew. From a Jewish perspective on the historical contexts, it looks as though others, who for whatever reason may have been interested in formulating a new teaching or a new movement, might have conflated historical account and theological dictum in the process of composing what would become the Christian Scriptures. Still, scriptural texts are not history books. Although history is indispensable to religious testimony, the aim of Scripture is not so much to record an accurate report of events as it is to sound the depths of the soul in its relation to God and humanity. Because Scripture, therefore, sets out to articulate the ineffable, it often relies on mythological accounts of historical events. The Christian Scriptures are no exception.

HISTORY AND MYTH

No one who rightly understands the Gospels takes them for a mere history book. Although the truth of the Gospels must rest upon a historical truth, like any other Scriptures, they are more about the life of the soul than about the history of an individual or of a period. For a Christian, that is the whole point of engaging the Gospels: to seek the salvation of the soul through a belief in Jesus as Christ and Savior, not to gather information about a Jew from the Galilee or to learn a history lesson.

There are, however, texts referring to Jesus that are intended to transmit a certain history. The first Roman authors to mention Jesus, for example, are the historians Tacitus and Suetonius. But the most notable historical account of Jesus from the period is the *Testimonium Flavium* of Josephus Flavius in his *Jewish Antiquities*. The writing of the *Jewish Antiquities* dates from the early 90s CE, some sixty years after the death of Jesus. Written without the benefit of other historical accounts or documents, it is likely based more on sixty years of popular perception than on archival research. Interestingly, in his history titled *The Jewish War*, written shortly after the destruction of the Temple in the year 70 CE, Josephus makes no mention of Jesus or John the Baptist or any other of the major figures in the Christian Gospels. And in the extant editions of the work, it appears that the *Jewish Antiquities* was edited by later Christians to suit the Christian doctrine.

This is what Josephus is alleged to have said about the historical Jesus:

> Now there was about this time Jesus, a wise man *if it be lawful to call him a man,* for he was a doer of wonders, *a teacher of such men as receive the truth with pleasure.* He drew many after him *both of the Jews and the Gentiles. He was the Christ.* When Pilate, *at the suggestion of the principal men among us* [that is, the Jews], had condemned him to the cross, those that loved him at first did not forsake him, *for he appeared to them alive again the third day, as the divine prophets had foretold these and a thousand other wonderful things about him,* and the tribe of Christians, so named from him, are not extinct at this day. (*Antiquities* 18:63–64)

The portions of this quote written in italics are what James Tabor identifies as "likely interpolations added by Christian copyists over the centuries in an attempt to make Josephus support faith in Jesus as the Christ."[10] Indeed, there is no evidence from Josephus or anyone else from the period to suggest that the Jewish historian was a Christian. Not surprisingly, some of the interpolations that Tabor refers to entail the reinforcement of the deicide charge against the Jews.

Among the Christian cultures, the oldest existing editions of Josephus's text are three Greek manuscripts dating from the eleventh century. Just as interesting from the historical standpoint is the tenth-century Arabic translation of the same passage from Josephus's *Antiquities*: "At this time there was a wise man who was called Jesus, and his conduct was good, and he was known to be virtuous. And many people from among the Jews and other nations became his disciples. Pilate condemned him to be crucified and to die. And those who had become his disciples did not abandon their loyalty to him. They reported that he had appeared to them three days after his crucifixion, and that he was alive. Accordingly they believed that he was the Messiah, concerning whom the Prophets have recounted wonders."[11] Whereas the Christian version places the blame for the execution of the Nazarene on "the principal men among us," namely the Jews, who "suggested" to Pilate that he should crucify Jesus, the Muslim version simply states that "Pilate condemned him to be crucified." Of course, like the Christians, the Muslim redactors of Josephus may have had their own agenda. Still, they appear to leave intact Josephus's comment on the crucifixion of Jesus, even though the Koran denies that his crucifixion ever took place (see *Sura* 4:157).

The Talmud also contains an account of a certain figure whom some have taken to be Jesus. He is called "Yeshu," an acronym for *yemach shemo vezikhro*, meaning "may his name and memory be obliterated." The name, of course, is similar to *Yeshua*, the Aramaic name of Jesus. According to one talmudic account, a certain Yeshu was arrested for sorcery and for inciting others to renounce Judaism. Because he had connections with Roman officials, the government spent forty days seeking witnesses to speak on his behalf. When no one stepped forward, he was stoned to death on the eve of Passover. But nowhere in any account of Jesus is there any indication that he incited anyone to renounce Judaism, that he had connections with Roman officials, or that he was stoned to death. The same account mentions five disciples—Matai, Nekai, Netzer, Buni, and Todah—who were also executed (see *Sanhedrin* 43a). Here too there is no resemblance to any other sources about Jesus and his disciples. Another talmudic passage thought to refer to

Jesus is a single line from the sage Shimon ben Azzai, who said, "I found in Jerusalem a book of genealogies; therein it was written that a certain man was the bastard son of a married woman" (*Yevamot* 49a). But, while Jesus may have been conceived prior to Mary's marriage to Joseph, there is no indication that he was the illegitimate child of a married woman. Therefore it would seem that these sources do not refer to Jesus.

More frequently regarded as Jesus is the disciple of Joshua ben Perachiah, who was also called "Yeshu"; the medieval sage Judah Halevi, for instance, mentions him in the *Kuzari* as Jesus of Nazareth, a student of Joshua ben Perachiah (*Kitav al khazari* 3:65). Joshua ben Perachiah's teacher was Yose ben Yochanan, the religious leader of Jerusalem, who in turn was a disciple of Antigos of Socho, a sage whose teachings were echoed in the teachings of Jesus. For instance, he taught, "Let your house be open wide, and treat the poor as members of your household" (*Mishnah Avot* 1:5). Under the reign of Alexander Yannai (103–76 BCE), Joshua ben Perachiah was forced to flee to Alexandria, and his disciple Yeshu followed him. When they were able to return to Judea, Joshua ben Perachiah dismissed his disciple Yeshu for judging a woman solely by her physical appearance (*Sotah* 47a; *Sanhedrin* 107b). The dating alone, however, would preclude the identification of Joshua ben Perachiah's errant disciple as the historical Jesus. Once again, it appears that what has often been taken to be a talmudic reference to the historical Jesus is not.

Exactly what can be said about the historical Jesus is subject to much speculation. But we do know something about the time in which he lived (he died around 30 CE at about thirty-three years of age). The Roman conquest of Jerusalem in 37 BCE brought to an end approximately 120 years of an independent Jewish rule of Judea under the Hasmoneans. The Romans appointed Herod king of Judea, and Herod cooperated fully with his benefactors. Because Herod ruled according to the will of the Romans, and not in keeping with Torah, his appointment created considerable resentment among the Jews of Judea. The Sanhedrin lost its political power, and Herod's love for pomp and splendor imitated the inclinations of all the Hellenistic kings in the east. Herod was a builder of cities and elaborate buildings, among which was the newly renovated Temple, so that when he died in 4 BCE, he left behind a vast legacy of engineering and architectural accomplishment. His death was followed, however, by internal political turmoil; subsequently the region came under a more direct Roman rule.

Under the Roman procurators, the Jews enjoyed some measure of autonomy, particularly in their religious affairs, as long as they remained peaceful. There are no reports of widespread bloodshed until the reign of Pontius Pilate (26–36 CE). From Pilate onward, however, messianic ferment and messianic movements, including apocalyptic visions of the last days, became increasingly prevalent and increasingly violent. At the time Judea was teeming with a variety of religious movements and political factions, including the aristocratic Sadducees, the oral-tradition-based Pharisees, the mystically inclined Essenes, and the politically militant Zealots. It was in such a climate of religious and political turmoil that Jesus appeared on the scene.

The texts that contain the most elaborate accounts of Jesus are, of course, the Gospels. But, as already noted, the Gospels are Scriptures, not historical accounts. Therefore the Gospels contain much in the way of myth and symbol, of allegory and parable. Because the Gospels were written some fifty to eighty years after the death of Jesus, there was plenty of time for Christian lore, as well as historical circumstance, to influence these scriptural accounts. With regard to the historical contexts, we need only point out the obvious. The Gospels were written in a Roman world at a time when the Christian movement was seeking adherents among the Gentiles without arousing too much wrath from the Romans. The Romans had recently fought a difficult, bitter war with the Jews and were engaged in a severe oppression of the Jews. In the Gospels, then, the Romans are presented in the most positive light possible, while the Jews are often cast in an equally negative light. Thus the story of Jesus is told in such a way as to absolve the Romans of any guilt for the most heinous of crimes—the murder of the Son of God—and to lay the blame for that crime squarely upon the enemy of the Romans: the Jews. The Gospels' deviation from a more probable history—namely that the Romans executed Jesus because he was a political threat, as they had executed many others—is more an instance of tampering with history than of generating myth.

Among the mythological elements in the Gospels is the genealogy of Jesus, from Abraham to Joseph; its aim is to demonstrate that Jesus was a Jew from the House of David, which is the royal messianic line of the king of the Jews (Matthew 1:1–16; in Luke 3:23–38 the genealogy begins with Adam). As this genealogy indicates, the tribal affiliation of the Jews was determined by the father's lineage. According to Christian doctrine, however, Joseph was not his father; God was his father. Therefore a Jew might ask: What makes him part of the tribe of Judah and the House of David? Still, one might make a case from Jewish law that if a child's father is unknown, he belongs to the tribe of his adoptive father. And since the time of the Assyrian invasion of the Northern Kingdom in 722 BCE, ten of the tribes had been scattered, so that many Jews could claim to be from the tribe of Judah.

Be that as it may, most of the elements of myth found in the Gospels are quite familiar to the popular cultures of Christian societies. To be sure, myth is always more familiar to us than history; myth conveys a spiritual truth more central to the life of the soul than the truths of history. The point of the mythological aspects of the Gospels is to show that Jesus is the Christ, Son of God, sent into this world to be offered up in sacrifice and to rise from the dead, so as to redeem us from our sins. Here we must distinguish between mythological elements of the Gospels and their stories of miracles performed by Jesus. Although the performance of miracles may be invoked as proof that someone is sent from God, they do not prove that Jesus is the Messiah. People throughout history have allegedly performed miracles, and one may regard many of those accounts as part of history; they are at least subject to historical investigation and verification. Supernatural powers do not a Messiah make. Indeed, whenever Jesus miraculously healed someone, very often it was the faith of the believer, not the power of Jesus, that brought about the healing (see, for example, Matthew 8:13). And when Peter declared to Jesus his belief that Jesus was "the Christ, the Son of the living God," Jesus answered, "Flesh and blood have not revealed this to you, but my Father who is in heaven" (Matthew 16:16–17). Where faith is concerned proof is irrelevant.

In the Gospels, as in other religious texts, myth concerns not the supernatural but the theological. In the distinctively Christian myth, and not so much in the parables of Jesus, we find the expression of an ultimate reality that is foreign to the spiritual truth articulated in the mythological elements of Jewish Scriptures. The primary aim of the Christian myth is to show that Jesus is the Son of God, a category that is alien to Jewish thought and absent from Jewish texts. The Aramaic *bar-elahin*, which may be translated as "son of God," appears in the Book of Daniel (3:25), but it is a reference to the fourth figure in the furnace with Shadrach, Meshach, and Abednego as a "divine being" or an "angelic being," and not to the Messiah; certainly nowhere do the prophets conceive of the Messiah as the Son of God.

Here, then, are a few examples of the mythological elements of Christian Scripture that attest to the status of Jesus as the Son of God:

1. The conception of Jesus by the Holy Spirit (Matthew 1:18–25), and Gabriel's announcement to Mary that she would be the Mother of the Son of God (Luke 1:26–35).

2. The story of the shepherds (Luke 2:8–17) and the three wise men, who recognized from the start what the Gospels set out to "prove," namely that the child born to Mary was the Son of God (Matthew 2:7–11).

3. The baptism of Jesus, a ritual based on the Jewish use of the *mikveh* or ritual bath; in its Christian form, however, it is quite alien to Jews. Here we have an affirmation from God Himself that Jesus is His Son, as was declared by a voice from heaven upon his baptism (Mathew 3:17; Mark 1:4–11; Luke 3:21–22; cf. John 1:29–34).

4. Jesus' forty days in the wilderness, when Satan tempted him to betray his mission as the Son of God and the angels came to minister unto him (Matthew 4:1–11; Luke 4:1–13).

5. The Transfiguration of Jesus that took place when Peter, James, and John ascended Mount Tabor and saw Jesus radiating light and speaking with Moses and Elijah; as in the account of his baptism, the episode ends with God's declaration that Jesus is His Son, in whom He is "well pleased" (Matthew 17:1–5; Mark 9:2–7; Luke 9:28–35).

6. The account of Caiaphas asking, "Are you the Christ, the Son of God," and Jesus answering, "It is as you have said" (Matthew 26:63–64; Mark 14:61–62; cf. Luke 22:70). Historically speaking, this would be incomprehensible both to Caiaphas and to Jesus, as the phrase *Son of God* appears nowhere in the Hebrew Scriptures or in Jewish thought, particularly as a defining feature of the Messiah.

7. The story of Jesus' taking the place of Barabbas on the cross (Matthew 27:16–22; Mark 15:7–11; Luke 23:18–20; John 18:39–40) and the subsequent cry of the Jews that the blood of Jesus should be upon them and their children (Matthew 27:25). Barabbas, whose name means "son of the father," is Everyman, for whom Jesus, as the Son of God, is substituted in atonement for the sin inherited from Adam. Just as every human being inherits the sin of Adam, so do the Jews who later rejected Jesus inherit the sin of his murderers.

8. The tearing of the veil covering the Holy of Holies in the Temple, accompanied by an earthquake, upon the death of Jesus (Matthew 27:51; Mark 15:38; Luke 23:45). This is calculated to demonstrate the end of Judaism and the advent of a new Covenant. Thus this incident is followed by the Romans' declaration, contra the Jews' refusal, that "truly this was the Son of God" (Matthew 27:54; Mark 15:39; Luke 23:47).

9. The story of Mary Magdalene and Mary the Mother of Jesus going to his tomb only to encounter an angel, who declared that he had risen from the dead

(Matthew 28:1–7; Mark 16:2–6; Luke 24:1–7; John 20:1–14), thus demonstrating the conquering of death itself attained by the Son of God.

10. The testimony regarding Jesus' ascension into the heavens to rejoin his Father (Mark 16:19; Luke 24:51).

Although the authors of the Gospels were not, strictly speaking, theologians, the mythic elements of the Gospels became essential elements of what would become Christian doctrine. Let us now take a look at some key points of the doctrine and how it was formulated.

THE FORMULATION OF CHRISTIAN DOCTRINE

Christian thinking developed in a Hellenistic world ruled by Romans. The first attempts to articulate Christian beliefs and to spread the Christian word were written in Greek, as Greek was the language of the literate at the time, just as Latin would later become a universal language of the literate. What, according to Christian teaching, is "in the beginning," first and most fundamental? It is the *logos* (John 1:1), as Greek philosophy had taught. Just as the Hebrew language had shaped Jewish thought, as any language shapes any way of thinking, so did the Greek language and its worldview influence Christian thinking, beginning with the word *logos*, a word that means "word," "reason," "thought," "first principle." Forming the basis of speculative systems, it is a word that is as central to philosophy as philosophy is to theology. Indeed, this Greek philosophical influence on Christian thinking is what makes Christian thought far more theological and systematic than Jewish thought.

Among the Greek philosophical systems that Church Fathers such as Clement of Alexandria (d. 215), Origen (185–254), and Augustine (354–430) attempted to synthesize with Christian teachings was Neoplatonism. Developed in the third century, particularly in the writings of Plotinus,[12] Neoplatonism is based on the idea that all things emanate from the nameless One and that the highest reality is a contemplative, spiritual reality, not the physical, material, concrete landscape of this world. The

Neoplatonic influence on Christianity shows itself particularly in the enmity between the spirit, which is forever willing, and the flesh, which is always weak (cf. Matthew 26:41). As soon as the Divine Being becomes the Incarnation, the human being loses his carnal being; as God is made flesh, so the human is made spirit. Perhaps that is why Christians have had relatively little interest in the day-to-day, flesh-and-blood life of Jesus: What matters is not how he lived but who he is, or rather, the *concept* of who he is. Thus, in keeping with Neoplatonism's emphasis on concepts and contemplation, we have the Christian emphasis on the content of belief derived from certain theological categories. Of course, there are also crucial differences between Neoplatonism and Christianity: The Neoplatonic One never so loved the world that He gave His only begotten Son to be offered up in sacrifice for its sins.

Because Christianity's accent falls on belief, the aim of the Church Fathers' philosophical approach to Christian teachings was to develop a systematic set of beliefs that could be called a doctrine. In 325, Constantine called for the first ecumenical council at Nicea, so that Christianity might have an officially sanctioned statement of doctrine. Beginning with the Council of Nicea, there arose a series of official creeds that succinctly stated the basic tenets of the Christian doctrine. This is the Nicene Creed:

> We believe in one God, the Father, the Almighty, maker of heaven and earth, of all that is, seen and unseen. We believe in one Lord, Jesus Christ, the only son of God, eternally begotten of the Father, God from God, Light from Light, true God from true God, begotten, not made, of one Being with the Father. Through him all things were made. For us and for our salvation he came down from heaven: by the power of the Holy Spirit he became incarnate from the Virgin Mary, and was made man. For our sake he was crucified under Pontius Pilate; he suffered death and was buried. On the third day he rose again in accordance with the Scriptures; he ascended into heaven and is seated at the right hand of the Father. He will come again in glory to judge the living and the dead, and his kingdom will have no end. We believe

in the Holy Spirit, the Lord, giver of life, who proceeds
from the Father and the Son. With the Father and the Son
he is worshiped and glorified. He has spoken through
the Prophets. We believe in the holy catholic church and
apostolic Church. We acknowledge one baptism for the
forgiveness of sins. We look for the resurrection of the
dead, and the life of the world to come.

The Apostles' Creed is briefer but basically the same:

> I believe in God, the Father, almighty, creator of heaven
> and earth. I believe in Jesus Christ, His only son, our
> Lord. He was conceived by the power of the Holy Spirit
> and born to the Virgin Mary. He suffered under Pon-
> tius Pilate, was crucified, died, and was buried. He
> descended to the dead. On the third day he rose again.
> He ascended into heaven and is seated at the right hand
> of the Father. He will come again to judge the living and
> the dead. I believe in the Holy Spirit, the holy catholic
> church, the communion of saints, the forgiveness of sins,
> the resurrection of the body, and the life everlasting.

The Athanasian Creed (written between 381 and 428) sets
forth the doctrine of the Trinity and the Incarnation and states
that anyone who does not believe in that doctrine is condemned
to eternal damnation. Thus wielding the keys to the kingdom
articulated in the doctrine, the Church came to wield more and
more power. To be sure, wielding power is often an underlying
interest in the institutional formulation of doctrine.

In the time of the formulation of Christian doctrine, the
difficulty that the Jews had was not only with the content of
the doctrine but also with the very notion of doctrine. Even
under the Hasmoneans, when the Jews enjoyed a measure of
political power, they had no officially sanctioned creed; perhaps that is why under the Hasmoneans we have the beginnings of the political and theological tensions between the
Sadducees and the Pharisees. When the Christians were articulating their doctrine and defining the heresies, the Jews were
redacting their oral tradition into what would become the Talmud, an endeavor that unfolded between the years 200 and

600, with later additions and redactions. Emphasizing how to live rather than what to believe, the Talmud contains no doctrine, no statement of a creed. Whereas the Christian accent on belief necessitated the formulation of a doctrine for Christians to believe in, the Jewish insistence on action necessitated the passing on of a teaching—of laws and statutes—that Jews could live by, regardless of whether they had any political power. The Christians asked, "What do we believe?" The Jews asked, "What do we do?"

Couched in the Christian creeds is a theology that is unintelligible to Jewish teaching. The primary concepts that define the creeds—Incarnation, virgin birth, Son of God, the Trinity, and so on—are not contrary to Jewish teaching; they are unintelligible to Jewish thinking. It is not for nothing that as early as the second century Marcion, a devotee of Paul's writings, taught that the God of Abraham had no connection to the God incarnate in Jesus, even though his claim was later deemed heretical. By the fourth century, between myth, history, and political reality, what might have once possessed a trace of Jewish teaching had been emptied of that teaching. With regard to historical considerations, one important point that the creeds have in common is that they became increasingly widespread as Christianity became increasingly powerful. A religion rooted in the content of belief not only must articulate that content, but it must also insist that others affirm the belief, if it is to endure in the world, even though it may deplore the things that are of world. When a religion has a vested interest in its prominence in the world, as Christianity had when it became the official religion of the Roman Empire in 385 under the emperor Theodosius, it must see to the official exclusion of all other doctrines and creeds, since they pose an implicit threat to Christian power. Thus Christian power led to a systematic oppression of the Jews by decree, just as Christian doctrine led to a systematic oppression of Judaism through a reading of Jewish Scriptures that is foreign to Judaism.

The oppression of the Jews that followed in the wake of Christian creed and political power lasted as long as the Christians had power. What ensued were not just a few pronouncements by this official or that but oppressive policies of the

Christian state and enactments of canonical law,[13] which all but amounts to "divine law." Here are a few examples:

1. Jews prohibited from eating with Christians, Synod of Elvira, 306.

2. Jews required by law to observe Christian feasts and fasts and to attend sermons calculated to persuade them to convert, 425.

3. Jews forbidden to read their sacred texts in Hebrew, Code of Justinian, 529–553.

4. Jews forbidden to show themselves in the street during Passion Week, Third Synod of Orleans, 538.

5. Order for the burning of the Talmud and other holy books, Twelfth Synod of Toledo, 681.

6. Pope Leo VII urges principalities to expel Jews who refuse to be baptized, 937.

7. Jews forbidden to be plaintiffs or witnesses against Christians, Third Lateran Council, 1179.

8. Jews required to wear Jew badges, Fourth Lateran Council, 1215.

9. Construction of new synagogues prohibited, Council of Oxford, 1222.

10. Compulsory ghettos, Synod of Breslau, 1267.

11. Jews forbidden to earn academic degrees, Council of Basel, 1434.

Equally numerous and infamous are the expulsions of Jews who rejected the Christian doctrine, all of which were either ordered or sanctioned by the Church. One recalls, for example, the expulsions from France in 1182, England in 1290,

Bern in 1294, parts of Germany in 1350, Hungary in 1367, Strasbourg in 1381, Mainz in 1420, Austria in 1421, Zurich in 1424, Cologne in 1426, Saxony in 1432, Augsburg in 1439, Wurzburg in 1453, Breslau in 1454, Warsaw and Cracow in 1485, Spain in 1492, Portugal in 1497, Regensburg in 1519, and so on. None of these expulsions was due to any action committed by the Jews; no, the Jews were driven from their homes solely because of the content of their belief.

Since Christian doctrine was central to Christian power, Jewish Scriptures, which were necessary to the messianic prophecies that legitimized Jesus, had to be either repressed or revised. Whereas the Oral Torah was banned and burned, the Written Torah, and with it the writings and the prophets, was reinterpreted to suit Christian doctrine. The plural *Elohim* in the Hebrew Bible, for instance, is taken to refer to the Trinity, the Binding of Isaac prefigures the Crucifixion, David's assertion that he was conceived in sin (Psalms 51:5) becomes evidence for the doctrine of inherited sin, the *alma* or "young woman" who would give birth to the Messiah (Isaiah 7:14) is mistranslated into the "virgin" of Christian doctrine, the Suffering Servant of Isaiah 52 and 53 is identified as Jesus, and the ingathering of the Jews, a prophecy that runs throughout the teachings on the Messiah, is relegated to an eschatological scenario in which the Jews will return to Israel, where they will have one last chance to accept Jesus Christ, the Son of God, as their Lord and Savior—or be eternally damned. Just to be sure that their appropriation of the Word was complete, the holy tongue of the Jewish Scriptures was replaced by the holy tongue of the Roman Church: Latin. And just to be sure that their power was secure, for centuries only the properly initiated had access to the word. Thus Christianity and Christendom became as *Judenrein* as possible, under the historical circumstances.

ANTISEMITISM AND ANTI-JUDAISM: IS THERE A DIFFERENCE?

If the mythological dimensions of the Gospels distance Jesus from his Jewish essence, the formulation of Christian doctrine makes the distinction between the Christians and the Jews absolute. While the question of the necessity of antisemitism or Jew hatred in Christian thought will be examined in detail in the following chapter, by now it is clear that in the transition from a Christian Gospel containing Jewish elements to a Christian doctrine purged of those elements, Christianity became not only distinct from Judaism but also opposed to it. Because Judaism is precisely what Christianity replaces, anti-Judaism had to become a defining feature of Christianity. Instead of the Torah of Moses, we now have the Blood of the Christ. Instead of the question of what must be done, we have the question of what must be believed. Instead of the commandments that guide our actions each day, we now have the grace that frees us from the law. Instead of the demand to study, so that we may know the *what* and the *why* of the law, we now have the faith through which alone we are justified. Thus, as Rosemary Radford Ruether has maintained, "anti-Judaism has been 'the left hand of Christology.'"[14] Not surprisingly, it did not take long to go from the anti-Judaic teaching that the "Old Covenant" of Judaism had been superseded by the New Covenant of Christianity, to a distinctively Christian hatred of those who cling to the Old Covenant.

In its early forms, one may have been able to distinguish between Christian antisemitism and Christian anti-Judaism. After all, Paul's polemics with James and the Christian Church in Jerusalem, which consisted almost entirely of Jews, were likely characterized not by a hatred of the Jews but by a desire to get at the truth of the new Christian teaching. Paul surely did not regard the Jews as the minions of Satan or as inherently evil. While it is true, as noted in the previous chapter, that Paul viewed the Jews as "the children of the flesh" and declared that "it is not the children of the flesh who are the children of God" (Romans 9:8), he did not engage in the antisemitic discourse of hatred found in the writings of the Church Fathers. To be sure, he was himself a Jew who grew up with Jewish teachings and tradition; whether he was an observant Jew who adhered to those teachings is difficult to say. Nevertheless, the seeds of the Jew hatred that would, in part, define Christian belief were soon planted in the Gospel of John (which was written some 35 to 40 years after the death of Paul), where the Jews are deemed the "children of the devil" (8:44). Thus the Jews embody the very evil that Jesus came to overcome. And is evil not to be hated (see Romans 12:9)?

Proceeding from this precedent, the theologians who would become the Fathers of the Church developed a *systematic* teaching of contempt for Jews and Judaism. By the time of the infamous "golden-mouthed" Saint John Chrysostom (347–407), antisemitism and anti-Judaism were all but indistinguishable. One might object by pointing out that nothing would have pleased Chrysostom more than to see the Jews flock to Christianity. But one also wonders whether the denizens of the "den of Satan" are capable of receiving redemption in Christ, when, in the words of the Saint, not only their synagogues but also "the souls of the Jews are the dwelling places of demons."[15] Such a view of the Jew endured for centuries thereafter. For example, as Mark Cohen has noted, "when Archbishop Abogard wrote to inform the Carolingian king Louis the Pious (778–840) how much damage his favoritism toward the Jews had done to the faithful of Christianity, he underscored their venality by calling them *vasa diaboli*, 'vessels of the Devil,'" in keeping with the teachings of the Gospel of John (8:44).[16]

Similar views can be found among other Christian saints and sages, priests and pontiffs:

1. Justin Martyr (ca. 100–ca. 163): The Jews should "rightly suffer," for they have "slain the Just One."[17]

2. Tertullian (160–230): "The Jews form the breeding ground of all anti-Christian actions."[18]

3. Saint Hippolytus (170–230): The Jews will forever receive God's just punishment for having murdered Jesus.[19]

4. Origen: "The calamities they [the Jews] have suffered [are] because they were a most wicked nation, which although guilty of many other sins, yet has been punished severely for none as for those that were committed against our Lord Jesus."[20]

5. Saint Cyprian (200–258), from his *Three Books of Testimonies against the Jews*: "The man of Righteousness was put to death by the Jews" (14); "there is a new dispensation and a New Law, with abrogation of the Law of Moses" (15); "now the peoplehood of the Jews has been canceled" (6).[21]

6. Saint Gregory of Nyssa (ca. 335–ca. 395): Jews are "confederates of the devil, offspring of vipers,… utterly vile,… enemies of all that is good."[22]

7. Saint Ambrose (ca. 340–397), upon the burning of a synagogue: "I declare that I set fire to the synagogue, or at least that I ordered those who did it."[23]

8. Saint Augustine: "The Jew can never understand the Scriptures and forever will bear the guilt for the death of Jesus."[24]

9. Saint Jerome, translator of the Hebrew Bible into Latin (ca. 340–420): "If you call it [the synagogue] a brothel, a den of vice, the Devil's refuge, Satan's fortress, a place to deprave the soul, an abyss of every conceivable disaster or whatever you will, you are still saying less than it deserves."[25]

10. Peter the Venerable, abbot of Cluny (ca. 1092–1156): "Truly I doubt whether a Jew can be really human…. I lead out from its den a monstrous animal and show it as a laughing stock in the amphitheater of the world."[26]

11. Pope Innocent III (ca. 1161–1216): "The Jews' guilt of the crucifixion of Jesus consigned them to perpetual servitude, and, like Cain, they are to be wanderers and fugitives."[27]

12. Saint Thomas Aquinas (1225–74): "It would be licit… to hold Jews, because of their crime, in perpetual servitude."[28]

From these few familiar examples one can see that by the time of the Middle Ages, Christianity, antisemitism, and anti-Judaism were inextricably interwoven. The expulsion of the Jews from every country in Europe, the many decrees issued against them, the mass murder of the Jews from the Crusades to the blood libel pogrom in Kielce—all of it attests to a definitive link between devout Christian belief and unabashed Jew hatred, the occasional calls for mercy notwithstanding. By the time of the Middle Ages, the Christian rhetoric of hatred had been transformed into a pattern of slaughter that continued into modern times and culminated in the Holocaust. While the saints and sages cited above are Catholics, the Protestants of the sixteenth century proved themselves to be no better with regard to the "Jewish question." One recalls, for example, Martin Luther's infamous remarks on the Jews in *On the Jews and Their Lies*, such as: The Jews are "murderers of all Christendom, with full intent, now for more than fourteen hundred years, and indeed they were often burned to death upon the accusation that they had poisoned water and wells, stolen children, and torn and hacked them apart."[29] Add to this John Calvin's statement that the Jews "prostitute" their "souls to Satan."[30] It is no wonder that in the Augsburg Confession of Philip Melanchthon, Jews are placed in the category of the "ungodly" (Article XXIV).[31]

This pattern persists in our own time, particularly in Russia and Eastern Europe, where the same Christian hatred of the Jews has its own modern history. In 1791 we have the decree of Tsarina Elizaveta II, in accordance with which the Pale of Settlement was established to confine the Jews to a region in southeast Poland and Ukraine; later it extended from the Baltic to the Black Sea. In 1804, Alexander I issued a decree forbidding the use of Hebrew and Yiddish in all schools (a policy later adopted by the Soviets). The infamous Russian May Laws of 1882, passed in the wake of the massive pogroms of 1881, regulated where Jews could live, what they could own, and when they could work. And in 1898, Konstantine Pobedonostsev, head of synod of the Russian Orthodox Church since 1880, declared that the Jew plague would be cured with one-third of the Jews converting, one-third emigrating, and one-third being killed. Lest one suppose that this distinctively Christian antisemitism ended with the Soviets or with the establishment of a "democratic Russia" in 1991, we need simply note that in 1997 the Orthodox Church asked for an investigation to see whether the tsar's family was a victim of the worldwide Jewish conspiracy. And when in 1998 the former Soviet general Albert Makashov of the Communist Party called for the murder of Jews and other anti-Jewish measures, the Russian Church maintained its familiar silence.

Nor is this a phenomenon restricted to the "backward Christians of Eastern Orthodoxy," as some liberal Christians in the West might like to think. In fact, the more liberal and sophisticated the Christians, the more inclined they are toward an anti-Israel—and by implication an antisemitic—way of thinking. In recent times, for instance, the liberal Protestants have had their representatives among such groups as the Presbyterians and other like-minded Christians, whose call for divestments or a boycott of Israel belongs to the millennial tradition of Christian Jew hatred. In some ways this form of antisemitism is even more insidious than the traditional, frank, and open Jew hatred of the Roman Catholic, Eastern Orthodox, and Protestant churches. The claim that they object only to Israeli "oppression" of the Palestinians does not wash, since those who engage in this discourse know very well how it plays into the hands of Jew haters of every stripe. They are far more vocal about the Israeli "occupation" of Gaza than they ever were about the Syrian thirty-year occupation of Lebanon, the Egyptian occupation of Gaza, or the Jordanian occupation of the West Bank. They wring their hands far more about Israeli soldiers at checkpoints than about Palestinian homicide bombers on buses; they speak with much more indignation about the Israeli security fence than about the daily Palestinian rocket attacks on Jews. Either they are ignorant or they are simply antisemitic, in keeping with the teachings of their sacred tradition. And people holding a doctorate of divinity degree cannot plead ignorance.

Thus, whatever the differences separating Catholic, Protestant, and Orthodox Christians as they have represented themselves over history, Jew hatred is a tie that binds them together. A major challenge facing the next step in Jewish-Christian dialogue is dissolving both the anti-Judaism and the subsequent antisemitism so deeply rooted not only in Christian history but also in Christian theology. Because this connection has become definitive, the relation between Jews and Christians must be redefined, if the dialogue between the two is to go anywhere. In our view, that redefinition has yet to take place. Since the historically problematic relation between Christians and Jews in rooted not in mere prejudice but in the fundamental tenets of Christian doctrine, we must address certain theological issues, certain theological differences, between Judaism and Christianity, if the relation is to be rectified.

FOUR

THEOLOGICAL ISSUES

By now we can see that the historical developments in Jewish and Christian thinking about their teachings have profound theological implications; in both traditions, metaphysical categories and historical realities are inseparable. Both maintain that God is involved in history and that history, therefore, is one of the avenues of revelation. Related to this view are other views that the two traditions share in their thinking about God, world, and humanity, particularly within the contexts of what distinguishes their thinking from the modern and postmodern thinking traceable to the Greek speculative tradition. Although there are definitive differences between Judaism and Christianity in their views on God, world, and humanity, there are also some similarities in their implicit opposition to certain aspects of speculative philosophy. Those similarities might provide some common ground to be developed in the Jewish-Christian dialogue.

Both Christianity and Judaism understand God to be the Creator of heaven and earth, for example, and not an Aristotelian "unmoved mover," "first cause," or "first principle" that possesses all the superlatives of being. It is this Greek thinking that misleads us into referring to God as the Supreme Being; strictly speaking, both Christianity and Judaism view God not as the Supreme Being, but as the One who is beyond the categories of being, both immanent and transcendent. Conceived as sheer perfection, the Aristotelian god is utterly indifferent and in need of nothing. To be sure, part of such a god's perfection lies precisely in its indifference: Because it lacks nothing, it cares for nothing. As Aristotle asserts, it neither loves nor is in need of love (see, for example, Aristotle's *Eudemian Ethics*, VII, 1244b). From the standpoint of the ontological thought we inherit from the Greeks, in the end being has no inherent meaning; being is simply *what* is there, not *who* is there. The Greek god may operate according to principles of reason, from which one might even deduce a certain morality, but it does not command love or prayer or anything else of the material world.

Indeed, if one may speak of a soul in the Greek speculative tradition, this world is precisely what the soul must escape, as Plato argued (see, for example, Plato's *Phaedo*, 80a–81a), so that we may abide in the midst of the "pure idea," the first principle itself. Although Christianity has been influenced by this Greek thinking, it still views the soul's relation to God in terms of loving relation, and not in terms of a conceptual principle. From both Jewish and Christian standpoints, we do not cry out, "Father!" to a conceptual principle or to some primal event in the past. The first cause does not ask what God asks Adam and each of us: "Where are you?" (Genesis 3:9). Nor does it ask what God asks Cain: "Where is your brother?" (Genesis 4:9). And: "What have you done?" (Genesis 4:10). Abraham, Job, and Moses do not argue with an unmoved mover; to be sure, the attempt to move God that characterizes prayer in Judaism and Christianity is absurd from the Greek ontological perspective, since everything that is comes about through an ineluctable law of necessity. Deaf and dumb, what the Greeks call "being"— even in the mode of Supreme Being—is an "it" whose silence is but the rumbling of nothingness.

One can see that Christianity and Judaism have some strong ties in their opposition to this god of the philosophers. Both take very seriously the questions that the Creator puts to humanity. Both understand those questions to be rooted in love, just as the act of creation is rooted in love. And both see that creation implies a relation or a covenant—a dialogue of prayer and good deeds—between Creator and creature.

Because God is the Creator of being from beyond being, He is more than all there is and yet abides in the midst of all there is, at once transcendent and immanent. This world is rather like a sponge in the midst of the ocean of divinity, both saturated and surrounded by God. Because God cares and even *suffers*, He can be moved by the life that He has created. Indeed, contrary to the Unmoved Mover, He is the Most Moved Mover, and He is moved not just by prayer but also by how we treat one another. Judaism, in fact, takes this "doing" to be a form of praying.[1] Because every human being is created in the image and the likeness of the Holy One, each of us has an essential connection to the other. Bearing a trace of the holiness that is prior to being, the human being is a breach of being: Simply stated, according to Jewish and Christian thinking, people are not animals ruled by instinct. Rather, they are children of God, chosen for a specific task in the world, and given the capacity for *decision*—a break in the chain of cause and effect—in order to pursue that task. Which means: Their choices are meaningful in the light of their having already been chosen by the Holy One. Therefore human beings have ethical obligations to one another that precede the contexts of their actions and exceed the scope of their reason. And those obligations are *absolute*.

Jewish and Christian notions of the holiness of the human being are alien to the ontological categories of speculative thought. Identifying being with thought, speculative philosophy tends to have a much higher regard for people who possess philosophical acumen and ethical integrity than for those who do not. From the standpoint of Jewish and Christian thinking, however, the value of a human being lies outside of anything that speculative thought can conceive. We may esteem, honor, and admire moral integrity, intellectual insight, athletic ability, professional accomplishment, courage in the face of danger, and simple loving-kindness. But the notion of holiness tells us that the value of a person is determined by none of these things of the world, by nothing that can be weighed, measured, counted, or otherwise calculated by circumstance or observation—not even by moral character. Holiness exceeds all circumstance. Hence, from the standpoint of Jewish and Christian teaching, a human being has *infinite* value—or rather a human being is *holy*—whether he or she is moral or immoral, intelligent or stupid, strong or frail, rich or poor, brave or cowardly, nice or mean, old or young, fat or thin. And that infinite value implies an infinite responsibility to and for our fellow human being.

Further, emerging from the Greek speculative tradition, modern and postmodern ontological thinkers know nothing of Holy Writ; they view the Bible, for instance, as just another text subject to deconstruction and reductionist analysis, nothing more than a quaint and curious volume of forgotten lore. In both the Christian and Jewish traditions, on the other hand, the absolute nature of our responsibility to and for one another is articulated in a canon of Holy Scriptures, some of which the two traditions share, even though they approach them quite differently. Both traditions understand their Scriptures to address the eternal life of the soul in its relation to the Holy One, although here too there are significant differences in the nature of that understanding. Still, from what has been noted, the two traditions may have enough common ground for a genuine theological dialogue in the future, particularly in the light of the postmodern, relativistic, and nihilistic thinking that is fundamentally opposed to and even hostile toward both Christianity and Judaism. There are other threats as well, not the least of which is to be found in a Muslim fundamentalist terrorism that justifies the destruction of any tradition that is not fundamentally Muslim. But in order for a dialogue to be built on this theological common ground, some basic theological differences between the two traditions must be addressed. To be sure, dialogue requires difference: No one ever attained wisdom from an echo.

In this chapter we shall explore some of the differences between Jewish and Christian theological thinking, differences that have led to the necessity of antisemitism in Christian thought. Properly understood, however, it need not remain a necessity; properly understood, antisemitism may in fact be viewed as the sin against the Holy Spirit. Indeed, Christians have made some theological progress in this regard. Vatican II is a case in point, and in this chapter we shall examine its implications. But progress is never without controversy. Therefore we shall conclude this chapter with a consideration of the tension between the theology and politics that may create divisions within the Church.

FUNDAMENTAL DIFFERENCES BETWEEN JEWISH AND CHRISTIAN TEACHING

Although, as noted, the similarities between Jewish and Christian thinking are significant and promising, the differences are also significant. We have alluded to the difference in how the two traditions approach Scripture. The general aim of the Jewish Scriptures is to present an edifying account of the historical, covenantal relation between God and the Jewish people in the contexts of creation, revelation, and a promised redemption. The general aim of the Christian Scriptures is to convince the reader to *believe* that the one path to the salvation of the soul lies in Jesus of Nazareth, the Son and the Incarnation of God, whose blood was offered up to cleanse humanity of its inherited and inherent sin. While the Jewish Scriptures are more than three times the length of the Christian Scriptures, the word *faith*, according to *Cruden's Complete Concordance*, appears about one hundred times more frequently in the Christian Scriptures than in the Jewish Scriptures. This would suggest that, contra Christianity, Judaism is more about engaging in a certain action than adopting a certain creed.

"All have sinned and fall short of the glory of God," as Paul states it (Romans 3:23). *All* have sinned, from infants to elders. Two things are essential to the remediation of that inherent sin: (1) the blood sacrifice of Jesus and (2) faith in the blood sacrifice of Jesus—that is the underlying message of the famous verse in John 3:16, as it is commonly understood, words spoken by Jesus himself: "For God so loved the world, that [1] He gave His only begotten Son, that [2] whosoever *believeth* in Him should not perish but have everlasting life" (emphasis added). What the Christians take to be essential to salvation—namely human sacrifice, albeit a human who is also divine—is both alien and abhorrent to Jewish thinking. Without *faith* in the one offered up in sacrifice, from a traditional Christian perspective, even Mother Teresa's altruism is not enough to attain salvation, for "man is justified *sola fide*—by faith alone—without the deeds of the law" (Romans 3:28; see also Galatians 2:16). It is not that Christians think we can act in any way that we please; indeed, belief should result in certain actions. But, generally speaking, the difference is this: For Christians, behavior derives from belief; for Jews, belief derives from behavior. Thus in Judaism man is justified by deeds alone, even if the faith is not quite there.

When the Israelites affirmed their devotion to Torah at Mount Sinai, they declared, "We will do, and we will hear" (Exodus 24:7); the Christian formula seems to be something like, "We believe, and we shall do." To elaborate on what was stated earlier, the general aim of the Hebrew Scriptures' account of God's involvement with humanity is to show that human beings, both Jews and non-Jews, must *act* in a certain manner toward one another, regardless of the content of their belief. God does not ask Cain how he feels or what he believes; He asks him what he has *done*. To be sure, the Christian Scriptures teach that "if it has no works faith is dead" (James 2:17), but the deeds derive their value from the faith, not the faith from the deeds. In Dostoyevsky's Christian masterpiece *The Brothers Karamazov*, for example, Ivan comes to the realization that if there is no God, then nothing is true and everything is permitted.[2] Jewishly speaking, it is the other way around: If nothing is true and everything is permitted, then there is no God. That is to say, when we are not God's witnesses—*with our hands*—it is *as if* there were no God (see, for example, *Pesikta de-Rab Kahana* 12:6; see also *Sifre* on Deuteronomy 33:5). From a Jewish standpoint, faith is not primary because faith alone will not draw God into this world; the two things essential to the Christian *as a Christian*—blood and faith—are nonessential to the Jew.

The scriptural teachings of Judaism accentuate far more than human belief. Their aim is to create an opening for the divine presence to enter this realm, here and now, through our thoughts, words, and deeds. Jewish teaching, therefore, leaves plenty of room for Mother Teresa's having a place with God—not because she followed the "Jewish faith," but because she treated others with loving-kindness. She is one of the *Chasidei Umot Haolam*, the "righteous among the nations," whose righteousness lies in their actions, not in their beliefs. Indeed, *chasid*, meaning "righteous" or "pious," is a cognate of *chesed*, which is "loving-kindness," and it is always something enacted: What, indeed, can it mean to speak of loving-kindness apart from loving actions? An ancient concept in Judaism, the notion of the righteous among the nations is foreign to Christianity; a person may refuse to convert to Judaism and nonetheless remain righteous, but, traditionally, one cannot reject Jesus and be counted among the righteous.

Although Christians often see Judaism as judgmental and legalistic, in contrast to the loving and forgiving nature of Christianity, it was Christianity that invented eternal damnation—not for failure to treat one's fellow human being with loving-kindness but for failure to have faith in the cross. The mainstream Jewish teaching is that, after a time of purification, every soul ends up on some level of proximity to the Holy One.[3] According to Christian theology, those who reject salvation in Jesus are destined for the "lake of fire and brimstone," where "they will be tormented day and night for ever and ever" (Revelation 20:10); there is no comparable verse in the Hebrew Scriptures. This eternal damnation is for those who do not *believe* in the salvific power of the blood of God that was offered up to God to redeem humanity from its tainted essence. "In flaming fire," writes Paul, God takes "vengeance on those who do not know God, and on those who do not obey the Gospel of our Lord Jesus Christ" (2 Thessalonians 1:8–9), where "obey" means "believe in." From a Jewish perspective, the purification of Gehinnom, as painful as it may be, is an act not of divine vengeance but of divine love, as when a mother cleans her child's wound so that it may heal.

Related to the differences in the emphasis that the two traditions place upon faith are the differences in how each understands the status of the Holy Word and the Covenant it articulates. In Judaism we have the commandment that every Jew should be thoroughly versed in the Covenant of Torah, not only in order to know his or her obligations but also in order to hold God to *His* obligations and, if necessary, to enter into a dispute with God. Indeed, Abraham's first conversation with God after sealing the Covenant of Circumcision was an argument over the fate of Sodom and Gomorrah (Genesis 18:17–33); it is the one place in the Scriptures where we see *God thinking to Himself*: "Shall I hide from Abraham what I am about to do?" (Genesis 18:17). Thus, before Jacob was named

Israel, Abraham lived up to the meaning of "Israel," that is, of *Yisrael*: "He who struggles with God."

Because every Jew is commanded to study Torah every day in its original language, over the centuries the literacy rate among Jews has generally been much higher than among Christians, who for hundreds of years relied on their priests and their preachers to tell them what the Scripture says. Hence the sculptures and the stained glass windows in Christian churches relate Bible stories through visual images. Even when the Protestants insisted upon a universal access to the Word, it meant translating the Scripture into German, for example, as Luther did, which in turn meant subjecting the believer to the interpretations of the priest, preacher, or translator; Luther did not declare, "Now we must all learn Greek and Hebrew." Since Christians maintain that we are justified by faith alone, the study of the texts is desirable but not indispensable for the life of the soul. And, with faith theologically understood as acceptance,[4] Christians have not generally encouraged questioning or arguing with God.

Because Christian theology does not insist that every Christian engage the holy texts on a daily basis, in Christianity there is no real notion of a *Lashon Hakodesh*, of a "Holy Tongue." Nothing in the Christian understanding of Latin, Greek, or Old Church Slavonic compares to the traditional Jewish view of the Holy Tongue. In Judaism, Hebrew is the Holy Tongue not because it is the language of prayer or even because it is the language of Torah; rather it is the language of Torah because it is the Holy Tongue: God created the Hebrew letters and words before He created heaven and earth. According to Jewish mystical teaching, heaven and earth are made of the Hebrew letters (see, for example, *Sefer Yetzirah* 1:1). Anyone who has seen what goes into the creation of a Torah scroll realizes that the *Sefer,* or the "Book," is revered among Jews as perhaps among no other people. The scrolls must be handwritten on a halakhically prescribed parchment with a specific type of ink. They are kept in a holy ark along the wall of the synagogue that faces Jerusalem. They can be used only if every letter is perfect. And the words must be vocalized in a prescribed manner when read before the congregation. Why? Because "in each and every letter," says the Baal Shem Tov, founder of Chasidism, "there are worlds" (*Keter Shem Tov* 1). Therefore Jews do not study the Torah in translation. Those worlds are at stake in how we handle the scrolls, how we utter the Hebrew words, and, above all, how we live by the words. *This world*, then—and not just *my soul*—is at stake in the fulfillment of the Word.

Where is the Christian commentary on the Latin letters? Or on the Greek letters? Where are the volumes written on the letter *A*, the first letter of the alphabet, or on the letter *I*, the first letter in the King James Version of the Bible? Where are the scribes who pray each time they put a quill to scroll? Where is the *concrete, worldly, ink-and-parchment* reverence for the Word? There is none.

The accent on *this* world is another major difference between Jewish and traditional Christian theology. One instance in which the influence of Greek thinking shows up in Christian teaching is in Jesus' assertion that "my kingdom is not of this world" (John 18:36); therefore Thomas Aquinas insists that no true happiness can be attained in this world.[5] Such a view is alien to Jewish thought. From a Jewish standpoint, we do not go to a "better place" when we die; no, *this* is a better place, because only in this world can the soul attain its ultimate wholeness, which includes its *physical* dimension, the dimension of *nefesh*, which is in the blood (see Deuteronomy 12:23). *This* world is a better place, because only in *this* world can we perform the *mitzvot* commanded by Torah—which are not only "commandments" *from* God but are also "connections" *to* God: The word *mitzvah* is a cognate of the Aramaic word *tzavta*, meaning "link" or "connection." Through the *mitzvot* we attain the *tikkun haolam*, the "mending of the world," that is at stake in our actions and for which we are accountable. Without the mending of this world, creation itself remains incomplete. Therefore the messianic time unfolds in this world and is rooted in actions that are of this world.

One way to think of this difference between the two traditions in this regard is this: Christians labor to get into God's kingdom, while Jews labor to get God into *this* kingdom. The traditional Christian deemphasis and even denigration of this world has made room in Christianity for the monastery and asceticism, which are also alien to Jewish thinking. "To be carnally minded," says Paul, "is death, but to be spiritually minded is life and peace" (Romans 8:6); hence Paul's injunction to "mortify your members which are upon the earth" (Colossians 3:5). Jewish theology does not make this distinction between the carnal and the spiritual; the carnal *is* spiritual, imbued as it is with the divine sparks of the divine utterance from which it is made (see, for example, *Talmud Bavli, Makkot* 24a). Whereas Catholic priests are expected to be celibate, in keeping with the Pauline injunction (see 1 Corinthians 7:32–38), the Talmud teaches that a Jew is not a man until he is married (*Yevamot* 62b). Indeed, in Hebrew the word for "holiness," *kiddushin*, also means "marriage." Therefore part of the observance of the holiest day, the Sabbath, entails not just eating heartily but also lovemaking between husband and wife.

This view of marriage and the conjugal relation, through which a human being is brought into the world, is related to how the two traditions view the essence of the human being. Which brings us to another point of difference mentioned earlier, namely the views regarding the essence of the human soul. Thinking from the premise that every soul is connected to God and is, therefore, on some level holy, Jews affirm every day in their morning prayers that *nashamah shenatata bi tehorah hi*, "the soul You have placed within me is pure." Sin, therefore, is something we commit, not something we inherit. And, according to the mystical tradition, it affects only the lowest of the five levels of the soul.[6]

From a Jewish standpoint, for instance, children are not in need of redemption—they are the source of redemption, as the great sage of the eighteenth century, the Vilna Gaon, maintains.[7] In the Midrash, Rabbi Assi teaches that children begin their study of Torah with the Book of Leviticus because "children are pure, and the sacrifices are pure; so let the pure come and engage in the study of the pure" (*Vayikra Rabbah* 7:3). To be sure, all of creation, says the Talmud, is sustained thanks to the breath of little children (see *Shabbat* 119b). And because every soul is inherently pure, ultimately every soul has a place with God. Christianity, on the other hand, teaches that, due to Adam's sin, every soul is tainted from birth (see Romans 5:12–21). Indeed, our inherent sin is what necessitates the crucifixion of Jesus, whose blood alone can cleanse the soul that *believes* in him, as affirmed in John 3:16. By contrast, Judaism teaches that such a sacrifice is not necessary for atonement; according to the Talmud, any person can attain atonement through his or her own *deeds* of loving-kindness (see, for example, *Sotah* 14a).

The issue of atonement brings us to one of the most fundamental of the theological differences between Christianity and Judaism: how the two traditions view the Messiah. The difference does *not* lie in the fact that that Christians believe the Messiah has come, while the Jews continue to await his advent. The distinctions, rather, are rooted in the basic theological categories that define the two traditions. If both traditions are indeed messianic traditions, their messianisms are radically different. Here one truly begins to wonder whether Christians and Jews worship the same God or mean the same thing when they speak of God. Jews, for example, do not worship a Triune God who can impregnate a virgin and become incarnate in a human being. And they do not conceive of a Messiah who must be tortured and slaughtered, according to the will of God, as a redemption or a price paid for the sins of humanity.

The basic Christian theological view of the Messiah is expressed in the Apostles' Creed cited in the previous chapter: Jesus Christ, the Son of God, was conceived by the power of the Holy Spirit and born to the Virgin Mary. He was sent into the world to be crucified as an atonement for the sinful essence that pervades humanity. Having atoned for the sin inherent to our being, he conquered death and thus rose from the dead on the third day after his crucifixion. Having ascended to heaven, he will return one day to judge all of humankind according their faith in him as the Christ, the Son of God, part of the Trinity of the Father, the Son, and the Holy Spirit.

Because, according to Christian theology, at the core of his or her being every human is tainted with sin, the Christian Messiah cannot be sired in the usual human manner. His mother must herself be pure, a virgin conceived through an immaculate conception, and his father must be God Himself. Thus in his essence the Messiah is *both* human *and* divine, the incarnation of the Holy One, the only-begotten Son of God. For in the Christian view, no other sacrificial offering is sufficient for transforming the sinful *essence* of humanity. And *only* this sacrificial offering made in an act of infinite love can attain that transformation; thus the Christian articulates his or her partaking of that offering in the sacrament of the Eucharist. Further, because sin is associated with death—Adam became mortal through his sin—the Messiah who atones for sin through the crucifixion also conquers death through the resurrection. Once this task is completed with the cry of "It is finished" (John 19:30), history becomes a matter of waiting for the Last Judgment, when the believers will be separated from the nonbelievers. The logic is sublime and profound; but it is not Jewish. Indeed, nothing could be farther from Jewish teaching concerning the Messiah.

With regard to Jewish views on the Messiah, there are many talmudic and midrashic teachings, and they are often confused and conflicting.[8] A few things, however, are clear. The one whom the Jews await is not the son of God any more than any other human being is a child of the Holy One.[9] He is neither the incarnation of God nor part of a triune divinity; the Midrash, in fact, speaks of his mortal death, saying that when the Messiah dies, the "world to come" will be ushered in (see *Tanchuma Ekev* 7). Further, he is not born of a virgin, who in turn requires an immaculate conception. Indeed, from a Jewish standpoint, the conception of any human being can be "immaculate," since in marriage the sexual union that produces a child is itself holy, as is the one born from that union. And because we do not inherit Adam's sin, we are born innocent and untainted. Therefore the one whom we await is not one whose blood will be offered up in order to cleanse us of our *inherently* sinful being. His kingdom is in this world and of this world, and *we* can hasten his coming through prayer, Torah study, and acts of loving-kindness—that is, through the observance of the mitzvot. The Talmud, in fact, teaches that the Messiah is in our midst in every generation (see, for example, *Sanhedrin* 98a), so that we need not await his coming; rather we must make it possible for him to manifest himself. That is the ultimate purpose of the mitzvot of Torah.

With the coming of the Messiah we shall see the consummation of Torah as something lived in the thoughts, words, and deeds of all humanity. For his ability to draw Torah into the world will be so great, that the Word of the Holy One will become part of every human heart (Jeremiah 31:33), and justice and righteousness will reign throughout the world (Isaiah 9:6). Swords will be beaten into plowshares, and "nation will not lift up sword against nation" (Micah 4:3). Most prevalent of all the prophecies is that the Jews will be returned from their exile.[10] From the standpoint of Jewish theology—as well as from the evidence of history—none of these prophecies is fulfilled in Jesus of Nazareth. More significantly, however, the categories of Jewish thinking cannot accommodate the Christian categories that shape Christian thought, nor can Christian thinking accommodate the categories of Jewish thought—particularly in this decisive matter of the nature of redemption. Thus there may be a certain animosity between the two. At the very least, there is a high potential for a conceptual disconnect in dialogue to arise whenever the topic of redemption comes up.

As far as animosity between the two traditions is concerned, here too there is a difference. The Jewish animosity toward Christianity—the association of the cross with forced conversion, torture, and murder, for instance—lies much more in the actions than in the beliefs of the Christians. As we have seen, the Jews understand righteousness more in terms of actions than in terms of beliefs. From the other side, the Christian animosity toward the Jews lies not in how the Jews treat the Christians, but in the Jews' conscious, conscientious, and explicit rejection of any belief in salvation through the blood of the Nazarene. The Christian animosity toward the Jews is far more a matter of theology than of ethics. Therefore, it seems, traditional Christian theology is, in part, defined by an anti-Judaic stance: It *has* to be anti-Judaic in order to be Christian. And from being anti-Judaic it is just a step or two before becoming antisemitic. Let us consider why.

THE THEOLOGICAL NECESSITY OF ANTISEMITISM IN CHRISTIAN THOUGHT

Although the millennial Christian hatred of the Jews cannot be justified, we can note a few points that will perhaps make it "understandable." First, there is the ancient charge of deicide. As the story of the crucifixion is related in the Christian Scriptures, the blame for the murder of the Son of God clearly falls upon the Jews. Pilate poses the rhetorical question, "What evil has this man done?" (Matthew 27:23), and when the Jews insist that Jesus be crucified, Pilate washes his hands of all liability in the matter, declaring, "I am innocent of the blood of this righteous person" (Matthew 27:24); the Blood of the Lamb is upon the heads of the Jews and their children (Matthew 27:25). And there can be no crime worse than murdering God (whatever that might mean). That the Crucifixion came about in keeping with the divine will and nothing could have been done to change it is irrelevant. Not only are the Jews the murderers of God, but they are the *unrepentant* murderers of God: Even when offered forgiveness and salvation in Jesus—even when confronted with irrefutable evidence that he is the Redeemer—they still refuse that redemption.

The Jews refuse salvation in Christ, moreover, while knowing better than anyone else how to recognize the Messiah. After all, they wrote the book, as it were, on that topic; no one knows the prophecies of the Messiah better than they. Therefore they *must* see who he is, and yet they *still* refuse him. (Never mind the fact that, from the standpoint of the Jews, they reject Jesus as the Messiah precisely because they *do* know the prophecies inside and out.) And who but one who is inherently evil—who is demonic and utterly contemptible—would reject salvation through the blood of the Son of God, when all the evidence, all the truth, all the love and forgiveness are right before his eyes? Hence the demonic *evil* of the Jews. Hence the satanizing of the Jews and the teaching of contempt became a natural theological move on the part of Christian thinkers, from Saint John Chrysostom to Martin Luther.[11]

One teaching that has long been theologically essential to Christianity is the doctrine of supersession, which, as Franklin Littell has correctly observed, "already has an exterminationist ring."[12] And Darrell Fasching insists that "if no interpretation other than the myth of supersession can be derived from the New Testament and embraced in practice by Christians, then Christianity is immoral and obscene."[13] According to this doctrine—and essential to the Christian notion of a *new* covenant—the Covenant of Abraham and the blood of circumcision have been superseded by a new Covenant, by the Covenant sealed in the blood of the one crucified at Golgotha. This teaching is opposed in Pauls's assertion that God has not cast away His people, the Jews (Romans 11:1). And yet it is expressed in the Christian Scripture's comment on Jeremiah 31:31,[14] where it is written, "In speaking of a new covenant [the prophet] treats the first as obsolete. And what is becoming obsolete and growing old is ready to vanish away" (Hebrews 8:13). Therefore the Jews should vanish—presumably by becoming Christian—for the sake of the their own souls. Thus Christianity paints itself into a theological corner: If the only path to salvation lies in the New Covenant of the blood of Jesus, as it is written in the Christian Scriptures (for example, Acts 4:10–12), then anyone who consciously and conscientiously says no to that path is damned, beginning with the Jews. The peoples of other traditions, to whom the prophets and the Gospels may be either altogether unknown or only vaguely understood, may appeal to that mitigating circumstance. With regard to peoples of distant lands who have not received the "good news," theologians such as Karl Rahner cut them some slack in this matter, arguing that, in their own way, they follow Jesus, even if they are not cognizant of the fact.[15] Not so the Jews: They have no mitigating circumstances. And their contempt for the self-evident truth makes them contemptible.

So why are the Jews so stiff-necked in their refusal of salvation in Jesus? For one thing, essential to the Covenant transmitted to the world through the Jews is the idea that the Covenant of Torah is set and eternal *as it stands*; hence there can be no new covenant, as it is written: "You shall not add to the word which I command you, nor take from it; that you may keep the commandments of the Lord your God which I command you" (Deuteronomy 4:2). Also essential to the covenantal teaching of Torah is the principle that the mitzvot are humanity's *only* link to God. In its traditional supersessionist mode, Christianity rejects theses teachings from the Torah. They are alien to the tenets of the Christian "new covenant," with its emphasis on the faith in Jesus Christ that *alone* brings salvation to the human being: "For by grace you have been saved through faith, and that not of yourselves; it is a gift of God, not of works..." (Ephesians 2:8–9). A Christian, then, *has* to oppose himself to anyone who refuses the grace that brings salvation through faith, particularly and primarily the Jews. And his or her acts of loving-kindness are of no help.

Perhaps in addition to this theologically grounded antisemitism, there is also a reason rooted in the psyche, namely the longing to have the matter of redemption *settled*. Situating the hatred of the Jews in the contexts of the Jewish wait for the Messiah, antisemitism may well lie in a theological anti-messianism, where messianism is understood in terms of working to hasten the coming of the Messiah. Just as abolitionism ends with the accomplishment of freedom from slavery, so does messianism end with the accomplishment of redemption, as defined by Christian theology. If the Jews did not kill Christ Jesus historically, they certainly kill Christ Jesus theologically, simply by insisting that he is not the Anointed One who brings peace on earth and goodwill toward all humanity. Thus the "wandering" Jew turns out to be the waiting Jew and therefore the hated Jew, for the Jew's wait unsettles those who would have things settled by declaring the redemption to have been accomplished. Rooted in a longing for resolution, antisemitism is a longing to be relieved of the endless waiting and the endless doing, of the infinite responsibility that devolves on the ego.

How long shall we wait? According to a commentary on Isaiah 63:4 in the *Pesikta Rabbati* (compiled in the ninth century), we have another 365,000 years (1:7). Which is to say: The wait is infinite. In the endlessness of the wait, we encounter "the one" known in the mystical tradition as the *Ein Sof*, the "infinite one" or "the one without end." Jews do not pronounce the Holy Name, because to utter the Name would be to determine the end. Thus, said Rabbi Shmuel ben Nachman, in the name of Rabbi Yonatan, "Cursed be the bones of those who calculate the end. For they would say, since the predetermined time has come, and yet the Messiah has not come, he will never come. Nevertheless, wait for him" (*Sanhedrin* 97b). In that *nevertheless* lies the *Ein Sof* not only of the wait but of the one whom we await.

The word for "wait" in this talmudic passage is *chikah*, which also means to "expect": even if he will never come, impatiently *expect* him. Therefore do not calculate the "end"—hasten it. Indeed, in the Talmud it is written that there will be no Messiah for Israel, because those days have already passed, in the time of Hezekiah (*Sanhedrin* 99a); the point is not to put an end to the wait and the expectation, but to underscore its infinite duration. Just so, it is written in the *Sifre* on Deuteronomy 3:23, "Says the Torah: Whether You redeem us or not, whether You heal us or not, we shall seek to know You." Our task is not to know God, but to *seek* to know God, to know God in the mode of "not knowing" that constitutes the open wound of the infinite wait. In our morning prayers, then, we are enjoined to seek God's face, even though we can never behold God's face. That seeking *is* God's face.

Much like Shmuel ben Nachman, Rav maintains that all the dates for the ultimate redemption have passed (*Sanhedrin* 97b). Once again, however, the teaching is not that we should leave off with waiting; rather, it is that now only *we* can bring the Messiah, for only *we* can wait infinitely, through the continual effort to meet an infinite responsibility to and for the other person. Only we can wait, and not God, because only we operate within the narrow confines of time. Jewishly speaking, time itself is made of that waiting. Perhaps better: Time is the tarrying of the Messiah. That the Messiah tarries is what gives meaning to life, and the dimension of meaning is the dimension of time.

From the standpoint of Jewish theology, the Messiah does not end history—the persistent wait for the Messiah *is* history, inasmuch as the meaning of the Messiah lies in the wait for the Messiah. That wait is constitutive of time because it is the opposite of killing time: It is time experienced as the drawing nigh unto the Holy One that Emmanuel Lévinas describes when he says, "Time is the most profound relationship that man can have with God, precisely as a going toward God…. 'Going towards God' is meaningless unless seen in terms of my primary going towards the other person. I can only go towards God by being ethically concerned by and for the other person,"[16] and not through a "leap of faith." Because "all the dates for the ultimate redemption have passed," I cannot wait: I have to *move now*. That is, my waiting must consist of this movement that is an urgent "going towards God," towards the One who both recedes and draws near as I approach, who is *in* the approach itself. And, although each is responsible for all, I am *more* responsible than the others; for *I* am the one who must bring the Messiah.

Perhaps the Christian antisemite hates the Jew because the very presence of the Jew signifies the infinite responsibility that makes the wait for the messianic redemption infinite. Perhaps, in a word, the antisemites hate the Jews because the Jews disturb their sleep. The presence of the Jews is a constant reminder that we are forever in debt and that redemption is always yet to be decided. There is no settling the accounts; no payment will do, because payment is always due. For this reason, says Franz Rosenzweig, "The existence of the Jew constantly subjects Christianity to the idea that it is not attaining the goal, the truth, that it ever remains—on the way. That is the profoundest reason for the Christian hatred of the Jew."[17] The hatred of the Jews is the oldest hatred, because the challenge from the Jews is the oldest challenge to the personal autonomy and the personal salvation that we seek, as we curl up in the comfort of relying upon our own reason and looking out for Number One: For much of Christianity, salvation is primarily a personal matter that concerns *me*. And my ego insists that everyone else be like *me* in his or her belief.

From the perspective of Jewish theology, on the other hand, I am responsible not only for my own salvation but also for the salvation of the entire human community—not by proselytizing people but by elevating the level of holiness within the community through an adherence to the commandments of Torah. As noted in chapter 2, this concern for communal salvation is rooted in the episode from the Torah, where God tells Moses, "I shall destroy them and make a great people of you" (Exodus 32:10), and Moses answers, "If You do that, then erase my name from Your Book" (Exodus 32:32). And, it will be recalled, this community of salvation includes "all the nations of the earth," (Genesis 12:3). Contrary to traditional Christian theology, Judaism does not divide the world into the damned and the saved on the basis of belief. This point is illustrated most perfectly in the story of Jonah. For a Christian, to bring the people of Nineveh to God would mean converting them to Christianity; for the Jew Jonah, it does not mean converting them to Judaism—it means leading them to realize that their treatment of one another is an expression of their relation to God, the Creator of heaven and earth, without whom life has no meaning. And so the Jew waits, not for the world to adopt a certain creed, but for the world to take on a certain character.

In Judaism there is no curling up in the solitude of the Kierkegaardian Single One, where my faith and my salvation are my own affair. Inasmuch as each of us is responsible for a total responsibility, each of us bears a trace of the Messiah. If that is the case, then, says Lévinas, "in concrete terms this means that each person acts as though he were the Messiah… . It is my power to bear the suffering of all. It is the moment when I recognize this power and my universal responsibility."[18] From a Jewish standpoint, then, Jesus cannot do it for me. *I* am the one who must mount the cross. And that, quite understandably, is precisely what, with notable exceptions, the Christian would avoid, since Jesus has taken his or her place.

In the Christian tradition, antisemitism necessarily arises when the fixed formulas and ready answers of the creed are challenged by the prospect that the creed is not enough. Longing for a final solution, the antisemitic drive is to have the last word, settle the matter of redemption, and slip into the egocentric sleep of salvation, a sleep that would draw everyone else into the confines of its slumber. Here we realize, with Lévinas, that "antisemitism is the archetype of internment."[19] In Christian supersessionism, it is a radical internment, a theological internment. But the Jew continually and stubbornly breaks free of the internment. Thus Christians begin by assimilating and end by annihilating the Jew, who disturbs their sleep with the insistence that the wait for the Messiah lies in an interminable service to the other person. Every transgression, the Jew insists, is counted and entered in the ledger. And there are no guarantees.

If this is the constant reminder posed by the Jew, who would not want to free himself of that reminder? And what better means of justifying the elimination of the Jew than theology?

Jean-François Lyotard rightly points out that the Jews were murdered in Auschwitz not because of their race but because of their constant testimony to Christendom's failure to create a world in which faith can be transformed into loving-kindness and redemption can thus be realized. "'The jews,'" as he puts it, are for this reason "the irremissible in the West's movement of remission and pardon. They are what cannot be domesticated in the obsession to dominate."[20] And if they cannot be domesticated, they must be annihilated. Thus Lyotard outlines the history of the antisemitism that has characterized Christianity as well as modernity: "One converts the Jews in the Middle Ages, they resist by mental restriction. One expels them during the classical age, they return. One integrates them in the modern era, they persist in their difference. One exterminates them in the twentieth century"[21]—which is the final, postmodern, and perhaps post-Christian solution to the Jewish question. And what is the Jewish question? It is the eternal irritant that began with the questions put to Adam and his firstborn: Where are you? Where is your brother? And what have you done?

Here we have the difficulty facing Christian theology, especially in the aftermath of the extermination of the Chosen People in the heart of Christendom. Because Christian theology needs the Hebrew Scriptures, it continually confronts the Jewish Covenant that is both indispensable and undermining to Christianity; without the Covenant of Abraham there can be no Christianity, yet the Covenant of Abraham declares that there can be no "new" covenant. Which brings us to a critical question: What are the implications of the institutionalized Christian hatred of the Jewish people, through whom the Covenant of Abraham comes into the world? And this brings us to a corollary question, a staggering question: Is antisemitism the sin against the Holy Spirit?

Antisemitism as the Sin against the Holy Spirit

In chapter 1 we noted the theological courage shown by Franklin Littell, who maintains that in the post-Holocaust era antisemitism is not merely one among the many sins of racism, bigotry, prejudice, and the like. No, says Littell, antisemitism is *blasphemy*, the "sin against the Holy Spirit."[22] But *blasphemy* is a very strong word, and Littell does not use the term lightly. Why blasphemy?

It is likely that Littell could not have attained his insight without recognizing certain problematic aspects of a modern ontological outlook that is *philosophically* hostile toward Judaism and revealed religion and that contributed to Nazi thinking. In 1923, Herman Schwarz, a "prominent" German thinker influenced by Meister Eckhart and Jacob Boehme, distinguished himself by becoming the first philosopher to publicly support the Nazis. He was followed by Bruno Bauch, Max Wundt, Hans Heyse, and Nicolai Hartmann, all of whom were Kantian Idealists; then there was the noted Hegelian Theodor Haerung and the Nietzscheans Alfred Bäumler and Ernst Krieck. The most renowned of them all, of course, was Martin Heidegger.

It was no surprise, therefore, when Nazi economist Peter Heinz Seraphim insisted that the National Socialist ideology was based on much more than prejudice or racial hatred; the racial foundations, he maintained, were based on an all-encompassing philosophical outlook—a *Weltanschauung*—not on ethnic or religious difference.[23] Which is to say: The Jew is not the "other"—the Jew is the "evil," the ultimate threat to the modern autonomous freedom, which defines itself in terms of autonomous reason and personal resolve rather than in terms of the heteronomous adherence to Torah. Those who have the will and the power to act upon these philosophical ramifications will do so by purging the world of the Jew. Thus a point made in chapter 2 becomes even clearer: The Nazis were not antisemitic because they were racists. It is just the reverse: they were racists because they were antisemitic. The difference lay in how the two, Nazis and Jews, understood the value of a human being. And blasphemy against God is always blasphemy against the human being. But there were few, if any, among the leaders of European Christendom who leveled this charge.

In their blasphemy the Nazis maintained that a human being has value through (1) an accident of nature, that is, being born Aryan and (2) summoning from within himself a certain will to power. The Jewish (and Christian) teaching concerning the human being is that (1) each one is created in the image and likeness of the Holy One, (2) each one has his or her origin in a single one, in Adam, and (3) each is bound to the other through blood and through a common tie to God. Nothing could be more opposed to Nazi ideology or to modern and postmodern Western philosophy. The Nazis were antisemitic for the same reason that Western ontological thought is antisemitic. As we saw in chapter 2, the infamous ideologist Alfred Rosenberg understood that the Aryan "race" was threatened not merely by Jewish blood but by Jewish teaching, that is, by Judaism. And so we see what the Nazi antisemite is anti.

It is easy enough to see that the Nazis' antisemitism is blasphemy. But what about Christian antisemitism? One parallel between the two lies in the Jew's threat to the individual's autonomous freedom. In a commentary from the Mishnah, for example, on the verse, "And the tablets were the work of God, and the writing was the writing of God, graven [charut] upon the tablets" (Exodus 32:16), it says, "Do not read charut ('graven') but cherut ('freedom'), for no man is free save one who is engaged in the study of Torah" (Avot 6:2). No man is free save one who has chosen the path for which he was chosen. Both modern thinkers and Christian theologians, beginning with Paul (see Romans 8:2; Galatians 3:24–25), however, reject this Jewish view that freedom comes only through the law of Torah; in both cases the Jew threatens personal freedom by insisting on a divinely imposed obligation to adhere to a divine law.

Nevertheless, modern speculative thinking differs significantly from Christianity: Whereas modern and postmodern thinkers take freedom to derive from the self, Christians believe it derives from divine grace. Still, as soon as Jesus is used to set up a diametric opposition between law and grace (see John 1:17; Romans 3:24), the Christian is stuck with an either/or dilemma: Either the Judaism, which opts for Torah, is evil, or Christianity, which opts for grace, is evil. A similar parallel can be found in the differing views on the holiness of the human being. With the doctrine of inherited sin (see Romans 3:23; 2 Corinthians 1:9),[24] Christians oppose the Jewish view that every child born is holy, infinitely precious, and unsullied by sin with the view that only after baptism or redemption through the blood of the Godman does a human being take on an absolute, untainted value. Still, whereas anyone can be baptized and become a Christian, only one who is born an Aryan can be an Aryan. And that is a crucial difference.

If Christian antisemitism is blasphemous, it is not for the same reasons that Nazi antisemitism is blasphemous. Still, even in its Christian variation, antisemitism is blasphemy and a "sin against the Holy Spirit." The Holy Spirit is God's presence in the world, and that presence rests upon Scripture, prayer, and acts of loving-kindness. If antisemitism leads to acts of cruelty against the Chosen of God, it is because it is based upon a denial of Scripture, which determines that the Jews are the Chosen of God, the ones with whom God has specifically entered into an eternal Covenant (see Numbers 18:19). In both instances it amounts to a removal of the divine presence from the world. Even from a Christian standpoint, blasphemy is a denial of God and His Torah, and any hatred of the Jews or desire to eliminate the Jews, whether by extermination or by conversion, amounts to a denial of God and His Torah. For, according to the Christian Scriptures, which include the Torah, the Jews are the Chosen of God, God's light unto the nations. As God's Light, the Jews are God's Torah: said the Koretzer Rebbe, a disciple of the Baal Shem Tov, "God and Torah are one. God, Israel, and Torah are one."[25] Christians can and must find a way to subscribe to a similar view, without abandoning their Christianity. They could perhaps make a beginning with Paul's declaration that God has not cast away His people, the Jews (see Romans 11:1). Each time the Christians consigned to the flames the folios of Talmud or the scrolls of Torah, each time there was a call for restrictions on Hebrew prayers and Hebrew tomes, each time accusations of the blood libel or of poisoning the host were leveled at the Jews, the effort to rid their world of the Jews amounted to an effort to rid their world of God. That is why antisemitism, whether Nazi or Christian, is blasphemy.

But is antisemitism truly a *sin against the Holy Spirit*? Once again Littell uses an extremely powerful term. Does he really want to go that far? He certainly cannot be accused of not realizing what he is saying; few Christian thinkers know what they are saying better than Franklin Littell knows. And very few Christian theologians approach Littell's shocking audacity and sheer courage in making such a statement. For that reason, Christian theologians interested in a next step for Jewish-Christian dialogue might benefit from a consideration of Littell's statement. The sin against the Holy Spirit is in a category by itself; as pointed out in chapter 1, Jesus teaches that the sin against the Holy Spirit *cannot be forgiven* (Matthew 12:31)! Even the blood of the slaughtered Lamb of God is not enough to wash away that sin. If Littell and Jesus are right, the cross is not enough to wash away the Christian sin of antisemitism that permeates Christian theology. And if it permeates Christian theology—if Christian theology is necessarily antisemitic—then Christian theology is necessarily blasphemy and a sin against the Holy Spirit. Thus in the post-Holocaust era Littell brings Christian theology to a most fearsome impasse: Christian theology can be Christian and thus escape blasphemy only if it is not Christian in the traditional, historical sense defined by the sages and saints of Christendom. Or have we said too much?

Even as we write these lines, we tremble. And if we are trembling, the Christians must be either reeling or outraged or both. For the Christians, it seems, are faced with a theological reformulation of their own identity, in such a way as to theologically allow the Jews room for salvation through Torah, and not through the crucifixion and resurrection of Jesus Christ. In short, Christian theologians can avoid the blasphemy of anti-semitism only by committing what until now would be viewed as another blasphemy, namely by adopting the view that for the Jews, Jesus is *superfluous to salvation*.[26] This move would require a new and different understanding of such teachings as "None comes unto the Father except by me" (John 14:6) and "other foundation can no man lay than that is laid, which is Jesus Christ" (1 Corinthians 2:11). Try as we may, the Jewish-Christian dialogue cannot dispense with theology; even if we confine our joint efforts to issues of social justice and responding to the threats of a nihilistic postmodernism, theology is never far beneath the surface. And Christians may have taken a first half-step toward moving beyond what Littell deems a sin against the Holy Spirit with Vatican II.

THE MEANING OF VATICAN II

The Second Vatican Council, convened by Pope John XXIII in 1962, was a crucial event in twentieth-century religious history, initiating an unprecedented process of theological self-critique and issuing a watershed document *Nostra Aetate* (*N.A., In Our Time,* October 1965). *N.A.* emerged in the wake of the Shoah as the Church's response to Christianity's post-Auschwitz credibility crisis. Why had an overwhelming majority of the baptized seen no contradiction between Catholic teachings on Judaism and being active or passive accomplices of National Socialism's "final solution?" Why had so many Christians committed apostasy during the time of testing? Realization that the Shoah problematized the Christian tradition itself was slowly beginning to dawn. Michael Phayer emphasizes that "the Holocaust, not tradition, was the formative event that occasioned the church's somersault."[27] That somersault is a response not only to the Church's own supersessionism but also to the various forms of supersessionism that the modern world has endured.

We have already noted the genocidal undertones of the Christian theology of supersession, which contends that the "Old Israel" has been displaced by the "New Israel" (the Christian Church). Here we point out that supersessionism generally leads to hatred, violence, and mass murder: Such horrors arise not so much from religion as from supersessionism, both religious and ideological. Muhammad, for instance, asserted that Islam displaced both Judaism and Christianity and proceeded to spread the new faith by means of the sword. In the secular world of modernity, both Marxism and National Socialism have made supersessionary claims; the former claim led to the enslavement of millions, the latter resulted in the Holocaust. Thus Vatican II's *aggiornamento* or "updating" of the Church heralded a new beginning both ideologically and theologically.

John XXIII is alleged to have explained the meaning of *aggiornamento* to a visitor by "going to the nearest window, opening it wide, and letting in the fresh air."[28] The liberal theologian Hans Küng commented that the pope had "in 5 years...

renewed the Catholic Church more than his predecessors had in 500 years."[29] There is great irony, however, in the fact that, according to Monsignor Louis Capovilla, the pope's private secretary and confidant, "it never entered Pope John XXIII's mind that the Council ought to be occupied also with the Jewish question and with antisemitism."[30] Furthermore, there was intense resistance in the Curia (the Vatican bureaucracy) and among the orthodox and the conservative prelates to any attempt at reassessing the Church's supersessionary theology of Judaism (see below).

Jules Isaac raised the issue of the Church's teaching of contempt in a private audience with the pope in 1960. Isaac's goal was to eliminate falsehoods about Jews from Catholic teachings. He suggested that the pope establish a committee to study the "Jewish question." Responding, the pope said "I thought of that from the beginning of our meeting." The pope then asked Isaac himself to speak with Cardinal Augustin Bea, the distinguished Jesuit biblical scholar whom the pope named to head a special Secretariat for the Promotion of Christian Unity and who was himself sympathetic to John's view. Isaac's meeting with the pope is one of the first authentic post-Holocaust Catholic-Jewish dialogues.

Isaac had no illusions about the enormity of the task that he faced. His unedited memoirs, found posthumously, leave no doubt about the gravity of his mission:

> How in a few minutes was I to make the Pope understand that at the same time as a material ghetto, there had been a spiritual ghetto in which the Church gradually enclosed old Israel; that there had always been a Catholic "teaching of contempt (*mépris*)" towards the Jews, but now that tradition faces a growing counterpressure, a *purificato* in the Church, so that between the two contrary tendencies, Catholic opinion is divided, remains wavering; the head of the Church, a voice from the summit, could show the good path by solemnly condemning the teaching of contempt, as in essence, anti-Christian?[31]

The fact that Isaac persisted and that John XXIII was receptive constituted an enormous step forward in Catholic-Jewish relations. The pope was personally committed to rectifying the Church's teaching of contempt. He ordered the word "perfidious" omitted from the Good Friday liturgy. Furthermore, as Phayer notes, John XXIII "had all negative attributes about Jews, e.g., 'veiled hearts' and 'blindness,' supplanted in the official liturgy with positive phrases –'the people to whom God first spoke.'"[32] John was truly Isaac's hoped-for "voice from the summit." This voice was necessary but not, however, sufficient. In articulating its post-Holocaust theology of Judaism, the Church would have to confront its own role in sowing the seedbed of the Shoah, especially in perpetuating the infamous "deicide" accusation against the Jewish people that stems from a literal reading of the Gospels.

But the Second Vatican Council was beset by a host of problems: bureaucratic, political, and theological. Conservative elements closely associated with the Roman Curia sought to block any attempts at reform. Reflecting on Vatican II, Andrew M. Greeley observes that "new wine was being poured into old wineskins, and the old wineskins burst."[33] This is clearly seen in the areas that initially prompted the convening of the council: liturgical reform, ecumenism, Christian unity, and birth control. Here the Church's centuries-old doctrines were being challenged and, in many cases, ignored by the faithful, who nonetheless chose to remain Catholic.

To return to the impact of the council on Jewish-Christian dialogue, it is important to note that Rabbi A. James Rudin terms the Second Vatican Council a "kind of *Brayshit*,… the beginning, albeit an impressive one, of a long effort to eradicate every vestige of antisemitism within the Catholic Church."[34] Yet, *N.A.* is both a theological watershed and a flawed document that cannot free itself of the Church's centuries-old animosity toward Judaism and the role of the Jewish people in history. On the one hand, *N.A.* recognized that the Church could no longer pretend that modernity never happened; Catholicism could ignore the world only at its own peril. Moreover, the document appeared to overturn the long-standing Catholic contention that "outside the Church there is no salvation," implying recognition of religious pluralism, that is, the validity of what is "true and holy" in Hinduism, Buddhism, and other religions, including Islam.

The document's most dramatic statement, however, lies in its brief note four, which deals with Judaism. On the one hand, note four articulates a new and hopeful vision of the relationship between Catholicism and Judaism, while seeking to rectify the Church's baneful historical record of injustice toward its "elder brother." But the statement on the relationship of the Church to the Jewish people reveals the depth of the teaching of contempt within the classical sources, namely the Gospels, and the *Adversus Judaeos* tradition of the Church Fathers. The Church's theology of Judaism could reach consensus only by embracing the theological ambiguity of Paul's Letter to the Romans, chapters 9–11, and by ignoring its own history of promulgating religious antisemitism. In short, note four embodies the mixed signals that the Church sends in its relationship to Judaism, reifying the bifurcation between creeds, which continue to proliferate in a largely positive manner (see below), and actions in the world, which continue to be hurtful to the Jewish people and harmful to the dialogue.

Irving Greenberg contends that *N.A.* is a bellwether of one of the "great religious purifications of all times," the determination to remove the "cancer of hatred" found in a literal reading of Gospel accounts of the Jews. He rightly notes that the "Holocaust dramatized how these vicious portraits can be used to set up the Jews for genocide and to justify mass murder; at the least, these degrading accounts encouraged Christian bystanding."[35] Greenberg attests that the council fathers had two theological choices. They could have communicated Gospel polemics and modern Scripture research. This choice ran—and continues to run—the risk of undermining the naïve faith of the masses. Alternatively, the council could have challenged the Gospel's own *Adversus Judaeos* tradition as "an example of the texts of terror that every religious tradition carries from the past—and distanced them."[36] This position was opposed by traditionalists and threatened to disillusion the faithful.

The council ultimately settled on a third option. This view hinted that the Jews never forfeited their election. Further, *N.A.*

called for teaching the Gospels in a way that does not present the Jews as cursed for the crime of deicide. Jews should not be "spoken of as rejected or accursed as if this followed from Holy Scripture." Neither all Jews at the time of the Passion nor Jews of today are guilty of crimes committed during the Passion. Finally, the Church "deplores all hatreds, persecutions, displays of antisemitism leveled at any time or from any source against the Jews."

This view had the advantage, argues Greenberg, of leaving "the Gospels' authority untouched." Consequently, on the one hand, *N.A.* acknowledges the spiritual ties linking Christians ("people of the New Covenant") and Jews. Furthermore, the salvation of the Church "is mystically prefigured" in the exodus from Egypt. Additionally, the statement acknowledges that the Church received the revelation of the Old Testament through the Jews, "with whom God in his inexpressible mercy established the ancient covenant," and—following Paul—the Church remembers that it is nourished "from that good olive tree onto which the wild olive branches of the gentiles have been grafted."

Note four is, however, triumphalistic and ahistorical. For example, the document attests that "Jerusalem did not recognize God's moment when it came," and Jews not only failed to accept the Gospel, but many opposed the spreading of it. Jewish authorities, the text continues, pressed for the death of Christ. Furthermore, Vatican II embraces the supersessionary stance of the Constantinian Church, asserting that the Church is "the new people of God." Church triumphalism reaches its apogee in *N.A's* contention that "Christ… has through his cross reconciled Jews and Gentiles and made them one in himself." In Greenberg's words, this third choice "left the Gospels' authority untouched. However, it left open the door for people like Mel Gibson, Tridentines who reject Vatican II's reforms, to continue to use the Gospel story to portray Jews as the hateful, spiritually decadent, and blind people who killed God, albeit not fully knowing what they did."[37]

N.A. emblemizes the Church's tendency either to gloss or to ignore history when discussing antisemitism. For example, the document does not reflect on the role of the Church's own teachings as a major source of Judeophobia, especially as it crystallized in the infamous "deicide" accusation. Yet historically it was precisely this accusation, Jews as "Christ-killers," that infused both theological and cultural hatred of Jews. Littell emphasizes the destructive role played by the deicide lie: Even though the lie was "based upon an antisemitic distortion of the record of Jesus' trial and condemnation, many of the Church Fathers went on to indulge in a 'high minded' boasting of precisely the kind that Paul warned them against."[38] He rightly notes that the "theology of boasting triumphalism... culminated in Christendom's murder of European Judaism."[39]

The deadly persistence of this accusation is well documented and need not be repeated here. On the personal level, however, it is significant that Alan Berger's late mother-in-law, Rozalia Benau, an Auschwitz survivor, recalls that on her return from the death camp, her "neighbor" said to her, "You see, Rozie, this is what you get for killing Jesus." The Church seeks to distance its anti-Judaism from what it terms the thoroughly modern neopagan (Nazi) regime, which based its Jew-hatred on a pseudoscientific premise that distinguished between the Aryan and allegedly inferior races. Yet Rozalia Benau's neighbor was neither a "thoroughly modern neopagan" nor a believer in Aryan supremacy. Rather she had been infected by the Church's teaching of contempt for Jews and Judaism as it was focused on the deicide charge.

Commenting specifically on the Council's statement dealing with the persecution of the Jews, Gary Wills succinctly observes, "The Council dismissed history." More than three decades later *We Remember: A Reflection on the Shoah* (see chapter 5) "rewrote" history.[40] It is precisely this tendency that has contributed to the cognitive dissonance between Church pronouncements and the Jewish historical experience. Long ago, Martin Buber remarked on this fateful discrepancy in an observation about the Jewish people: "Standing, bound and shackled in the pillory of mankind, we demonstrate with the bloody body of our people the unredeemedness of the world."[41]

Nostra Aetate's ambivalence toward the Church's own past is most noticeable in the debate about whether the word *deicide* should be included in the final draft. The word was inserted—

and removed—three times. Phayer notes that opposition came from three sources: pastoral, theological, and political. Focusing on the theological dimension, orthodox churchmen argued that including the word *deicide* would, as Greenberg suggests, "give the impression that the Gospel account of Jesus' crucifixion was inaccurate or renounced by Council action." Further, the word *deicide* itself "created confusion by suggesting that God could be killed."[42] These verbal and mental gymnastics aside, the real issue for the Jewish people was the seriousness of the Church's intent. Abraham Joshua Heschel reacted strongly to the news that Pope Paul VI had personally approved the deletion of specific reference to deicide in the final document. Heschel wrote, "The deicide charge is the most dreadful calumny ever uttered. It resulted in rivers of blood and mountains of human ashes.... It is absurd, monstrous, and unhistorical, and the supreme repudiation of the Gospel of love. The weakening of the document in any of its aspects...would remain for all times as one of the major contributions to antisemitism."[43]

Phayer notes three reasons why a strongly worded statement on relations with the Jews proved difficult. First, many of the council fathers "did not understand the thinking of the small and isolated seminal groups that had been rethinking Christian-Jewish relations during the previous decade." The impact of Pope John XXIII's death in 1963, prior to the issuance of *N.A.*, silenced the "voice from the summit" that was crucial for the success of a strong statement on Catholic-Jewish relations. "Finally," writes Phayer, "international politics swirled around the existence of an Israeli state in Palestine, making any statement on Jews a lightning rod for controversy."[44]

Assessing the impact of *N.A.* on Catholic-Jewish relations in the light of the past forty years, we note two contrary trends. On the one hand, Rabbi Rudin rightly contends that *N.A.* has led to "more positive (Catholic-Jewish) encounters since 1965 than there were in the first 1900 years of the Church."[45] Furthermore, the decades following the promulgation of *N.A.* have witnessed the appearance of Vatican documents that, refining its broad outlines, substantively advanced and enhanced the process of Catholic-Jewish dialogue. One example is *The Implementing Guidelines* dealing with liturgy, teaching, and education that emerged in the seventies. A decade later two important documents were issued: *Notes on the Correct Way to Present Jews and Judaism in Preaching* and *Catechesis in the Roman Catholic Church* emphasized the historical relationship between the two faith communities and New Testament portrayals of Jews. *The Bishops' Criteria for Evaluation of Dramatization of the Passion*, a document issued by the United States Conference of Catholic Bishops, required that presentations of the passion be based on the findings of historical scholarship and avoid negative stereotyping of the Jewish people. We note that the Gibson film violated every one of the bishops' criteria.

Significant documents dealing particularly with the Shoah and Catholic-Jewish dialogue were issued in the decade of the nineties. Proclamations were made by the Belgian, French, and Polish episcopates that explicitly asked forgiveness and specified the Church's sin of silence during the Holocaust. Amidst great fanfare the Vatican issued *We Remember: A Reflection on the Shoah* in 1998. *We Remember* is much better known than the Episcopal statements, but it is less specific and far more controversial (see chapter 5). Two years later *Dabru Emet (Speak the Truth)*, a statement crafted by four Jewish intellectuals and signed by more than two hundred academics and rabbis, was published in several leading newspapers, including the *New York Times*. The intention of *Dabru Emet* is to acknowledge the change in Catholicism's theology of Judaism. Like *We Remember, Dabru Emet* also generated much controversy (see chapter 5). At the dawn of the twenty-first century, the Vatican, in *The Jewish People and Their Sacred Scriptures*, attested to the validity of the ongoing Covenant that God made with the Jewish people, although, as Rabbi Rudin notes, the book was not translated into English in a timely manner. *Walking God's Paths*, a DVD with study guide, appeared in 2004. This helpful DVD consists of six fifteen-minute discussions featuring Christian and Jewish scholars explaining how the two communities can understand and positively relate to one another after the Shoah.

As we have seen, however, the reforms initiated by *N.A.* have not yet proven sufficient either in overcoming antisemitism or in addressing the type of popular religious enthusiasm unleashed by films such as *The Passion of the Christ*. Furthermore, negative stereotypes of the Jews in literary portrayals such as Chaucer's *The Prioress Tale*, Shakespeare's *The Merchant of Venice*, and Charles Dickens' character of Fagin in *Oliver Twist* are so deeply ingrained in Western culture that constant and vigorous educational efforts are required to combat this hatred. In addition, the ferocious culture war that is raging encourages a Manichaean worldview that in the name of religion condones such negativity. In reference to *N.A.*, we believe that the assessment of Gary Wills is accurate: "Hopeful Catholics and generous Jews settled for this imperfect document,… since it did represent progress, given the terrible conditions that preceded the Council, and it could be the basis for building new attitudes."[46]

We now stand a biblical generation removed from the promulgation of *N.A.* The gains made have been undeniable. We think of the mutual goals of social justice, elimination of poverty, environmental concerns, and the vastly improved quality of human relations between Catholics and Jews. However, *N.A.* failed to mention the Holocaust, the state of Israel, or—as noted—the word *deicide*. Nagging doubts remain. What is the Church's intention? What will be the course of future dialogue efforts? Unanswered questions about each partner's definition and expectations of the dialogue hang in the balance. It seems to us, especially in the wake of the controversies generated by exposure of old theological wounds and the "great awakening" of fundamentalist religious expression in America and elsewhere that there are five areas of primary concern.

First, there is the matter of papal leadership. John XXIII was clearly committed to helping the Church achieve a *chesbon hanefesh* concerning its relationship to the Jewish people. His life situation had brought him face-to-face with the horror of the Shoah. Pope Paul VI, although carrying through the Second Vatican Council, lacked his predecessor's commitment to improving relations with the Jewish people. Paul preached a Passion Sunday sermon in 1965, several months prior to the declaration of *N.A.*, in which he accused the Jews of deicide. George Bull terms John XXIII "the accelerator" and his successor "the brake" in the attempt to articulate a credible post-Auschwitz Catholic theology of the Jewish people. Thus, within the forty-year period of the reign of three different popes—Pius XII, John XXIII, and Paul VI—there were three distinct attitudes toward the Church's relationship to the Jewish people.

John Paul II appeared to follow in John XXIII's footsteps, at least concerning the importance of Catholic-Jewish dialogue. Will Pope Benedict XVI and succeeding "voices from the summit" be personally committed to the dialogue? Or will this effort simply take a backseat to more pressing concerns, such as the conservative backlash against the reforms of Vatican II, the Church's rapidly growing African and Asian ministries, and the Vatican's strained relationship to Islam? In other areas of Vatican II reforms, both John Paul II and Benedict XVI seem to have slowed the pace of reform. The irony here is that both men were in the progressive or liberal camp when they attended the Second Vatican Council. Jews tenaciously recall what happened to the Jewish people when Joseph's memory was unknown to a new pharaoh. We do not suggest equivalence between ancient Egyptian rulers and contemporary popes. However, we wonder if a similar outcome awaits Catholic-Jewish dialogue with the passage of time and the assumption to the throne of Peter by one whose concerns lie elsewhere. The calamity here is not pogrom but rather neglect, which, in turn, might possibly lead to re-embracing old hateful stereotypes.

Memory looms large in Catholic-Jewish dialogue. The generation that witnessed the horrors of the Holocaust and the promulgation of *N. A.* is rapidly disappearing. On the other side of the coin, more people have been born after the promulgation of *N.A.* than were alive at that time. Consequently, the Church's theological "somersault" has already begun to recede in memory. Professor Mary C. Boys attests that most Christians in the mainline Christian world "are at best only dimly aware of the substantial rethinking of the past thirty-five years." Furthermore, she observes, "anti-Judaism is still prevalent in the Christian community."[47] Boys's perceptive comment attests to the staying power of the cancer of antisemitism.

The second issue is antisemitism, the longest-lasting social pathology. Littell distinguishes three types of this pathology: theological, cultural, and political. The first is associated with the Church Fathers and "the victory of Hellenistic thought and Roman law." Cultural antisemitism, he writes, "was built into the language and images and instincts over centuries of 'Christendom.'" Political antisemitism is "an ideological weapon" employed by modern totalitarian regimes. The most dangerous, deeply rooted, and hidden sources of the evil are "theological and/or cultural."[48] *N.A.* sought to address the theological dimension of antisemitism, however incompletely. Yet the document left untouched the deep-seated issue of cultural antisemitism. Worse still, there was no discussion of the devastating effects when theological and cultural antisemitism merge. Of the myriad examples relevant here, we point to a vicious political cartoon that appeared in *La Stampa* (April 3, 2002) during the second Intifada after Fatah gunmen invaded and barricaded themselves inside the Church of the Nativity in Bethlehem (see p. 27). The drawing depicts an infant Jesus replete with a halo peering out of a manger; the cannon of an Israeli tank is aimed at him. The infant asks, "Are they here to kill me again?" We question how effective any Church document or creedal formulation can be in the face of such deeply ingrained teaching of contempt. A massive and continuous educational effort is required to address this issue.

The third issue concerns language itself. Judaism and Christianity may be *separated* by a common language. At the outset, we note that Catholicism speaks of "theology." Judaism, for its part, refers not to theology in the formal sense, but to *Yirat Shemayim* ("fear of heaven"), which requires moral behavior and the doing of *mitzvot*. Although both communities refer to repentance and forgiveness, they understand these terms in different ways. Catholicism speaks of *metanoia* (changing one's heart). Judaism speaks of repentance or return *(teshuvah)*, which involves a turning away from sin and toward the Torah. Moreover, the Jewish tradition attests that there are two types of sin, each of which requires a different agent of forgiveness. There are sins committed by one human against another *(beyn adam l'adam)* and sins committed by humans against God *(beyn adam le makom)*. Only the person sinned against can forgive the sinner, and only God can forgive trespasses against the divine. Consequently, the Jewish understanding of forgiveness requires a personal, one-to-one encounter. There is no notion of corporate forgiveness in Judaism. Therefore, when the Church asks forgiveness from the Jewish people, it is seeking what is theologically impossible.

Forgiveness is the central issue raised in Simon Wiesenthal's story *The Sunflower*.[49] In Wiesenthal's book Karl, a fatally wounded Nazi, asks Simon, a Jewish concentration camp inmate, to forgive him for murdering a Jewish family. Simon cannot halakhically or spiritually forgive Karl, who in his youth had been an altar boy in the Catholic Church. We bracket the question of why his Catholic upbringing did not interfere with Karl's becoming a murderer of Jews. Focusing instead on the issue of forgiveness, David Blumenthal applies this principle to Catholic-Jewish dialogue. He observes that Judaism has "no spiritual or halakhic mechanism" that would enable Jews to formally "forgive" either the Church or "the community of Catholics" for centuries of the teaching of contempt that prepared the ground for the Holocaust.

Judaism can, however, apply the notion of *mechila*—"forgiving the other's indebtedness"—if such forgiveness is warranted. David Blumenthal relates *mechila* to the dynamics of Catholic-Jewish dialogue, noting that three conditions are necessary: "First, desisting from the sin of persecuting Jews, including desisting from teaching doctrines and supporting popular attitudes that encourage or even tolerate the persecution of Jews; second, making appropriate restitution where there are material claims that can be compensated; and third, the reform of character through intellectual-moral analysis, remorse, and confession."[50] The Church, in short, needs to begin living its own theology. The only practical way to achieve this goal is through action dealing with antisemitism in a clear and consistent fashion, condemnation of, and refusal to deal with, terrorists, and making accessible Vatican archives dealing with the Church's World War II activities.

The fourth issue concerns Israel. On the one hand, the Vatican has moved dramatically beyond *N.A.*, which, as noted above, omitted any mention of the Jewish state. The Vatican has established diplomatic relations with Israel. Moreover, Pope John Paul II's visit to Israel in 2000, unlike that of Paul

VI thirty-five years earlier, involved meeting the Israeli prime minister and president, a pilgrimage to the Western Wall, and a visit to Yad Vashem. On the other hand, it is uncertain whether the Vatican appreciates the deep and abiding role of Israel as a vital component of Jewish identity even for many Jews who do not consider themselves religious in the Orthodox sense. The Church apparently limits its perception of Israel to a political entity rather than a country bearing theological significance. This is precisely the argument made by Cardinal Bea at the Second Vatican Council.

The meaning of Vatican II for Catholic-Jewish dialogue is pivotal, yet ambiguous. The council boldly sought to confront the issues of the teaching of contempt, supersession, and deicide. Yet, *N.A.* was less a bold confrontation than a tentative first step. Indeed, Father Thomas F. Stransky contends that the amendments to the chapter on Jewish religion resulted in *N.A.*'s being transformed "*from* a bold proclamation *to* a bold argument" (emphasis added).[51] As we have noted, theological triumphalism retained pride of place in note four, for example, in the Christian self-definition: "The Church is the 'new people of God.'" Furthermore, the Church's post-Holocaust theology of Judaism was beset by an antisemitic bias on the part of conservatives of both the Latin and Eastern Church, as well as by Arab hostility toward the Jewish people in general and the state of Israel in particular.

The Shoah, although not mentioned in *N.A.*, is the great hovering presence in Catholic-Jewish dialogue. While certain sensitive Christians had begun to confront the Shoah's impact on Christianity, the issue was acknowledged neither by Pope Pius XII, the wartime pope, nor by Pope Paul VI, successor to John XXIII. Perhaps the earliest public recognition that the Holocaust was a massive credibility crisis for the Christian faith came from Alexander Donat, a Holocaust survivor. Donat put the matter starkly. "How," he enquires, "can Christianity survive the discovery that after a thousand years of its being Europe's official religion, Europe remains pagan at heart?"[52] Not to acknowledge this question means that there was neither a general recognition of the Church's credibility crisis nor the possibility of the need for repentance.

The record of Pope Paul VI, upon whom fate had thrust the role of carrying out the Second Vatican Council, exemplifies the moral blindness that made it impossible for the Vatican to recognize the relationship between the Church's historic teaching of contempt and the Shoah. Paul's reign was marked by secrecy and an increasing belief that the Church had been taken over by Satan. His attitude toward the Jews was at best ambivalent. For example, John T. Pawlikowski reports that Paul, as Giovanni Montini, Vatican secretary of state, "had a conversation in 1945 with Gerhard Riegner, during which he doubted Riegner's word that 1.5 million Jewish children had actually perished during the Holocaust."[53]

Nevertheless, *N.A.* set in motion a process by which Christianity, or specifically Catholic Christianity, could begin a process of serious reflection on the dark legacy of Auschwitz for humanity and for human understanding of the role of God in history. If in fact Jews and Christians are both favored of God, what does the Holocaust say about such a deity? The irony is that after an initial period of denial, the Catholic pendulum appears to have swung in the opposite direction. Pope John Paul's beatification of Edith Stein, a Jewish woman who became a Carmelite nun and was murdered by the Nazis because she was a Jew, touched off a debate over whether the Church is seeking to hijack the Shoah. This, in turn, has more recently opened the question of who "owns" the tragedy, and exemplifies what the philosopher John K. Roth terms "Holocaust politics."[54]

A CHURCH DIVIDED: THEOLOGY AND POLITICS

The intertwining of theology and politics has both an internal and external component. Internally, the theological struggle was—and is—between conservative and progressive elements. While the situation is complex and cannot simply be reduced to labels, George Bull helpfully describes the theological difference between the two groups: "The conservative tends to emphasize the Church's possession of the whole truth as expressed in set formulae, is unwilling to countenance the idea of the development of doctrine, emphasizes the unity rather than the diversity of the Church, takes his stand on the dogmatic definitions of Trent and Vatican I, and… tends to look to the past—namely, to the thirteenth century—for the measure of the present."[55] The Curia, composed primarily of conservative or orthodox elements, fought to uphold a medieval worldview that contends that modernity or any element of change—and the Jews were foremost among those identified with change—is dangerous.

Representatives of this body sought to sabotage the strongly worded statement on the Jewish religion and successfully blocked the word "deicide" from *N.A.* Perhaps no statement better exemplifies the resistance to change than that of Cardinal Ottaviani, a leader of the conservative bloc who, reacting to John XXIII's death, observed that now he could die a Catholic.[56] Furthermore, a political flap with serious theological overtones developed over the appointment of Dr. Chaim Wardi by the World Jewish Congress as "unofficial observer" at the first session of the Second Vatican Council. Stransky notes a twofold flaw in this move. Bea's secretariat had been neither consulted nor informed about the appointment. Furthermore, while the secretariat had invited other "*religious* communities, albeit only Christian, to have official observers, in the case of the Jews, the Vatican was dealing with a *political* body, the State of Israel." In a signal of things to come, Arab diplomats bombarded the secretariat of state with "vociferous protests."[57]

The progressives, led by John XXIII, believed that the post-Auschwitz Church was deeply in need of reformulating its theology in a more profound and deeper way. Moreover, the Church needed to identify itself as a pilgrim Church rather than as an ideologically driven absolutist institution untouched by the concerns of its laity throughout the world. This meant an emphasis on ecumenism, both within and outside the Christian world. The ensuing theological "somersault" was especially prominent in the Second Vatican Council's attempt to formulate a credible post-Holocaust theology of Judaism. Yet even Cardinal Bea, who was personally committed to a strong statement on the Jews, could not abandon the superseding myth. For example, on the one hand, he stated that the destruction of Jerusalem was not solely due to the crucifixion. Rather, he saw it as a warning of the apocalypse awaiting the end of human history. On the other hand, Bea stated that the Jews' function of preparing for the kingdom of God had ended with the coming of Jesus and the establishment of the Church.

The intermingling of Church politics and theology reached its zenith in the process that eventuated in the watered-down version of *N.A.*'s note four. On the one hand, Arab governments waged a *jihad* against any statement absolving the Jews of "deicide." According to the biblical account, argued the Arabs, Jews were punished for the crucifixion of Jesus by being condemned to eternal exile. If the council "exonerated" the Jews, there would be no reason for them to be punished. Consequently, the establishment of the state of Israel would be implicitly recognized by the Church. This was—and is—anathema to most Arab states and explains the crude and repulsive antisemitic statements of the Syrian president and his foreign minister in their "welcoming" remarks to Pope John Paul II on his 2001 visit to that country (see p. 27).

One of the abiding ironies of Vatican II is Pope Paul VI's visit to the Middle East. Paul's journey sought to cool inflamed relations between Arabs and Jews and to assure the Arabs that he would not act against their interests. The pope's visit to Israel was brief and lacking in any formal acknowledgment of the Jewish state. His snub did not, however, reassure the Arabs, who had threatened retaliation against Christians living in Arab lands if the word *deicide* appeared in *N.A.* Arab electronic media, in response, accused the Jews of attacking them as they had attacked Jesus two thousand years earlier. Thus Islam, which believes that it has superseded both Judaism and Christianity, raises the Christian deicide accusation against the Jewish people despite the fact that, as noted in the previous chapter, the Koran denies that the crucifixion ever took place (see *Sura* 4:157). The Arabs' position, therefore, is based on their blatant Jew hatred, about which the Church maintains a deafening silence.

Conservatives and the orthodox hierarchy also opposed any reference to the word *deicide*. Including this word, they argued, would undermine the faith of the masses in two ways; it would imply either that the Gospel accounts were wrong, or that the council was rejecting the Gospels. Moreover, as noted above, "deicide" contends that it is possible to murder God, which would also sow confusion among the faithful. In addition, the conservative bloc wanted a statement that would make it clear that "at least *some* Jews were implicated in the Crucifixion" and that this resulted in their punishment. Pope Paul VI insisted that Bea's secretariat amend the statement on the Jews owing to the objections. Bowing to theological and political pressure, the secretariat capitulated and removed the "offending" word, although stating, as we have noted, that neither all Jews then, nor Jews of today are guilty of killing Jesus. Rabbi David Polish, speaking for many in the Jewish community, described the statement as "a unilateral pronouncement by one party which presumes to redress on its own terms a wrong which it does not admit."[58]

In conclusion, we wish to emphasize two points. The Church did indeed perform a theological somersault in self-critically reflecting on its tortured and torturing theology of Judaism. This move was unprecedented in the history of Catholic-Jewish relations. But the revolution was far from complete. James Carroll summarizes the situation: "Neither the fathers of Vatican II nor Pope Paul VI was prepared to examine the foundational assumptions of Christian faith, the prophecy-fulfillment structure of salvation history, the construction of a Passion narrative requiring the Messiah to be rejected by 'his own,' and atonement Christology itself, as this all implied a denigration of the Jews. Instead, acting from good intentions, Church Fathers hoped to renounce the denigration, but without facing what made it inevitable."[59] We believe that this process continues as an underlying cause of the Church's insistence on sending mixed signals concerning Catholic-Jewish dialogue. Those who contend that there is only one true Church—for example, the 2000 document *Dominus Ieus*, authored by the then-cardinal Ratzinger, and challenged by Cardinal Walter Kasper—fly in the face of Vatican II reforms concerning Catholicism's relationship to other Christian and non-Christian denominations.

The Church exemplifies what Lévinas describes as a *totalizing institution*. This means that despite impressive gestures on the part of Pope John Paul II, such as holding a concert at the Vatican as a memorial to Holocaust victims, which can be understood as the continuous exfoliation of *N.A.*, the issue is not only theological. It is also ethical. Or, rather, a theology that lacks a strong ethical commitment is by definition deficient. For Lévinas, the Holocaust is less a question of "Where was God?" Rather, the central query is "Where was man as an ethical being?" Personal ethics and social justice are prior to any totalizing institution. Consequently, the concept of the Church as magisterium that is sinless cannot address or even acknowledge the role it played in fomenting hatred of Jews. *N. A.* did give expression to the Church's somersault. And the way ahead is of course the only way for the dialogue to proceed. But the path is strewn with obstacles such as fundamentally different ideas about the meaning of history, the definition of memory and personal responsibility, and the role of each community in God's salvific plan.

FIVE

CAN THERE BE A JEWISH-CHRISTIAN DIALOGUE AFTER AUSCHWITZ?

The question of whether a post-Holocaust Jewish-Christian dialogue is possible is a serious one. Before saying, "Yes, of course it is possible," we should remind ourselves that prior to the Holocaust there had never been such a dialogue. One might recall the establishment of the National Conference of Christians and Jews (NCCJ) in 1928, an organization that did in fact foster better relations among Protestants, Catholics, and Jews. But in this case "better relations" simply meant "friendlier relations," which generally came at the expense of any genuine theological dialogue or understanding. As Hubert G. Locke has pointed out, serious discussions of the tensions between Judaism and Christianity were not part of the NCCJ's agenda. "It was almost as though there was a deliberate attempt to avoid serious theological dialogue," says Locke, "as if that would threaten or possibly shatter this new and fragile alliance between two historically hostile forces. For the past almost eight decades, therefore, Christians and Jews in America have been unfailingly polite to one another while meticulously avoiding, except in the rarest of settings and circumstances, discussions of substance about the historical and theological gulf that separates one community from the other."[1] We believe that, for the most part, this is still the case.

What Locke takes to be but a single gulf is actually two, as we have seen in the last two chapters: Although there are connections between them, the historical gulf is distinct from the theological gulf. The historical gulf is easy enough to see; after centuries of oppression, expulsion, and slaughter in predominantly Christian lands, it is understandable that there might be a certain animosity or suspicion between Christians and Jews. In some ways the relation between Christian perpetrators and Jewish victims has an intimacy that makes better human relations between Christians and Jews a matter of some urgency. No one is particularly concerned about relations between Christians and Confucians or between Jews and Jains. What had already been a historical rift between Christians and Jews became an unfathomable abyss when nearly half of world Jewry was annihilated in the millennial heart of world Christendom. The Holocaust, therefore, raises issues concerning the human capacity not only for evil but also for reconciliation. Two thousand years of Jew hatred that culminated in the murder of the 6 million cannot be put right in just a few decades.

Further, while the matter of simply getting along is difficult enough, dialogue is an even greater challenge. We can be polite, courteous, and even kind to each other without having to enter into the agony and the labor of dialogue. In order for dialogue to happen, we must attain a certain level of *trust*, which requires something more than mere courtesy—it requires a willingness to become *vulnerable* to one another, when, from their experience with the Christians, history warns the Jews to do just the opposite. Dialogue also demands a certain level of *courage*, the courage to *change*, even though our traditions contain absolute truths that resist change. Finally, dialogue calls for a certain level of *understanding*, which requires something much more complicated than knowing how the other feels—it requires knowing how the other *thinks*.

This is where the theological gulf comes in. From what has been said in the preceding chapters, we can see that the chief obstacle to Jewish-Christian dialogue in this regard does not lie in differing opinions or viewpoints; nor is it simply a matter of obtaining more information about each other's history, culture, religion, and so on (all of which, of course, is very important). The primary challenge to serious theological discussion between Christians and Jews lies in *how* we think, not just in *what* we think. To a large extent, the differences between the modes of thought lie in how the two traditions have regarded Greek philosophy. In the previous chapter we noted that both Judaism and Christianity stand in opposition to certain Greek categories of thought; nevertheless, while Jewish thinkers have tended to resist the hellenization of Jewish thought, Christian thinkers have tended to incorporate Greek categories into their thinking. This tendency has made Christianity perhaps more susceptible to the totalizing ontological thinking that has arisen from the Greek tradition, where thought is equated with being, freedom is understood as autonomy, value is construed as will, and power is the only reality. In the modern and postmodern periods, however, both Jews and Christians have bought into such categories, replacing God with the *concept* of God, à la Hermann Cohen,[2] for instance, in an effort to "think being."

Thus we have a third gulf that threatens Jewish-Christian dialogue: the gulf between the participants in the dialogue and a surrounding outlook that characterizes modern and postmodern thought. It is an outlook that equates being with thinking, and not with the divine commandment to act or the divine inspiration of faith. "To think being," says Emmanuel Lévinas, "is to think on one's own scale, to coincide with oneself. And the way the ability to say *I* was understood in that adequate knowledge which equaled itself in equaling being, without being able to remain outside that adequate knowledge to weigh it down, was called freedom. But on that royal road as well, philosophers found they had been duped."[3] Franz Rosenzweig's indictment of philosophy's reduction of the world and human freedom to the "perceiving self" is even stronger: "Corresponding to the Copernican turn of Copernicus which made man a speck of dust in the whole is the Copernican turn of Kant, which, by way of compensation, placed him upon the throne of the world, much more precisely than Kant thought. To that monstrous degradation of man, costing him his humanity, this correction without measure was, likewise, at the cost of his humanity."[4] Refashioning himself after his own image, the human being loses his human image and ultimately dehumanizes the *other* human being. For he loses the holiness that defines the human, as taught in Jewish and Christian traditions.

The threat to Jewish-Christian dialogue, then, lies not only the historical and theological gulf that Hubert Locke identifies but also in a philosophical environment that is hostile toward the core categories of both traditions. This hostility that confronts both Christians and Jews may provide some common ground for dialogue. In the postmodern era, with its egocentric thinking, the death that concerns me—the death that I fear—is *my* death.[5] For the Jewish or Christian thinker, on the other hand, the death that concerns me is the death of the *other* human being—the widow, the orphan, and the stranger—not because I am sensitive but because I am *commanded*. Proceeding from the equation of thinking with being, the modern ontological thinker operates in an isolation of the sensitive self, where at best he or she is merely "alongside" the neighbor, with no *essential* tie to the neighbor. Grounded in a fear of God and a teaching concerning the connectedness of each human being to the other, Jewish and Christian thought is guided by a fear *for* the neighbor. For my neighbor is my *neighbor* inasmuch as through him I encounter the divine commandment to care for him. Contrary to modern and postmodern thinking, this religious thinking is not a thought *of something* but a thought *for someone*, in response to a transcendent commanding "voice." If Jewish-Christian dialogue is to happen, it must be driven by a divinely commanded thinking for the sake of another, in a time when there is a great deal of intellectual hostility toward such thinking.

One positive development that might come of Jewish-Christian dialogue is a surpassing of the devastating influence of the ontological tradition on Jewish and Christian thinking. Here each mode of thought, Jewish and Christian, may be of some help to the other. But is it too late? Are the historical and theological chasms that separate Christianity from Judaism too deep and wide for Jews and Christians to enter into a dialogue that can both affirm one another and oppose the postmodern threat? Have postmodern ways of thinking so estranged us from our own traditions that we have grown blind to our most fundamental teachings? If so, then what makes Jewish-

Christian dialogue *Jewish*, *Christian*, and indeed a *dialogue*? And where lies the bridge that spans the chasm?

These are some of the daunting questions that we shall address in this chapter. Once we have recognized the post-Holocaust challenges to Jewish-Christian dialogue, we shall go on to explore some tenuous avenues of hope for Jewish-Christian dialogue, particularly with regard to the documents *We Remember* and *Dabru Emet*. At the same time, in order to make clear some of the challenges to our trust and courage, we shall consider what some Jews, at least, have wanted to say but perhaps have been afraid to say.

POST-HOLOCAUST CHALLENGES

Jewish-Christian dialogue is desirable for a number of reasons. It might generate a life-affirming response to a certain postmodern nihilism and paganism as well as to the life-threatening ideologies of Muslim fanaticism. Therefore, at stake in Jewish-Christian dialogue is not only a better relationship between the two communities, but also an outlook regarding the sanctity of life that might benefit all of humanity. Like the Covenant of Abraham (see Genesis 12:3), Jewish-Christian dialogue might bring blessing to all the nations of the earth. Further, if we can clarify a few fundamental categories that shape our religious thinking, a Jewish-Christian dialogue might even make each party a little more intelligible to the other, so that we can better understand the nature of each other's religious thinking.

As noted in the previous chapter, among our shared categories are creation and commandment, revelation and holiness, salvation and absolute responsibility. Both traditions adopt, for example, the premise that the world comes into being through the action of a Creator, according to a certain design and purpose. Both have some sense of certain absolutes, such as the prohibition against murder, that are commanded by God and not merely deduced by reason. (Indeed, the Holocaust has demonstrated the bankruptcy of such rational deductions.) Both understand that a transcendent holiness enters the world through divine revelation, to sanctify our lives and to lead us to a purity of soul associated with salvation. And both insist upon an ethical responsibility to and for one another that cannot be abrogated. These shared categories that shape our religious thinking are huge, even though they allow for considerable debate on their nuances, particularly with regard to the status of divine commandment and its relation to revelation and salvation. In the light of the historical and theological tensions between the two traditions, however, we encounter a crucial question: Can there be—*ought* there be—a Jewish-Christian dialogue after Auschwitz?

Should the Jews simply say to the Christians, "Leave us and our children alone," and let it go at that? Indeed, this is Eliezer Berkovits' position. He maintains that, theologically speaking, "nothing could be less fruitful and more pointless" than Jewish-Christian dialogue: "As far as Jews are concerned, Judaism is fully sufficient. There is nothing in Christianity for them. Whatever in Christian teaching is acceptable to them is borrowed from Judaism. Jews do not have to turn to the New Testament for the 'two laws' [see Matthew 22:37–40]: Jesus was quoting them from the Hebrew Bible. And whatever is not Jewish in Christianity is not acceptable to the Jews."[6] While Berkovits's statements about the sufficiency of Judaism for the Jews are correct, they do not necessarily provide a reason to reject Jewish-Christian dialogue. Nevertheless, in both traditions, as we have seen, the theological is interwoven with the historical: In order for the Christians to leave the Jews alone—something that Christians have never managed to do—they would have to change the missionary elements of their theology. What is needed here is what Franklin Littell calls "the right of the Jewish people to self-identity and self-definition."[7] If Jews do not have this right, then they are justified in saying to the Christians, "Leave us and our children alone."

Some Jews are tempted to take such a stance, given the sea of Jewish blood spilled at the hands of Christians and the ongoing proselytizing efforts of certain Christian groups, who fund the activities of such insidious organizations as Jews for Jesus and Brit Hadashah. Indeed, for the Jews simply to be left alone would be a major improvement over what has been the norm throughout the centuries. These days, for the most part, Christians are no longer murdering Jews and are not likely to start up again (hopefully we do not speak too soon here). Outside of Russia and Eastern Europe, where the ancient Christian hatred of the Jews continues to take violent forms, Christians generally leave Jews alone, even though they remain relatively silent in the face of Arab Muslim and liberal intellectual assaults against the Jews. In our own time these factions, and not the Christians, are the ones who vilify us, vandalize us, attack us, and kill us.

There are, of course, liberal intellectual Christians who preach and even practice divestment from the one country where Jews enjoy a haven from antisemitism, but so far they call only for economic sanctions against the Jews. At the meeting of its 216th General Assembly in Richmond, Virginia, in 2004, for example, the Presbyterian Church, U.S.A., decided to initiate a process of phased selective divestment from multinational corporations operating in Israel.[8] Ironically, but perhaps not accidentally, this move is similar to that of European academics who demand a boycott of all Israeli academics and universities: no lectures, no publications, no visiting appointments, no fellowships, no entry for Israeli scholars and scientists into the glorious Western world. In chapter 1 we noted that some Israelis have been dismissed from academic positions in Europe solely because they were from Israel. What is the precedent for this? When were German, Soviet, Red Chinese, Iraqi, Iranian, Syrian, or Palestinian scholars ever fired because of where they were born? Only the Israelis enjoy this distinction. Only the Israelis fall prey to this antisemitism with little objection from the Christians.

All of this should sound very familiar. Who can forget that the first measures the Nazis took against the Jews were economic measures, beginning with the boycott of Jewish businesses in April 1933, an action taken with the tacit approval of the Christian churches of Germany? Who can forget the "isolated incidents" of violence against the Jews in the time of the Third Reich, just as similar incidents are taking place every day *again* throughout Europe—*again* with the tacit approval of the Christian churches? It is not for nothing that the chief rabbi of France has warned Jews not to wear their *kipot* in public, as the danger of being attacked is too great. It is not for nothing that the Vatican has issued no official statement regarding the *evil* of those who assault the Jews in Catholic France or Catholic Belgium. It is not for nothing that liberal Presbyterians, liberal Anglicans, and liberal European intellectuals find common ground with each other after all—and they find a small piece of common ground with the Nazis.

As for Israel, with its advancements in computer technology and medicine, one wonders how serious the Christians and liberal intellectuals can be about divestments and economic boycotts. The refusal to use Israeli products or inventions, for instance, would require a refusal to use Windows computer systems, Pentium 4 and Centrino processors, voice mail, AOL Instant Messenger, and cell phones, to name just a few items that Israeli scientists have produced. As in the area of computer technology, medicine is another field in which the Israelis excel. They have made unique advancements, for example, in the treatment of multiple sclerosis, paralysis due to stroke, breathing disorders, depression, Alzheimer's disease, smallpox, immune deficiency syndromes, movement disorders, and uterine fibroids, to name just a few areas of innovation in Israeli medicine. Shall we boycott the Israelis in these areas?

Some of the Israeli innovations in medicine have come in the wake of hundreds of terrorist attacks against the Jews. As a result of the Palestinians' bombing of their buses and burning of their children, for instance, the Israelis have become the world's experts in the treatment of burn victims. If a Presbyterian has a child who has suffered serious burns, God forbid, would he or she really want to boycott the Israelis' latest developments in the treatment of burn victims? Do those who persist in their hatred of the Jews really want no part of Israel's medical breakthroughs? Well, *do* they? The Palestinians refuse Israeli medical treatment of their children, so great is their hatred of the Jews.[9] Are the Presbyterians as committed to the Palestinian cause as the Palestinians are? Or are they content with something so ludicrous and transparent as taking their money out of companies that sell bulldozers to Israel?

Then, of course, there is the obvious point that the Palestinian economy is interwoven with the Israeli economy: To damage one is to damage the other. But it happens that, among some individuals and organizations, the plight of the

Palestinians is simply a convenient excuse for expressing their Jew hatred. In its post-Holocaust contexts, this bashing and boycotting of Israel is a stumbling block to Jewish-Christian dialogue. Why? Because it looks as if the antisemites' hatred of Israel and the Jews exceeds any benefits that they might derive from Israel. There are some courageous and vocal Christians such as Franklin Littell, John Pawlikowski, David Gushee, and John K. Roth, himself a Presbyterian who has voiced objections to Christian boycotts of Israel. With the exception of the evangelical leaders, however, Christian religious institutions have generally remained silent when it comes to an active support of Israel.

Thus, when Christians say to the Jews, "We want to talk," the Jews ask, "What have you done?" From a Jewish standpoint, the matter of *doing* something is a serious one for the future of Jewish-Christian dialogue. Roth is especially sensitive to this point. In an essay titled "Useless Experience: Its Significance for Reconciliation after Auschwitz," with his usual courage and insight, Roth takes to task "the Vatican's reluctance, if not refusal, to open fully its archives pertaining to the Holocaust and Pope Pius XII, whose reign (1939–58) included the years of the Holocaust and its aftermath. Scarcely any post-Holocaust rift vexes Catholic-Jewish relationships more than the question of whether Pius XII did all in his power to resist the Holocaust or, more seriously, whether complicity pervaded Vatican policies toward Nazi Germany. With the Vatican's plans to confer sainthood on the problematic pontiff already well along, the debate will not go away."[10] As we understand it, the identification of an individual as a saint requires the confirmation of a certain number of miracles; if that is the case, Pope Pius XII might have performed just one more miracle: He might have enjoined Catholic Christendom—which would have included Poland, the country where all of the annihilation camps were located—to say no to the Nazis. As for opening up the archives, Roth is quite right: A genuine Jewish-Christian dialogue requires a certain disclosure, not just to assuage the Jews but to lend the Catholic Christians an ounce of credibility.

What Roth says about "the problematic pontiff" who is a candidate for sainthood, the "post-Auschwitz Catholic" Harry

James Cargas makes even more problematic when he points out, "Pope Pius VII excommunicated the supporters of Napoleon and Pius XII himself, in 1949, excommunicated Communists from the Church, but never Nazis. No such action was ever threatened."[11] It is almost as if the Church had no particular problem with the murder of Jews. Other outrages, yes, as Cargas points out: supporters of Napoleon, the Communists, and people who get divorced. But the murder of the Jews? No outrage there. It is as if, like the Nazis, the Church associated Jews with Communists; it is as if the Church took seriously the teachings of its saints outlined in chapter 3, namely that there is something evil or satanic about the Jews. How, indeed, can the Church *not* take seriously the teachings of its saints? Cargas called for the posthumous excommunication of Adolf Hitler, Heinrich Himmler, Joseph Goebbels (all of whom committed the mortal sin of suicide), and other Nazi Catholics who died as Catholics in good standing. Of course, nothing was done or will be done to that effect. It is unprecedented. But then so is the Holocaust. So is Jewish-Christian dialogue. And it calls for something unprecedented to be *done*.

And now, as if matters were not complicated enough, we have in Benedict XVI a pope who was a member of the Hitler Youth and a soldier in the *Wehrmacht*. He was just a kid forced into service? Never mind! We are not talking about the CEO of a company or even the head of the Austrian government. We are talking about the *pope*! His appointment is indeed world-historical: no pope, however antisemitic, has ever been a former Nazi. Some Jews refer to him as "the Nazi pope," even though such an appellation may well be unjust; most Jews, in fact, seem to be supportive of the Vatican's selection of the new pope. Still, one wonders, much more urgently than with the last pope: What will Benedict XVI *say* about the slaughter of the Jews in the heart of Christendom and the rising antisemitism throughout the world? And what will he *do* about it? He has announced his determination to "re-Christianize" Europe; what will that mean for the Jews of a Europe plagued with a resurgence of antisemitism? He did have a moment of courage in 2006, when he publicly pointed out Islam's history of violence; but when the Muslims turned violent, he apologized for his statement. Is that the papal example of the courage of Christian conviction?

The fear—a fear that should haunt Christians as much as it does Jews—is that when the Muslims of Europe turn their violence on the Jews—as they have already begun to do—the pope will say little and do nothing. Indeed, the Church has gone from a pope who in his youth risked his life to save Jews to a pope who in his youth supported the murder of Jews. Does the Church now suppose that enough time has elapsed and enough survivors have died to make such an appointment run smoothly? Should the Jews now accept an invitation to enter into dialogue with Catholic Christians? *Ought* the Jews to accept such an invitation? And what concerns have the Catholics themselves expressed in this regard? Can they even be expected to voice a concern over the selection of the pope in the interest of Jewish-Christian dialogue? Is Jewish-Christian dialogue even on the agenda?

And so we wonder: What does this appointment mean for the significance of the late Pope John Paul II's world-historical visit to Israel in 2000, when he went to the Wall to pray for forgiveness and to Yad Vashem to memorialize the Jews murdered in the Holocaust? Indeed, what did all *that* mean? In this visit to the Jewish state we have an example of the astonishing upheavals in Jewish-Christian relations that characterize the post-Holocaust era. Never before would such an action on the part of a pope have been even remotely conceivable. And yet, as the pope stood on the grounds of Yad Vashem, Ehud Barak read, in Hebrew, these lines from the first stanza of "From among All the Nations" by Natan Alterman:

> When our children wept in the shadow of the chopping block,
> We heard not the warmth of the world,
> For You chose us from among the nations,
> You loved us and longed for us.[12]

These lines were followed by a round of applause, especially from the Christians of the world looking on. But many Jews and certainly most Israelis knew the rest of Alterman's famous poem, including these stanzas:

And day and night the ax devours,

As the Holy Christian Father in the City of Rome

Would not emerge from his sanctuary with the image of the
Redeemer

To stand for even a day in the midst of the pogrom.

To stand for even a day, not one single day,

In the place where for years, like a scapegoat,

A small child has stood,

Nameless,

A Jew.

And there is much ado about portraits and sculptures

And works of art to be protected from the bombs,

But the true works of art, the heads of the little ones,

In the end will be crushed against roadways and walls.[13]

These lines reveal what was between the lines of Barak's
greeting to the pope. They reveal not so much the lack of courtesy on the part of a host as the depth of the wounds within a
people. And they reveal what the current pope must respond
to, if there is to be a next step in Jewish-Christian dialogue.
Thus we have some sense of the historical challenges to a post-
Holocaust Jewish-Christian dialogue.

There are theological challenges as well, not only in the differences between Christians and Jews discussed in the previous
chapter, but also in differences among Christians and among
Jews themselves. It comes to this: Who speaks on behalf of
whom? The divisions between Protestants and Catholics, for
instance, are significant, as are the differences between Orthodox and Reform Jews. And we have not even mentioned the
evangelical Christians and the secular Jews. Even within all of
these movements there are broad spectrums of viewpoints to
be dealt with, both historical and theological. From the time of
Luther, there has been a history of the slaughter of Christians by
Christians themselves. And in the post-Holocaust era there is a
division between Christians who believe that in the aftermath

of Auschwitz, Christianity is faced with a profound rethinking of its teachings and traditions, and Christians who see the event as nothing more than an unfortunate aberration perpetrated by people who have no connection with "true Christianity."

Among the Jews there are divisions with regard to questions so basic as the matter of who is a Jew and what constitutes Jewish thinking. In the nineteenth century, for example, Jewish reformers set out to make Judaism more palatable by adjusting it to the times. It is reminiscent of the situation Emil Fackenheim describes in the time of the Maccabees. In 167 BCE, he notes, Antiochus's decree prohibiting Jewish observances "owed its inspiration to Hellenizing Jewish leaders who, long bent on 'accommodating traditional Judaism to the times,' at length enlisted non-Jewish government force. In their own eyes, these leaders were not traitors or apostates. They were a 'reform party,' concerned not to destroy Judaism but rather to preserve it. Yet had their efforts succeeded, they would have destroyed Judaism from within far more thoroughly than any external enemy."[14] In the wake of the German Enlightenment a "reform party" arose among Jews who suffered from an intellectual embarrassment over the revealed Judaism of Torah and Talmud. Then, as now, many Jewish thinkers were quick to reject "irrational" teachings such as those pertaining to diet, clothing, and liturgy, without first considering the rationale behind those teachings—or the implications of their rejection. They were comfortable with the idea that God forbids murder; but when it came to the question of whether God buried Moses, they would fidget in their seats. And so they sought a reasonable accommodation.

These tensions within Judaism and Christianity remind us that Jewish-Christian dialogue takes place in the contexts of a much needed Jewish-Jewish and Christian-Christian dialogue. To be sure, our attempts to seek a direction for Jewish-Christian dialogue might be of some help to those who seek better relations within the two traditions. In any case, the two examples of dialogical efforts we shall now consider are specific to a particular group of Christians and to a particular group of Jews; neither document pretends to speak for all Christians or all Jews.

PROMISE AND PERIL: *WE REMEMBER: A REFLECTION ON THE SHOAH*

The framework for meaningful post-Holocaust Christian-Jewish dialogue ostensibly crystallized in the promulgation of two key documents that appeared near the end of the twentieth century. *We Remember: A Reflection on the Shoah* was issued by the Vatican on March 12, 1998. *Dabru Emet (Speak the Truth): A Jewish Statement on Christians and Christianity* appeared as a full-page ad in the *New York Times* and *Baltimore Sun* in September 2000. Intended as guidelines for the future, each of these statements presents a distinctive angle of vision on the past and a hopeful projection for twenty-first-century Catholic-Jewish dialogue. Each speaks about the Bible, Covenant, God, history, and theology. Both documents are noteworthy for signaling a break with pre-Holocaust modes of how the two faith communities should view one another. Despite the promise contained in these documents, however, each appears fraught with peril and compels us to question how language is being used and the degree of historical and theological candor displayed after the Holocaust.

The great storyteller Rebbe Nachman of Bratzlav is well known for his aphorism "There is nothing so whole as a broken heart."[15] He is attesting that hope is possible only when the worst is known. In this reading, the true test of a broken heart is a willingness to confront and reject what is dangerous and hateful. This confrontation has, in turn, the power of legitimately allowing an individual, or an institution, to begin to change behavior having fully faced history. But, as we have seen, history for both Christianity and Judaism is laden with theological meaning. In the context of the post-Holocaust Christian-Jewish dialogue, this requires at least two principles: an unblinking look at supersessionary Church teachings concerning Judaism as sowing the seedbed of the Holocaust, and an articulation of the purpose of dialogue.

On March 12, 1998, eleven years after being announced, and timed to appear shortly before Passover and Easter, the Vatican issued its long-awaited public statement on the Catholic

Church and the Holocaust. Commissioned by Pope John Paul II, *We Remember* was prepared under the guidance of Cardinal Edward Idris Cassidy, director of the Commission for Religious Relations with the Jews.[16] In a prefatory letter to the document, the pope states his intentions to "help heal the wounds of past misunderstandings and injustices." The first Vatican document to explicitly mention the Holocaust, it intentionally employs the Hebrew term *Shoah* (catastrophe) in referring to the fate of European Jewry.

Rightly calling the Shoah an "indelible stain" on the history of the twentieth century, the pope expressed his fervent hope that *We Remember* may help shape a future free of the possibility of another Shoah. Historically speaking, the document is intended as, in Cardinal Cassidy's words, "another step on the path marked out by the Second Vatican Council in our relations with the Jewish people." The document calls for a "moral and religious memory" of the Holocaust and urges, especially for Christians, "a very serious reflection on what gave rise to it." *We Remember* reverberated throughout the Catholic and Jewish worlds; some applauded its boldness while others decried its timidity. Others still contended it went too far. While it may have helped to heal some wounds, the document exposed the festering nature of others. *We Remember* is simultaneously an absolute departure from, and an espousal of, mixed Church signals and missed opportunities.

To appreciate the significance, and the weakness, of *We Remember* it is helpful to briefly look at the post-Holocaust record of the Vatican, and especially the actions of Pope John Paul II. The Second Vatican Council, convened by Pope John XXIII, and concluded—in a far less bold manner—by his successor Pope Paul VI, and the Vatican implementing documents that followed, ostensibly ushered in a new era in Catholic-Jewish relations. Further, John Paul II, the first non-Italian pope in five hundred years, was personally committed to improving Catholic-Jewish relations owing to his own experience. As Karol Wojtyla, he grew up in Wadowice, a small Polish town near Krakow, and had Jewish friends who were murdered by the Nazis. Moreover, his 1986 visit to the main synagogue in Rome was unprecedented, as was the Vatican concert honoring the memory of the victims of the Shoah. Additionally, under the pope's guidance the Vatican granted diplomatic recognition to the state of Israel. As noted earlier, John Paul II also made a pilgrimage to Israel, where he visited Yad Vashem and placed a prayer acknowledging Christian anti-Judaism and sins against the Jews over the centuries in the Western Wall. He also publicly denounced antisemitism as a sin.

But *We Remember* is, in the words of Rabbi Irving Greenberg, "a split document emotionally and theologically."[17] We add that it also reveals the basic difference between Catholic and Jewish understandings of the meaning of history and the role of memory. The document embraces both the light of repentance and the darkness of traditional dogma concerning the unerring nature of the Church. The first two of the document's five sections are genuine calls for memory and repentance. Part 1, "Tragedy of the *Shoah* and the Duty of Remembrance," emphasizes that the Shoah is a "major fact" of the twentieth century (an official and public rebuke to Holocaust deniers and other antisemites). Condemning indifference to this fact, the document underscores both the "close bonds of spiritual kinship" between the Church and the Jewish people, and the necessity of the Church's "remembrance of the injustices of the past." Further, memory is imperative for the common future of Christians and Jews.

The second section, "What We Must Remember," makes three crucial points. First, the pain of the Jewish people during the Shoah is beyond the power of language to convey, and Jews were murdered solely because of their birth. Second, the immensity of the crime requires "moral and religious memory," and Christians especially need seriously to reflect on what gave rise to it. The third point is a statement and a question. Because the Shoah occurred in Christian Europe, it is imperative to ask about the relation between the Nazi persecution and the "attitudes down the centuries of Christians toward the Jews." We sadly note that the remainder of the document fails honestly to confront history and thereby is unable satisfactorily to respond to its own agenda. Consequently, the apparent encouragement of a Catholic self-theological critique after Auschwitz is honored all too often in a theological breach.

Coupled with its stated desire to rid the Church of antisemitism, *We Remember* embraces a reading of history that is at best disingenuous. Sections 3 and 4, "Relations between Jews and Christians" and "Nazi Antisemitism and the Shoah," are flawed by an absence of historical accuracy and theological candor. Three points stand out in particular: a reading of the dispute between the early Church and Jewish leaders that rests entirely on Paul's triumphalist distinction between *law* and *spirit*, and a subsequent description of the response of the German Church during the Holocaust; distinguishing between Christian anti-Judaism and Nazi antisemitism in a manner that completely absolves the Church of any impact of its bimillennial teaching of contempt; and the assessment of Pope Pius XII's response to the Holocaust.

We Remember insists on upholding the medieval notion of distinguishing between the Church and the errors and failures of its sons and daughters. The Church as magisterium is held blameless. It appears untouched by history and unaccountable for acts of evil perpetrated in its name. Consequently, the document acknowledges that "erroneous and unjust interpretations of the New Testament regarding the Jewish people and their alleged culpability… have (engendered) feelings of hostility toward this people." The Church's failure to examine in a theologically self-critical way what role its own teachings have played in the actions of its "sinful sons and daughters" exemplifies what one scholar terms "theological moral evasion."[18]

Focusing on its description of first-century, post-crucifixion relations between the early Church and the Jewish leaders, *We Remember* speaks of the occasional violent opposition "to preachers of the Gospel and the first Christians." Rabbi James Rudin comments that in using the words *violently opposed*, "the Vatican text transmits the not-so-subtle message of a moral equivalency between historic, often deadly, Christian persecution and denigration of Jews and Judaism and the anti-Christian attitudes and behavior of some Jews."[19]

The Vatican text is demonstrably false in its claims that Christian resistance to Nazism was active and vigorous. The example of the German Church is instructive. The document contends that the Church condemned racism and singles out in this context Cardinals Michael Faulhaber of Munich and Adolf Bertram of Breslau, as well as Bernhard Lichtenberg, provost of the Berlin Cathedral. While it is true that Faulhaber was not a National Socialist and courageously defended the Jewish origins of Christianity against attacks by racist Nazis in a series of Advent sermons during the winter of 1933, he also embraced the classical Christian position that the Jewish people were cursed for rejecting their Jesus. Robert Wistrich tellingly notes that "in 1934 [Faulhaber] would indignantly deny suggestions made abroad that his sermons constituted a defense of German Jews or a criticism of Nazi policy."[20] It is sobering to recall that Benedict XVI, John Paul II's successor, has written: "What moved me deeply (about Cardinal Faulhaber) was the awe-inspiring grandeur of his mission, with which he had become fully identified."[21] Cardinal Bertram, described by Michael Phayer as an "inveterate accommodationist, who wanted to avoid conflict with the state," for his part, sent Hitler a congratulatory fiftieth birthday telegram in 1939.[22] Lacking a clear, consistent, and unambiguous message from the Vatican about fighting antisemitism and resisting Nazism, German cardinals were free to follow their own inclinations about helping Jews.

Lichtenberg was the only true resister of those named. He prayed publicly for the Jews following *Kristallnacht*—one of the very few protests on the part of the German Church, was arrested by the Nazis, and sentenced to Dachau, but died en route to the concentration camp. Why, we wonder, did the Vatican statement not distinguish between Lichtenberg and the two cardinals whose behavior was in no way exemplary either from a normative Christian point of view or from the perspective of morality and ethics? Further, why did the statement omit reference to Gertrude Luckner, or any other woman resister such as Margarete Sommer? Silence, not protest, was the rule in German churches. Concerning the Vatican response to the onslaught of Nazism, *We Remember* cites Pope Pius XI, who died in 1939. Two years earlier his encyclical *Mit Brennender Sorge (With Deep Anxiety)* condemned the by-then obvious Nazi racism. The following year Pius XI, departing from his script and with tears in his eyes, told a group of Belgian pilgrims that antisemitism was intolerable. "Spiritually," he continued, "we are all Semites."

There is evidence that Pius XI had intended to publicly condemn National Socialism's despicable antisemitic behavior in the wake of *Kristallnacht* (November 9–10, 1938). He had commissioned the American Jesuit John LaFarge, known for his antiracist work in America, to prepare a draft of an encyclical on racism called *Humani Generis Unitas*, the *Unity of Humankind*. LaFarge and his coauthor, German Jesuit Gustav Gundlach, discovered that the draft of their manuscript had not been forwarded to the pope. Its transmission was sabotaged by Wlodimir Ledóchowski, the general of the Jesuit society. When the draft finally arrived, the pope was too ill to deal with the matter. Following Pius XI's death the text disappeared, only to be discovered years after the Shoah. Michael Phayer notes that while its views on antisemitism were "quite unexceptional culturally and theologically,... it did condemn both racism and racial antisemitism explicitly."[23] We wonder about the possible impact this document might have had on the course of events had it in fact been issued on the eve of the Shoah.

In *We Remember*, the section "Nazi Antisemitism and the Shoah" makes a sharp distinction between Christian anti-Judaism and Nazi antisemitism. On the one hand, it is true that National Socialism's Jew-hatred was based on a constellation of non-Christian ideas: nineteenth-century pseudoscientific racial theories; Darwinian biosocial assertions; and the alleged superiority of "Aryan" blood. However, the document refrains from inquiring into what conditioned people to accept such assertions. Theologically sanctioned accusations began with the Christian Scripture itself. Jews were portrayed as deiciders. The Patristic period witnessed the emergence of the *Adversus Judaeos* tradition. Accusations of blood libel, identification with Satan, and centuries of demonizing Jews and Judaism had left their mark. Popular culture in the form of art, literature, and theater incorporated these themes. It was no accident that Jews were targeted for the *Endlösung*.

We Remember also identifies Nazism as a "thoroughly modern neopagan regime" whose antisemitism "had its roots outside of Christianity" and which "opposed the Church and persecuted her members also." While this position has some merit, it commits two sins of omission. First, it exemplifies what Dr. Paul O'Shea terms "Catholic denialism," which refers to an unwillingness to accept responsibility for the Church's role during the Holocaust.[24] The Vatican document simply does not bear historical scrutiny. Nazism borrowed much from traditional Christian teachings and practices of contempt for Judaism. The historian Lucy Dawidowicz observed that there is a straight line from Luther, whose vicious pamphlet *On the Jews and Their Lies* advocated burning the synagogues and expelling Jews, to Hitler. Further, the assertion that Jews and Christians alike were victims of Nazism may be a step toward Christianizing the Holocaust. Certainly some Christians were persecuted for their opposition to the regime. Some American fliers also perished in the Holocaust at a camp called Berga. But to assert that Jews, who were singled out for murder because of their birth, and Christians, who were not, are alike as victims is to undercut the document's earlier assertion in section 2.

The document gets further into historical difficulty in asserting that many individual Christians helped their Jewish brothers and sisters while some did not. This simply lacks all credibility. The historical record shows that the reverse is true. Most Christians did nothing to aid Jews or to embrace the normative Christian teachings of charity and universal love. Complicity rather than compassion characterizes the response of the bystanders during the Shoah. Unfortunately, those who cooperated with the Nazis either actively or as passive bystanders were conditioned by the teachings and omnipresent cultural symbols of Christianity's contempt for Jews and Judaism. Recognizing those few Christians who did resist is, of course, a moral obligation. This is why Yad Vashem in Israel honors the *Hasidei Umot Haolam*, the "righteous among the nations," by planting trees along a designated Avenue of the Just. That there were so few who acted morally is a rebuke to the Church and to the millions who stood idly by.

The document's brief reference to the role played by Pope Pius XII during the Shoah is theologically and historically disingenuous. In the space of two sentences and two footnotes, the authors of *We Remember* have rubbed salt into old wounds, outraged critics, and enfeebled the Church's own call for the moral dimension of memory. Pius XII is credited with defying Nazism in his very first encyclical, *Summi Pontificatus*, issued on October 20, 1939, warning against theories that "denied the unity of the human race" and against the "deification of the state." Further, the pope is credited with saving hundreds of thousands of Jewish lives through his own actions and through authorizing rescue activities of his representatives. The document's largest footnote reports the praise of Jewish leaders concerning "the wisdom of Pope Pius XII's diplomacy" during the war.

The literature on the wartime role of Pius XII is enormous, much of it contradictory in nature, and doubtless inaugurated by the appearance of Rolf Hochuth's 1963 polemical play *Der Stellvertreter (The Deputy)*, which sharply attacked Pius XII's silence during the Shoah. A brief survey of selected scholarly analyses of Pius XII in relation to the Holocaust deserves our attention. Father John Morley's 1980 book *Vatican Diplomacy and the Jews During the Holocaust: 1939–1943* concludes that Pius XII's record was "not good." Michael Phayer's *The Catholic Church and the Holocaust, 1939–1965* (2000) is a sober look at Pius XII's persona and policies. Phayer concludes that the pope was moved by several considerations. Politically, his concern was for the physical safety of Vatican City. Personally, his preference was for diplomacy rather than public declarations. Theologically, Pius XII had an abiding fear of Communism and viewed Hitler and National Socialism as a bulwark against godless bolshevism.

In the same year, Susan Zuccotti's book *Under His Very Windows: The Vatican and the Holocaust in Italy* appeared. She concludes that Pius XII emphasized political and diplomatic responses, not moral teaching. The pope, she concludes, "was the leader of millions of Catholics who had been taught to look to him above all others for spiritual and moral guidance."[25] In this crucial hour, at a time when millions of Jews were being murdered, Catholics looked to Pius XII for "a word, a sign, an indication of how to respond." "The Pope's own countrymen," she writes, "similarly looked to him for guidance. They found little or nothing."[26]

John Pawlikowski contends that Pius XII was "committed to a *diplomatic* rather than a *prophetic* vision of the Church." This choice resulted from the pope's determination to "preserve Catholicism as an institutional force against the onslaught, as he saw it, of Bolshevism and liberalism." His concern about liberalism, notes Pawlikowski, stemmed from the Church's reaction against what it viewed as a "fundamental threat to the continuation of a European civilization in which Christianity would set the moral, cultural, and even the political tone."[27] It surely was not accidental that Pope Pius IX issued his *Syllabus of Errors* (1864), which listed eighty of the "principle errors of our times." The chief error is the assumption that the pope must "reconcile himself to and agree with progress, liberalism, and modern civilization."

A fatal dichotomy marks Pius XII's wartime response. "Words," notes Paul O'Shea, "were uttered in torrents for the safety of the Catholic world, for the preservation of Rome, for the peace of Europe and the world. But none were uttered for Jews *qua* Jews. The impotency of words, which never once stopped him from speaking for Catholics, stopped him from speaking clearly for the Jews."[28] O'Shea views the pope's failure to speak out as being rooted in his theological view of his mission as Christ's Vicar on earth, which "made him accountable to God for the preservation and salvation of the Catholic Church so that its mission could continue. Nothing, not even the deaths of millions, could be allowed to stand between the Pope and this God-given task."[29] Pius XII also inherited the Church's centuries-old teaching of contempt for Judaism. In this view, Jews were deicide people who, as Saint Augustine long ago taught, bore the mark of Cain. Therefore their fate would be in the hands of God. Consequently, for Pius XII, Jews in essence were less important than a host of other considerations; "lesser victims" than all others.

Some questions arise from this section of *We Remember*. Why, for example, is the Vatican so committed to absolving Pius XII prior to the completion of a comprehensive assessment of his record? Indeed, why has he been proposed for beatification while so much uncertainty exists? One part of the answer may lay in the aforementioned Hochuth polemic. The

Vatican initially agreed (October 1999) to open its archives to a specially constituted Catholic-Jewish team of scholars, whose task was to study documents pertaining to Pius XII's conduct during the Shoah. After the team submitted a list of questions that needed to be addressed, the archives were placed off-limits amidst mutual recriminations and charges of anti-Catholic bias (August 2001). James Carroll provides another clue to the Vatican strategy. He writes that "John Paul II has reasserted the idea of infallibility (inaugurated by Pius IX), on the one hand, while demonstrating an unprecedented and genuine sympathy for Jews, on the other." This, says Carroll, "is the great paradox of his papacy."[30] It also continues the notion of mixed signals which simultaneously encourages dialogue while asserting an incompatible theological absolutism that renders impossible any meaningful self-critique on the part of the Church.

The Vatican document, ostensibly focusing on the uniqueness of the Jewish experience during the Holocaust and condemning antisemitism and racism as being against the principles of Christianity, then lists other twentieth-century genocides. *We Remember* specifies the Armenians, the Gypsies, and victims in the Ukraine in the 1930s. Similar tragedies in America, Africa, and the Balkans are also deplored, as is the fate of the millions of victims of totalitarian ideology in Russia, China, Cambodia, and elsewhere. Additionally, the document refers, ambiguously, to the well-known "drama of the Middle East, where many human beings are still their brothers' victims." What does this mean? And why restrict this observation to the Middle East when sadly it describes the situation in much of the world?

Lumping other tragedies into this section, far from focusing attention on the specificity of each, tends rather to dilute each of them. Preferable is Elie Wiesel's attestation that "every tragedy deserves its own name." If the Holocaust is an "indelible stain" on the history of the twentieth century, then what are these other moral outrages? Curiously, the document omits any reference to the participation of certain high-ranking clergy in helping Nazi criminals escape to South America. The contention that only one Croatian archbishop—rather than the Vatican itself— aided the Nazi murderers exemplifies "Catholic denialism." What possible moral or theological warrant could account for such evil behavior? At the very least, it demonstrated the complete indifference of the Vatican toward the Jewish experience in the Holocaust. Why did the document not report on the Vatican's immediate post-Shoah failure to specifically condemn the destruction of European Judaism, or to excommunicate any of the high-ranking Nazis?

Further, if evil is ubiquitous, then everyone is its victim. Consequently, the Jewish people cease being Nazism's principal victim. Sergio Minerbi believes that Pope John Paul II intended to Christianize the Shoah. "The holocaust," writes Minerbi, "could become a Polish-Catholic martyrdom, the Catholic Church as a whole becoming thus a victim and not merely a witness of the holocaust, and therefore Pius XII would pass into history as the chief martyr."[31] As an aside, it is instructive to focus on three examples of sainthood/martyrdom: the elevation to sainthood of Pius IX, Father Maximillian Kolbe, and Edith Stein. A fourth case involves the wish to beatify Pope Pius XII. Pio Nono, a pre-Holocaust figure, was, as noted, not only the author of the infamous "Syllabus of Errors," which condemned modernity—a movement that the Church closely identified as being "Jewish." He also refused—despite worldwide protest—to return Edgardo Mortara, a six-year-old Jewish child who was clandestinely baptized by his nanny—unbeknownst to his parents—and forcibly removed from his home. The child was taken to the Vatican. Mortara subsequently became a priest.

Advocating reconciliation and the role of memory is antithetical to the actions that occurred during the pontificate of Pius IX. Upon hearing of the impending beatification, Gerhard Riegner wrote "the beatification of Pope Pius IX was a terrible shock for us." Riegner, the World Jewish Congress representative in Geneva, was informed in 1942 by a German businessman, Eduard Schulte, of the German plan to annihilate the Jews of Europe. He cabled this information to WJC colleagues in London and New York. For decades following the Holocaust, Riegner dedicated himself to improving and normalizing relations between the Church and Judaism. How, Riegner asks,

> ...is it possible to comprehend, after a solemn expression of repentance and asking pardon for all wrongdoings against Jews throughout history, the beatification of

> somebody who more than anyone else personified the most authoritarian and closed attitude in the Church and who strongly condemned all modern movements? How hold up as an example for veneration a person who reestablished the ghetto of Rome, who renewed all the discriminations of which the Jews were victims in the state and the church, and who concealed and defended the clandestine conversion and abduction of a Jewish child and his elevation to the priesthood? Are these acts indicative of "unconditional fidelity to revealed truth"?—John Paul II utilized this phrase in describing Pius IX.[32]

The cases of Kolbe and Stein also reflect the Church's ongoing practice of sending mixed theological signals. Father Kolbe performed an altruistic act in Auschwitz, voluntarily taking the place of a condemned prisoner who had a family. He was, however, also the prewar editor of a journal that espoused antisemitic views. Edith Stein, a Jewish convert to Catholicism, became a nun in the Carmelite order. She was taken to Auschwitz from Holland, not because of her being a nun. Rather, because of an act of Dutch resistance, all Jews in the area were rounded up and deported. Her Jewish identity condemned Stein. Making her a saint of the Church—Saint Benedicta of the Cross—wounds Jewish sensibilities and raises concerns about the reemergence of supersessionary and triumphalistic attitudes toward Judaism. As an aside, Pope John Paul II conferred sainthood on more people than any of his predecessors. Pope Benedict XVI, John Paul II's successor, has allegedly "fasttracked" the candidacy of John Paul II himself for consideration of sainthood.

To return to the Vatican document's inclusion of Pius XII as a hero of the Holocaust, it is, on the face of things, unsupportable. No evidence exists that he saved hundreds of thousands of Jewish lives. Nor do we yet have documents to attest that he acted in a consistent manner in order to aid the Jewish people. Moreover, the citation in footnote sixteen of *We Remember*, which lists Jewish leaders' praise of the pope's wartime actions, omits reference to the fact that these statements were motivated by political concerns, that is, by the hope that the Vatican would recognize the modern state of Israel. The Church is, of course, free to canonize anyone whom it sees fit. But this also sends a message that the person so designated has led a life worthy of emulation. Suspicions could have been allayed and trust built if the document had not been insistent on raising the unresolved issue of Pius XII—which merits a separate study—in a document that aims at repentance.

Section 5 of *We Remember* looks "Together to a Common Future." Employing the Hebrew word *teshuvah* in appealing for repentance, the authors again express deep sorrow for the "failures of her sons and daughters in every age." But the document gives no evidence of a connection between official Church theology which preached that Jews were deicide people and that Judaism had been superseded, and those failures for which sorrow is expressed. True *teshuvah*, in the Jewish tradition, requires a turning; turning away from sin and turning toward the teachings of the Torah. Further, this turning process is observable in changed behavior on the part of one who is a sincere penitent. While we do not believe or suggest that the Church needs to turn toward the Torah, we do argue that it should turn away from the continued sin of failing to acknowledge the Church as the source of teachings that fertilized the "spoiled seeds" of anti-Judaism and antisemitism, which, the document rightly states "must never again be allowed to take root in any human heart."

Comparing *We Remember* to the earlier statements of the Polish (1990, 1995, 2000), German (1995), French (1997), and Italian bishops (1998), there is a marked difference not only in tone, but also in theological and historical integrity. The French bishops elected to make their declaration at Drancy, "the antechamber of death." Cardinal Jean Marie Lustiger, whose Jewish mother perished in Auschwitz, was one of the bishops at Drancy. Both the German and French declarations admit the Church's moral failings, especially the sin of silence, during the Shoah. The Polish bishops' "Pastoral on Jewish-Catholic Relations" (November 2000) specifically addresses the moral failure of many Polish Catholics to aid the Jews during the Holocaust: "If only one Christian could have helped and did not stretch out a helping hand to a Jew during the time of danger or caused his death, we must ask forgiveness of our Jewish brothers and sisters."

The late Harry James Cargas authored an even earlier paper titled "My Papal Encyclical" (1989).[33] Cargas calls on the Church to admit errors on the part of Christian teachers, including the Church Fathers. Further, he admonishes the Church about the necessity of examining and rooting out from the Christian Scripture all teachings of hatred and the necessity of interpreting them in a nonhateful or hurtful manner. While not carrying the weight of the Vatican document, these five statements courageously engage in a theological self-critique. This offers a far firmer foundation for genuine dialogue than do statements that endorse theological and moral evasion, and we believe that this is in line with the meaning of Reb Nachman's paradox.

PROMISE AND PERIL: *DABRU EMET*

No Jewish response to the apparent overturning of the Church's teaching of contempt has had the public impact of *Dabru Emet*. Crafted by four Jewish studies professors—the late Tikva Frymer-Kensky of the University of Chicago Divinity School; David Novak of the University of Toronto; Peter W. Ochs of the University of Virginia; and Michael A. Signer of the University of Notre Dame—representing a variety of positions along the Jewish theological spectrum, the statement was signed by nearly two hundred rabbis and scholars. Like *We Remember*, the Jewish statement attracted much attention, praise, and controversy. *Dabru Emet* articulates the promise of a new beginning for Jewish response to Christian attempts at *teshuvah*. Judaism, the statement argues, need no longer instinctively fear Christianity. A new theological dawn has broken. Further, the declaration rightly declares that Jews may learn more about their own tradition by engaging in dialogue with Christians.

Dabru Emet, like *We Remember*, is intended as a "first step." As a first step and one that seeks to overcome Jewish defensiveness about interreligious dialogue, it does appear promising. Furthermore, the document, attests David Fox Sandmel, is designed to promote further conversation and study "first and foremost, within the Jewish community, and secondly, between Jews and Christians."[34] Sandmel, who is one of the editors of *Christianity in Jewish Terms*—a fleshing out of the *Dabru Emet* one-page statement—opines that studying together, Jews and Christians "gain understanding that can replace old fears and stereotypes with respect and tolerance… and in the process become better Jews and Christians."[35] This position may be normatively accurate. But it is seriously flawed on the factual level. It embraces the American belief that negotiation can narrow difference and result in harmony.

Dabru Emet overlooks two basic facts; the asymetrical relationship between Christians and Jews, with the former numbering approximately 1 billion worldwide whereas Jews number roughly 14 million. But the fundamental asymmetry transcends demographics: It is theological in nature. Christianity, attests Paul, is the "wild olive shoot" grafted onto the olive tree which, root and branch, is Israel (Romans 11:17–24). But the incarnation means that the promise of Judaism is fulfilled. Christianity needs Judaism. But Judaism needs for its fulfillment neither Christ nor Christianity. Further, despite all the talk about change, antisemitism, as Edward Flannery observed, "is not in its death throes. A civilization contaminated so long with a toxin so virulent could hardly be detoxified in such short order."[36] *Dabru Emet*'s optimistic assessment—while laudable in its intent—is purchased at a steep price: the peril of theological evasion and historical distortion.

Two introductory paragraphs note the important post-Holocaust change in Christianity's official statements about Jews and Judaism, and the necessity of a thoughtful Jewish response. There ensue eight one-sentence propositions, each followed by a short explanatory paragraph. The eight statements are:

1. Jews and Christians worship the same God.

2. Jews and Christians seek authority from the same book, the Bible (what Jews call "Tanakh" and Christians call the "Old Testament").

3. Christians can respect the claim of the Jewish people upon the land of Israel.

4. Jews and Christians accept the moral principles of Torah.

5.   Nazism was not a Christian phenomenon.

6.   The humanly irreconcilable difference between Jews and Christians will not be settled until God redeems the entire world as promised in Scripture.

7.   A new relationship between Jews and Christians will not weaken Jewish practice.

8.   Jews and Christians must work together for justice and peace.

The authors contend that *Dabru Emet* seeks to travel the path of rethinking "how Jews and Christians may relate to one another." Yet the statement reveals just how difficult it remains for the two traditions to "speak the truth" both to one another and to themselves. Papering over some differences and avoiding central and complex questions, the Jewish statement gives the false impression that there are no major theological differences between Christianity and Judaism. Further, the differences that do exist can be sidestepped in the name of interfaith harmony. Placing *Dabru Emet* in the context of one of the major pitfalls of interfaith dialogue over the last decades, Jon D. Levenson notes that given the history of religiously inspired contempt and animosity: "It is inevitably tempting… to avoid any candid discussion of fundamental beliefs and to adopt instead the model of conflict resolution or diplomatic negotiation. The goal thus becomes reaching an agreement, in the manner of two countries that submit to arbitration… to end longstanding tensions or of a husband and wife who go to a marriage counselor in hopes of overcoming points of contention…. Commonalities are stressed, and differences— the reason, presumably, for entering into dialogue in the first place—are minimized, neglected, or denied altogether."[37] The peril of this model is that the ultimate objective becomes "not just agreement but mutual affirmation." Mutually critical judgments that the two traditions have made about each other are "increasingly presented as merely the tragic fruit of prejudice and misunderstanding."[38]

Dabru Emet does have one nonproblematic assertion. Jews and Christians, the authors write, "must work together for justice and peace." We wonder what dialogical principle is furthered by this platitude. Moreover, why is working together for peace and justice restricted to Jews and Christians? What of Jews and Buddhists? Or Christians and Muslims? Or secularists and those who reject all faith positions? Should not all those interested be included in this imperative? Platitudes tend to yield only more platitudes. Refraining from examining the hard questions posed by antithetical theological positions and very different readings of history will not substantively further the dialogue.

Dabru Emet, following *We Remember*, elides historical and theological realities in contending that Nazism was not a Christian phenomenon. "Nazism itself," the authors attest, "was not an inevitable outcome of Christianity." Perhaps not, but the Nazis certainly made ample use of negative Christian stereotypes of Jews, which found a receptive contemporary audience. The statement then asserts that if the Nazis had completely exterminated the Jews, the regime would have "turned its murderous rage more directly to Christians." This claim ignores the central difference between Jews and Christians under National Socialism. As noted above, Jews were exterminated because of the "crime" of existing. It is true that Christians who resisted the regime were persecuted. But if they did not resist, and had no Jewish ancestors, they faced no danger of being sent to death camps. By equating the position of Christians and Jews, the statement gives the Church a theological pass rather than compelling discussion on why the majority of Christians under National Socialism were bystanders and, more than a few, murderers. In this, *Dabru Emet* accepts uncritically the similar assertion found in *We Remember*.

Theological difficulties are also evaded in the assertions that both faiths "seek authority from the same book" (*Tanakh* for the Jews and Old Testament for the Christians) and that "Jews and Christians worship the same God." Problems with the first point begin with language and end with theology. The very phrase "Old Testament" is itself supersessionary. Jews do not refer to their sacred text as the "Old Testament." The Jewish sacred text is called *TaNaKh*, an acronym standing for *Torah* (the Five Books of Moses), *Nevuim* (prophets), and *Ketuvim* ([other] Writings). Furthermore, Jews do not refer to, consult, believe authoritative, or, for the most part, even know the contents of the so-called "New Testament." Christians do read or, more accurately, *misread* the "Old Testament" as an introduction to, or preparation for, their "New Testament."

Dabru Emet further errs on the side of avoidance and evasion in neglecting mention of either rabbinic texts such as the Mishnah and Gemara, or the various authoritative councils in Christianity that defined basic creedal statements of belief. These texts and entities play a crucial interpretive role in determining biblical meaning and relevance for Jews on the one hand, and Christians on the other. People reading the Bible, whether *Tanakh* or "New Testament," without reference to subsequent interpretations are most likely to be fundamentalists who, ironically, are *the least interested* in interfaith dialogue and the most committed to evangelizing.

The assertion that Jews and Christians worship the same God is seriously flawed. *Shema Yisrael* – "Hear O Israel, the Lord our God, the Lord is One"—is the central Jewish confession of faith. For Christianity, the assertion of Jesus' divinity—as the Son of God—is essential. Indeed, as Michael Wyschogrod notes, the two most intractable theological differences between Jews and Christians are "the divinity of Jesus and Christianity's abrogation of Mosaic law—neither of which is mentioned in *Dabru Emet*."[39] The consequence of this evasion is deeply troubling for the future of Jewish-Christian dialogue. In attempting to achieve "theological reciprocity," the Jewish statement's reassessment of Christianity comes at the expense of acknowledging real theological differences. And dialogue, as noted, can occur only when there is difference.

We think here, in terms of the assertion about worshiping the same God, of an analogy from the world of Jewish mysticism. Gershom Scholem, the twentieth-century pioneer of the scientific study of Jewish mysticism, noted that there is no such thing as mysticism in the abstract. Each religious tradition has a particular path that its adherents follow in order to seek the mystical goal. "Why," Scholem inquires, "does a Christian

mystic always see Christian visions and not those of a Buddhist? Why does a Buddhist see the figures of his own pantheon
and not... Jesus or the Madonna? Why does a Kabbalist (Jewish
mystic) on his way to enlightenment meet the prophet Elijah
and not some figure from an alien world?"[40] The path to mystical experience, and to God, requires symbols and rites unique
to each tradition. Furthermore, the role of the guru or master
in each of these traditions is to assist the disciple in placing his
or her experience within the ritual/symbolic images of their
respective teachings.

In terms of the psychology and sociology of religion, *Dabru
Emet* makes the intriguing point that "a new relationship
between Jews and Christians will not weaken Jewish practice."
The authors of the statement are certain that Jews need not fear
assimilation, intermarriage, or conversion. In this context it is
significant to note that the *Dabru Emet* ad was suggested by two
professors at Christian schools, Signer and Frymer-Kensky. The
position of David Novak, a political and religious conservative,
illustrates a curious contemporary phenomenon: the unstated
but real partnership between conservative Jews and Christians
in their mutual opposition to what they view as rampant secularity in American culture.

In this context it is worth noting that some Orthodox
Jews—in a move that appears counterintuitive—supported
Mel Gibson's film *The Passion of the Christ*, not in terms of its
message, but precisely because they viewed it as a blow against
what they perceive as a triumphant secularism; it was a victory
for "their" side in the raging culture war. Novak specifically
notes the "dangers of secularity" for both Jews and Christians.[41]
Peter Ochs, for his part, also views secularity as a danger to the
dialogue. He writes, "Most folks are not aware of how much
religious Muslims, Jews, and Christians suffer from the antireligious prejudices of modern secular society."[42] The statements
by Novak and Ochs overlook two significant facts. First, during
the Holocaust, many people who claimed to be religious were
murderers. It behooves those who speak of religion after Auschwitz as a bulwark of moral integrity and respect for human
life to articulate precisely how they define religion. The second
point deals with who is in and who is out of the dialogue. Why

are secularists, derided as a group, automatically excluded? Is there nothing that informed and sensitive people can add to the deliberations about respect for the other?

The matter of "practical politics" also deserves mention. The vast majority of *Dabru Emet*'s signatories are Reform and Conservative rabbis who must deal with the fact of intermarriage in their congregations. The paradox for Reform Judaism is that while Hebrew is increasingly used in the prayer book, there is an urgent debate over whether a non-Jewish spouse can serve on the temple's executive committee. Jacob Neusner opines that the "urgency of the *[Dabru Emet]* statement" derives from the "practical politics of finding something to say on the subjects of Hanukkah/Christmas and Easter/Passover, not to mention the problem of little Moshe O'Reilly."[43]

More could be said about *Dabru Emet*. For example, it is obviously the case that Christians can support the state of Israel; some do, but others do not, as we have already noted with regard to Christian calls for divestment. Others, especially certain but not all evangelicals, express support out of highly suspect theological motives. Similarly, it may be asked: Who is the anticipated Messiah? Wiesel in his novel *The Gates of the Forest* writes, "All men are the Messiah."[44] It is doubtful if Christianity would embrace that concept. We believe that in its rush to embrace a type of theological homogeneity, *Dabru Emet* has impeded rather than advanced Christian-Jewish dialogue. This is not to say that the two faith communities have nothing in common. We have already pointed to some of the shared goals, especially in terms of social justice, human rights, and *tikkun olam*. And we happily note the new openness to meaningful theological discussion.

Christianity and Judaism are, however, different. This is precisely why dialogue is necessary. The aim is not to bring the two points of view about God, Scripture, Messiah, and Covenant into harmony, but rather to deepen understanding of both one's own tradition and that of the other. In this process what we expect minimally is a respect for the dignity and safety of the other. In a world confronting Muslim jihadists and religiously sanctioned violence, and where Israel is continuously under both physical and verbal assault—British prime minister Blair condemned suicide bombings in *Palestine* (August 26, 2005), evidently unaware that Israel exists, and Pope Benedict XVI "forgot" to mention Israel as a victim of terrorist suicide bombers (August 25, 2005)—it is more important than ever to embrace Reb Nachman's paradox. If the dialogue is to develop and mature in the twenty-first century, it must do so based on the type of hope that emerges from the fullness of a broken heart.

Saying Out Loud What We Are Afraid to Say

As has been the case throughout this book, we speak here from a Jewish perspective. Therefore when we address the matter of saying out loud what we are afraid to say, it concerns what some Jews are afraid to say to well-meaning Christians, not what Christians are afraid to say to the Jews. But that too may come to light in the Christian response to what we now say, as well as to what we have said so far.

Many of us who are involved in Jewish-Christian dialogue have long sensed that there are certain lines that must not be crossed, lest we stop speaking to each other altogether; as soon as the discussion approaches those lines, the dialogue often degenerates into chitchat. Why do some of us grow afraid to speak above a whisper, and then only to like-minded colleagues? We are afraid to offend, afraid to hurt. It is a fear based on the respect and affection of friendship. After all, if Christians such as John Roth, John Pawlikowski, and David Gushee have found the courage, integrity, and sensitivity to sit down with us and talk, who are we to say things that might hurt or offend or anger them? Generally speaking, Christians take a far greater risk than Jews do when entering into a Jewish-Christian dialogue. It is they who are saddled with a teaching of contempt for the Jews that was never regarded as heresy. It is they who have maintained that the Jews are eternally damned, not just for the murder of Jesus but, more seriously, for the conscientious and calculated rejection of Jesus as the Savior and Messiah. It is they who must make certain adjustments in their thinking and teaching about Christianity, perhaps to the point where it may no longer be recognizable as Christianity, if they want to view Jews as true partners in dialogue, and not just as the "yet-to-be redeemed."

Contrary to the Christians, the Jews need not abandon anything in their religious traditions or in the teachings of their sages in order to accommodate the Christians in a dialogue. The Jews do not view the Christians as "yet-to-be redeemed," simply because they have rejected Judaism. Indeed, the Christian rejection of Judaism is perfectly okay with the Jews and always has been. Contrary to the Christians, who have no concept of the "righteous among the Jews who reject Jesus," the Jews have always counted certain Christians *as* Christians among the "righteous Gentiles." While many Jews have hated and feared many Christians, associating the cross not with salvation but with annihilation, Christians have never had any reason to associate the Star of David with the same sort of butchery and brutality. Judaism has never had anything like the official, theological teaching of contempt championed by so many Christian sages and saints over the ages; nor have the Jews ever maintained that Christians, or anyone else, should be kept in misery in order to demonstrate the falsehood of their teachings, as Saint Augustine and numerous other Christian saints have taught with regard to the Jews.[45] Wherever the Jews have come to hate the Christians, it has been because of what the Christians have *done* to the Jews, both through violence and through proselytizing, and not for the Christians' rejection of Judaism.

The troubling issues, of course, do not end here. Christianity's contribution to the Holocaust lies not only in its antisemitic, supersessionist teachings or in its insistence that everyone find salvation in Jesus. It is also rooted in certain fundamental, defining elements of Christian doctrine, specifically the doctrine of inherited sin and the teaching that faith, *not deeds*, is the key to redemption from that sin. According to this view, the human being, in his very existence and essence, is entombed in a state of sin. We can rise from that tomb only by embracing a certain belief, namely that Jesus Christ, the Son of God, paid the infinite ransom not just for what we have *done* but also for what we *are*. If anyone should refuse that redemption, not only does he remain in the tomb—he is consigned to the flames. Thus the blood of Christ redeems the believing Christian from this terrible judgment for the crime of being—*which is the crime of the*

Jew, both from Christian and from Nazi standpoints.[46] Yes, the Christian and Nazi reasons for regarding the being of the Jew as criminal are different, and that is extremely significant. But the implications are basically the same: One way or another, the Jews must disappear from the face of the earth.

Because the Jews explicitly and with conviction reject the Nazarene as their redeemer from sin, they are locked into that essential, ontological sin and are therefore subject to a most severe judgment for their inherently sinful being. Says Paul, "Wherefore, as by one man sin entered into the world, and death by sin, so death passed upon all men, for all have sinned" (Romans 5:12). For those who refuse to be washed in the Blood of the Lamb, justice means paying a death penalty for being alive, as the Jews of Nazi-occupied Christendom did. To the extent that this Christian doctrine persists after Auschwitz, the distinctively Christian view persists that the nonbeliever's being—that is, the Jew, at the core of his or her being, from infants to elders—is unredeemed, sinful, and justly consigned to death.

Thus for reasons of Christian doctrine, and not because he had become an apostate, a papal nuncio remarked to Michael Dov Weissmandl in 1944, "There is no innocent blood of Jewish children in the world. All Jewish blood is guilty. You have to die. This is the punishment that has been awaiting you because of that sin [deicide]."[47] Deicide aside, however, the unredeemed sin of the Jew for being alive—the sin of rejecting the redemption offered through the sacrifice of the Son of God—remains. And so Hitler becomes the instrument of God's justice. Or was the papal nuncio speaking blasphemy? If so, according to which doctrine, according to the teachings of which Christian scripture or sage or saint? Is not the doctrine of our sinful state, inherited and redeemable only through faith in Jesus, a defining element of Christianity? Can the Christians eliminate it from their teaching without altering the essence of Christianity? With these questions going through his or her mind, a Jew attempting to enter into a dialogue with a Christian wonders: How is it possible to engage in dialogue with someone who thinks you are either damned or yet-to-be redeemed?

Other Christian teachings, and not the abandonment of those teachings, assisted the Nazis in their slaughter of the Jews and remain as obstacles in any Jewish-Christian dialogue. In the previous chapter we commented on Jesus' assertion that "my kingdom is not of this world" (John 18:36); as soon as the true kingdom and the true blessedness are relegated to another world, it becomes all too easy to grow deaf and indifferent toward the outcry in this world. If the Nazis seek to rule *over* the world, the Christians seek to rise *above* it; as for the Jews, they seek to dwell *in* it. And both the *over* and the *above* are opposed to this *in*. Although their reasons are quite different from those of the Nazis—reasons of faith and devotion to God, and not reasons of race and devotion to the Führer—the Christian position is not merely different from a Jewish mode of being *in the world*: It is antithetical to it. The Messiah has come: It is finished. There is no need for the good *deeds* that prepare the way for the Messiah's entry into this world; rather, according to Christian reasoning, through *faith* we must prepare to enter the Messiah's world, which is elsewhere. Therefore we may retreat to the monastery or to the convent and say our prayers, deaf and indifferent to the roar all around us.

In many Christian traditions, the ideal life, the pure life, the "spiritual" life is the celibate and ascetic life of the monk or the nun; in Judaism there is no way of life higher than the way of marriage and childbearing. For there is no loving God without loving people, and you cannot love people by shunning their company or by refusing to have children. Although Christians most assuredly are not Nazis, their view of the world and of the ideal life can play into the hands of the Nazis. For it can play into the hands of an indifference toward the condition of this world—and toward the plight of Jews in this world—as one turns away from this world to prepare to enter the next. This attempt to turn one's face toward God ends by turning one's back on humanity. The result can be a proliferation of the illness of indifference that contributed to the murder of the 6 million. Thus the Christian accent on the heavenly kingdom, and not on the earthly plight, can exacerbate the problem of Jew hatred as it plays out in this world. We do not envision the pope urging his priests and nuns to get married and have babies. It is not that we want the Christians to be like the Jews; rather, we want the Christians to adopt a teaching that declares the Jews to be who they are, without trying to kill them or convert them or to make them into their elder brothers or covenantal partners. The Jews are *not* "covenantal partners" with the Christians (whatever that could possibly mean); the Jews are covenantal partners with God.

As for the Jewish-Christian partnership in dialogue, it is possible only with a partner who does not want you to be like him or think like him but who understands that dialogue requires difference. Whereas a Jew would never attempt to convert a Christian to Judaism or suppose that a Christian's soul would be better off if he or she should become a Jew, can a Christian truly say to a Jew, "Do not convert to Christianity. It is no good for you. You are better off with your own teaching and tradition"? Can a Christian remain faithful to Christian teaching and denounce efforts to proselytize the Jews, declaring that the souls of the Jews are in a better state without Christianity? Can a Christian in the end say to a Jew, "You do not need Jesus in order to have a place with God. Jesus is superfluous to your salvation. For you, the Torah is enough"? Is this not blasphemy?

To be sure, whereas a Christian is immediately pleased to have a convert to Christianity, Jews are initially puzzled and at times even suspicious of their converts, even though in the end they honor them. Recognizing that each human being is created for his or her specific path, the rabbis see it as their duty to make three serious efforts to dissuade a proselyte from converting to Judaism; the practice is based on the story of Ruth the Moabite, whose mother-in-law told her three times that she should remain in Moab rather than follow Naomi to Bethlehem (Ruth 1:11–16). The Christian longing for universal assent to the doctrine has had murderous consequences, not just for the Jews but also for tens of thousands of people wherever Christianity has spread.[48] And those consequences ensue not just when Christians abandon their teachings, but precisely when they adhere to them. Thus the question arises: Can the Christians find a way to abandon the proselytizing teachings of their tradition, to the point where they might rejoice in, or at least support, the fact that a Jew rejects Christianity and remains faithful to his or her tradition? If the Christians are to rethink the notion of salvation and what it requires, to the point where Jesus is *unnecessary* to the salvation of the Jews, then what becomes of the Christian claim that Jesus is the Messiah? After all, according to traditional Jewish teaching, at least, the Messiah is by definition *indispensable* to the salvation of the Jews and everyone else. A Messiah meant only for the Gentiles, with the Torah sufficient for the children of Abraham, is inconceivable to the Jews. Can the Christians get rid of the necessity of salvation only through the Christ and still have Christianity? And even if they can dispense with that teaching, can the Jews get rid of it?

Just as there are difficulties for Jewish-Christian dialogue in these matters of doctrine, so are there difficulties with regard to implications of the historical contexts for dialogue itself. Dialogue, for example, requires coming together on a more or less equal footing. But Jews and Christians are not on an equal footing. Christians bear a far greater heritage of guilt for atrocities committed against the Jews than the Jews bear vis-à-vis the Christians. Jews and Judaism, moreover, are essential to the substance and truth of Christianity and Christian identity; Christians and Christianity, however, are absolutely unnecessary to Judaism and Jewish identity. While Jews may be "the significant other of Christians," as Henry Knight refers to them,[49] Christians are assuredly not the "significant other" of Jews.

Therefore many of us find it rather offensive, albeit well-intended, when Knight goes on to say, "They [the Jews] are our significant others, now reclaimed in more positive relation, as partners in our covenantal way."[50] Reclaimed? In the Christians' covenantal way? Most Jews recoil at being either claimed or reclaimed by Christians (again, whatever that means). We do not want to be reclaimed. Some will say that we want to be left alone; others will say that we want to be respected, whether because of or in spite of our difference. If we seek to be partners in dialogue, we neither desire nor understand what it means for Jews to be partners with Christians in a "covenantal way." Although Knight's remark can be understood as a statement of the Christian need for the Jews and Judaism, does it mean that the Christians must, in some sense, "return" to Judaism? Does the covenantal way pertain to the Covenant of Abraham? Whereas for the Jew, the covenantal way is the Brit Milah, the

Covenant of Circumcision; for the Christian, according to Paul, it is precisely the rejection of circumcision (see, for example, Galatians 5:2). If, on the other hand, we are indeed partners in the Covenant of Abraham, does it mean that with the advent of Jesus there is in fact no "New Covenant"? Is the notion of a New Covenant not a defining feature of Christianity?

The need to be needed is among the most basic of human needs, and Christians involved in Jewish-Christian dialogue need to be needed. But in what sense do the Jews need the Christians? One might say that in a time of worldwide antisemitism and Israel bashing, the Jews need the political support of Christians in order to assure the survival of the Jewish state and the Jewish people (the survival of one is bound to the survival of the other). That may be the case, but, as already pointed out, the Christian support of the Jewish state has been sporadic and lukewarm at best. And, as much as the Jews need the Christian support of Israel, the Christians need their support of Israel even more. It is one way—perhaps the only way—they can return to a concrete concern for this world. It is one way that might open up a path for Christians and Jews to follow together. The Christians are not in need of redemption—they are in need of a *teshuvah*, a movement of return to the Jewish essence of the One for whom Christianity is named. And that Jewish essence of their Savior can be found only in the Jewish people, who follow the path that the Nazarene followed.

Six

DIALOGUE IN ACTION

O n January 3, 2007, Jewish scholars Alan Berger and David Patterson met for more than three hours with Christian scholars John Pawlikowski (Catholic), John Roth (Protestant), and David Gushee (Evangelical) to engage in a Jewish-Christian dialogue. Among the most preeminent of today's Christian thinkers engaged in Jewish-Christian dialogue, all three had read the manuscript of this book up to this point. Because Alan Berger and David Patterson have largely had their say in the preceding chapters, much of what follows consists of the Christians' dialogical response to points that the authors have raised. Only in this way could this volume begin to take on the dialogical dimensions that we seek. All of the participants came together in good faith, trusting each other to be open and honest and to put even the most sensitive topics on the table, without fear of offense, in the interest of arriving at a deeper understanding of the questions raised and of the truth of our traditions. The topics covered are hardly exhaustive; there is much more ground to be covered. It is our hope, however, that the following pages may illustrate how a genuine next step in Jewish-Christian dialogue might be made.[1]

Getting Started: The Christians' Reply

David Patterson (DP):

> Let's start by giving the Christian scholars an oppor-
> tunity to respond to questions and issues pertaining to
> what they've seen in the manuscript. Does that sound
> all right?

John Roth (JR):

> That's fine, as far as I'm concerned.

DP: One more thing: Alan and I want to thank the three of
you so very much for being part of this. We're both very
grateful to the three of you.

David Gushee (DG):

> Speaking for myself, I'd like to say I'm grateful for the
> invitation, grateful for the kind words that you've said
> about us, and I hope to be constructive.

JR: I want to add, too, David and Alan, that this is an
immensely interesting manuscript, and I'm really glad
personally to have a chance to interact with it and with
the two of you on this.

DP: Thank you. Shall we get into it?

DG: Let's do it.

John Pawlikowski (JP):

> Well, the first point I would make is something that
> you say on page xii, regarding the dialogue coming
> to a standstill. In my judgment, that would be some-
> what overstated. I think that there's a way in which
> the inter-institutional dialogue has come to a standstill,
> not so much in terms of whether or not there are meet-
> ings that take place, because, in fact, there are. How-
> ever, as a participant in some of those, I don't see them

really advancing the discussion in any profound way. They've become almost, if I can put it this way, political exercises.

Nonetheless, I think there is an area where it hasn't come to a standstill, and that would be the more academic context. I see an increasing number of scholarly books in this area. We now have some twenty-six or twenty-seven centers dealing with Christian-Jewish relations at educational institutions throughout the country, and these are the ones that have joined the formal Council of Centers. There are others that are not part of this. I see a lot of interesting work taking place in the academic area, which at some point may filter into the more institutional. I just think you need a little nuancing on that point. It's primarily at the institutional level that there's been some change.

My second point would have to relate to your introduction to chapter 1. I would generally agree with you in terms of what you state about the asymmetrical nature of the relationship, particularly on the theological level. This is something that I actually raised in an op-ed piece that appeared in *Moment* magazine some years ago. The thesis I put forth is that if Christian theologians, scholars, are increasingly making an argument that there is an inherent bonding between Judaism and Christianity—something, in fact, on the Catholic side, John Paul himself said in some of his statements—does that not put some kind of pressure on the Jewish side to offer a response? The response could be, "Absolutely not, we don't agree with this," but it seemed to me very hard. What I was seeing was a certain applause for that development within Christianity without a real grappling on the Jewish side, as to whether that would have any significance for Jewish theological perspectives on Christianity. The other aspect of that question would be the scholarship that's emerging relative to the first century and even beyond, where it is clearer that the separation between Judaism and Christianity was a far longer process than we imagined even ten years ago, far more complex. And where there was continued religious interaction in some cases well into the second century and in a few places, even beyond that. Amy-Jill Levine actually said right here in Memphis when we were together at a conference a couple of years ago that she found some evidence as late as the fifth century, which I hadn't heard about. The interaction that was taking place, even though we don't know everything we would like to know about it, seems to indicate that there was some openness on the Jewish side to still considering these people who followed Christianity as somehow within the larger tent of Judaism. So at least some of the new scholarship would raise some new issues for Jewish theological perceptions, even though I generally agree there is a certain asymmetrical dimension to the relationship on a lot of fronts, including the theological.

Now, when you say that for Christians the cross symbolizes the passion and resurrection of Jesus, I would just say this: I think that's again a generally true statement, even though the cross has been interpreted in significantly different ways by different theologians. But certainly there's at least another trend, which is one that I have tended to follow and which has a richer possibility from the Christian side for constructive Christian theology of the Jewish people, and that's a greater stress on the incarnation rather than the passion and resurrection. There is a theological trend, historically, and not just in the contemporary period in Christianity. My only concern is that throughout the manuscript there are times when there is a little bit of stereotyping of Christianity. Now I realize it's an extremely complex reality, and you can't cover all the nuances.

When you get into the whole question of the Holocaust and so on, I certainly would applaud the idea that the Holocaust is a fundamental starting point for Christian theological reflection. One of my criticisms of colleagues who have been involved in this process on the Christian side, people like the late Paul Van Buren, or on the Jewish side, someone like David Hartman, is that they would reduce the Holocaust to something we mourn, but not something we build on theologically. I have a fundamental disagreement with that. For me the Holocaust has significantly altered the way we understand the God/human person/human community relationship. In that sense, there is a kind of theological relationship that the Holocaust forces both Christians and Jews into. Irving Greenberg has actually made the point that the Holocaust theologically challenges anybody who builds their understanding upon the biblical covenantal tradition. He would even extend that to Islam, to the extent that Islam also builds on Judaism and Christianity, so I do think that's very important.

However, I would just have one caution: I'm not one who quite accepts a straight line between classical Christian antisemitism and the Nazi reality. For me, the traditional Christian antisemitism wanted to make Jews miserable and marginal in human society. This also resulted in a considerable number of people actually dying as a result, there's no question about that. But I don't think it had the aim at total annihilation that was the main thrust of Nazism. I also think that Nazism was rooted in a biological theory of racial inferiority that was not there in Christianity. I've said in many of my writings that for me Christian antisemitism is the indispensable seedbed for the growth of Nazism, particularly in European society, but I'm not sure it would have emerged in the way that it did, with a philosophy of total annihilation, if there had not been this modern biological theory.

To finalize my initial comments: In many parts of the book you emphasize the ambiguity in the way Christians are responding to the dialogue with Judaism. That's a reality. With regard to the theological issues that have emerged from the Christian-Jewish dialogue, on the Christian side there is a fundamental unwillingness to confront them in many circles, and this is especially true at the institutional level.

DG: So much to say. I'll try to be very brief at this stage.
This was an engrossing book to read; it is the most
direct and no-holds-barred critique of Christians and
Christianity that I have read from a Jewish perspective. But I also thought it opened up the possibility of
dialogue at a deeper level. It took courage to write this
book, because it opens up the possibility of rejection,
of negative reaction. Like the part "Saying Out Loud
What We Are Afraid to Say," where you suggest that
on balance Christianity has been a negative presence,
basically, in the world. That's a pretty challenging
statement, and I appreciate your having the honesty
to say it.

When challenged at that level, most Christians I
know would simply harden into a defensive crouch and
say, "That's absurd," or "That goes way too far." And
this raises an interesting question about how much a tradition can be challenged before the general response of
a lot of people in that tradition is just to go into a hun-
ker-down mode and say, "No more criticism, no more
critique, no more reformation, no more change. We will
defend ourselves." I think this is a great issue in Jewish-Christian dialogue, in general. There is a challenge
that leads to reformation and repentance and change,
and then there is challenge that leads to shame, which
then hardens into anger and resistance, and I think that
some of the conservative responses to Jewish challenges
to Christianity post-Shoah reflect a kind of hunkering-
down based on shame, "No more criticism," and "We
will defend our glorious tradition," and that kind of
thing.

As an evangelical, I would know that evangelicals
are only minimally involved in this conversation in general. Partly because of the dynamics in our theological
tradition, which makes it hard for us to hear the criticisms. When scholars define evangelicals, they say there
are four main characteristics: (1) biblical authority, (2)
Christo-centrism, (3) an emphasis on evangelism and
missions, and (4) personal conversion and piety. So if

you look at those four characteristics, you see the problems immediately.

Biblical authority is going to be a problem in light of challenges to specific biblical texts, and when the issue goes to the truthfulness and even the morality of biblical passages, it is very hard for evangelicals and a lot of conservative Christians to embrace. As for Christo-centrism, it all has to do with what we make of Jesus, and I want to talk about that later.

Evangelism and missions are a key issue, perhaps *the* key stumbling block for evangelical engagement in this dialogue, because any claim that says your effort to bear witness to your faith in Jesus Christ is illegitimate in principle is going to go right into the heart of evangelical identity. It is very hard for an evangelical Christian to be opposed to personal conversion and piety and to those Jewish people who convert to Christianity; it is hard for an evangelical Christian to be opposed to anybody converting to Christianity. In fact, it is what we are trained to want of everyone. And so rethinking that is a tremendous challenge within our tradition.

In terms of evangelicals and the Holocaust, I would say this: Evangelicals in general are aware of the Holocaust; they are troubled by the Holocaust. The students that I teach want to study it; they want to learn about it. Their initial default setting is, as you say in the manuscript, to think that the Holocaust has really nothing to do with Christianity. Horrible Nazis killed the Jews. Pagan Nazis, who worshiped Satan and were into the occult, and all of that.

These horrible Nazis persecuted the Church, and so we lift up heroic resisters like Dietrich Bonhoeffer, and evangelicals have invested pretty deeply in Bonhoeffer. So evangelicals take the Holocaust seriously, but not as a challenge for Christian theology. For many it is an example of great evil, a reason to support Israel and to want to have fraternal relations with the Jewish people. But how this goes back to the New Testament or the cross or the resurrection or salvation by grace through faith—almost no evangelicals have engaged that discussion.

Evangelicals in America are among the most loyal supporters of the state of Israel that one could find. And people ask me about this a lot. One reason for that support is because of our immersion in the Scriptures, both Old Testament and New Testament, as we would call it. Because we still are a Bible-reading people, a Bible-memorizing people, and a Bible-studying people, we travel the dusty roads of Galilee and Jerusalem and so on. So there is a historical sense of connection to the Holy People and the Holy Land that remains very strong, and that's a real resource for Jewish-Christian relations. It has helped lead to a strong evangelical sense of identification with Israel, including the modern state of Israel.

There is also within evangelicalism the apocalyptic speculations of people like Tim LaHaye and Jerry Jenkins and the *Left Behind* series. People have been writing these various scenarios since at least the twenties. In the seventies, when I was cutting my teeth, it was Hal Lindsey and *The Late Great Planet Earth*, which many evangelical kids were exposed to in youth groups, as I was. All of this involves a scenario where history is coming to an end soon, Jesus will return soon, He will return to Israel, the Jewish people will have an opportunity to see Him again and convert, there will be some climactic final battle, and history will come to an end. I don't know how many people purchased the *Left Behind* series, but I think it was over 50 million people. Wildly successful.

There is a lot that is disturbing about these books, but evangelical support for that series and for that vision should be understood to be not unanimous. It's called premillennial dispensationalism. This particular strand of theology really emerged in the late nineteenth and early twentieth centuries and became the eschatological framework for Christian theology for a strong slice of the evangelical community. It is taken as Gospel by a lot of the most visible conservative evangelical leaders, which helps to explain their support for Israel. They believe that part of God's unfolding plan is the establishment of the state of Israel and that these events will unfold in the last days.

You don't have anti-Israelism, anti-Zionism, in the evangelical community in the way that is discussed in this manuscript. You do have real issues, though, as to whether the Jewish community really wants the support of evangelicals on the basis of a theological scenario that is both biblically problematic and involves a conversionist scenario. "We love you, we're waiting for you to convert." But it has led to a political alliance of convenience. So I guess that's what I'll say to start off. There are a number of issues in texts related to messianism, to Scripture, and to theology. I'll just stop there.

JR: First, I want to say, I think that Alan and David know of my affection and high regard for them. But I also want to say, especially having listened now to David Gushee and John Pawlikowski, that I'm really proud of my Christian brothers here, too. I'm learning a lot just listening, and I think the five of us together make a pretty good package for advancing a dialogue that may be stalled in some ways, but certainly isn't among the five of us.

I divided my notes into four parts: I had a section on strengths that I saw in *Jewish-Christian Dialogue*, a section on problems, a section on questions, and a section on passages from the book. I think the list of strengths is immense here, but I'm not going to dwell on that so much except to say that I really appreciate the boldness in the book. It takes up the theological issues and goes right to the heart of them.

Having made that point, I'll move on to problems and questions that pertain to some of the theological material. One of the problems in the book is that it often relies on what I would call dualistic, either/or distinctions that seem to me too strong. Here I'm in agreement with David Gushee's point that certain challenges in the dialogue may arouse resistance. I found myself vacillating overall between agreement with the book's arguments, on the one hand, and, on the other hand, some anger about them.

You make either/or distinctions that seem too strong. Doing versus believing, for example. Too often in your account, it seems to me, Jews are always doing things, and Christians are always just believing things. Another instance would be the idea that Jews emphasize the world versus the idea that the Christian point of view is otherworldly. There is also the view that Jews take a historical view versus the theological emphasis of Christians. Other dualistic, either/or dichotomies involve living time versus marking time, belief derived from behavior versus behavior derived from belief. These distinctions seem to me to be dualistic in a way that makes it hard for me to recognize my own Christian identity. If "dialogue" doesn't allow us to recognize our identities, then it may need to correct itself and go deeper.

Furthermore, there is a kind of litany that runs through the book, and I find it perplexing. For example, the authors say that some Christian theological ideas are "abhorrent," "unintelligible," "foreign," "alien," and "inconceivable" to Jews. As we get into conversation, I want to find out more about the abhorrence and the unintelligibility and the inconceivability of basic Christian theological ideas. One place where that will come to bear is on the trinitarian notion. The idea that God is one but in three persons. Christians don't find that to be inconceivable, and, for me, it's a puzzle as to why it would be inconceivable to Jews. I think the idea could be rejected, but inconceivable? That's another matter. So, again, I wonder: Does the book go too far in a direction that is dualistic, and therefore distorted in some way?

A second overall point would be that in the book there is an interpretive mood that understands Christianity as a blend of history and myth, but I don't find a comparable move being made about Judaism. It seems to me that Alan and David tend to read Judaism as more straightforwardly historical and not so much as mythical. For example, at one place you say, "In Judaism, God created the Hebrew letters and words before he created heaven and earth." Now I read that and think, "Now what kind of statement is that? Surely that's mythological." So to what extent is the Patterson/Berger reading of Judaism complementary to their reading of Christianity, which includes history and myth? It seems to me that once you introduce the mythical into any religious tradition, then you've opened up the possibilities for dialogue, but if you don't, then one tradition is going to be a blend of history and myth, whereas the other really got it right, and I think that difference may block dialogue.

A third point: There's a tone in the book that seems to suggest, "Jews win, Christians lose." For example, you say there's nothing specific or concrete that Christians must do every day in order to claim that they are practicing Christians or that they are working for the coming of the Messiah. The tone there says to me that Judaism is better than Christianity. But you could also say that Christians are expected to do certain things; it just depends, for example, on what their sense of vocation is. If I think of myself as a teacher and that's my calling as a Christian, then there are certain things I must do every day. I must prepare my classes. I must treat my students in a particular way. There's a whole list of things. It isn't as specific as a series of commandments that are detailed in terms of specific practices, but there would be a whole series of things I could list that I would be expected as a Christian to do every day.

Just two other points, and then I'll stop and see where we want to go next. I was struck by how little emphasis you place on the notion of resurrection, which increasingly for me, as a post-Holocaust Christian, emerges and looms very, very large as a key teaching within Christianity. For Christians, I think, to say that there is resurrection means that death does not win, that evil is overcome—maybe not completely, but evil doesn't have the last word. For me, the Christian understanding of resurrection emphasizes those themes. The book speaks very little about these matters but instead devotes a lot of attention to the notion of original sin, which arguably is a far less normative idea for Christians. The result is that the book lacks some balance with respect to what the Christian tradition maintains.

Finally, a concern about strategy: I'm worried that in the book, Alan and David, you often stress common ground between the two traditions, but only to take it away by saying that the differences are really the major thing that stands out. You may be right, but I'm worried that you've extended something with one hand only to pull it away with the other. And whether it's necessary to do that as much as the book seems to do, I'm not sure. I know my voice here is more critical at the outset, but that's because I think that John Pawlikowski and David Gushee highlighted a number of strengths that I saw in the book, so I didn't feel a need to reiterate them, but I did have these feelings of concern that I've tried to express in my opening remarks.

JP: I'd like to pick up on one point that both John Roth and David Gushee raise, because I think it is also a concern of mine. It is a fundamental question: What do you hope to accomplish by this volume? The danger is that if you come on too strongly in the critique, the reaction may be along the lines that David Gushee outlined, and John Roth expressed that he himself felt, namely, a bit of anger which can then lead to circling the wagons, and saying, "Well, we're not going to engage in dialogue." And on the Jewish side, your approach might simply play into the hands of those who say, "Dialogue is worthless for Judaism; not only worthless but dangerous, because it may undercut our self-identity, and therefore, we really don't want to engage in it."

So my guess is, knowing both of you, that you want to promote dialogue, but the danger is that if you come on *too* strongly and seemingly unappreciative of key Christian beliefs, the end result might be for even more moderate people within the Christian tradition to just sort of say, "Well, we can't talk to those people, if that's their attitude."

It's interesting what John said about resurrection. Because I did stress the incarnation. I'm not opposed to the focus on resurrection, but resurrection also raises an issue because one could say that there would have been no notion of resurrection in the Christian tradition if it hadn't already arisen in Judaism in the postbiblical period. And so, from a Jewish perspective, there is a theological linkage in a way; it's true that original sin may be something where there is a kind of theological separation, because I don't see original sin having the same theological emphasis in Judaism that it has had historically in Christianity.

The other thing would be that there's at least been some theological exploration on the Jewish side of certain themes, for example the notion of incarnation. One could argue that people like Mike Wyschgorod, Elliot Wolfson, and others have in fact written on this. Wolfson would say that he's found some notions in the Jewish mystical literature of the period. It seems to me that it at least ought to be acknowledged. You may disagree with it, but there's at least some discussion of those kinds of things on the Jewish side. And this would help, I think, with the tone, that there is some rethinking, because I would have that feeling that John has, that when all is said and done, one gets a sense from the manuscript that really there isn't much homework that Judaism needs to do in terms of its own self-identity. It's pretty well established, and pretty much where it should be, and there doesn't need to be major reform or major change. It's really on the Christian side. And so maybe some acknowledgment that there's a recognized need to also adapt within Judaism, not so much as a result of the dialogue with Christianity, but simply in terms of rethinking some of its sources and so on. That helps to create a more dialogical situation, rather than a more antagonistic situation that seems to emerge from the manuscript as it now stands.

DG: I remember when I read Eliezer Berkovits's *Faith after the Holocaust*. As a Christian it was like taking a guilt bath, you know. He was so negative.

JP: I dialogued with him when he was in Chicago.

DG: At one level, it is good for us as Christians to have to take a guilt bath now and then, because it is not as if the Holocaust has ever been fully assimilated in the Christian community, has ever been fully dealt with, or is that long ago, to hear what feels like a cry of outrage at not just the Holocaust, but at the history of mistreatment, sometimes needs to happen; it's the right thing to do, and we need to hear it, notwithstanding the possibility that it will lead many people just to hunker down. So, the tone has a certain kind of anger to it, a certain kind of polemic to it, but I interpreted that as, well, it's good to be exposed to this again. It's been a while since I've been exposed to this kind of tone, and that feels about right in light of this history.

DP: Well, one of the problems in the dialogical process that strikes me is that often it's too much about sameness and not enough about difference. Because difference is an uncomfortable thing, sometimes an enraging thing, to have to address. I think one point we want to make is that difference is good for dialogue, and difference generates possibilities for learning. It's difficult to learn from an echo. But if you are exposed to a challenging and very different point of view, then if you want to understand something, you have to listen to another perspective, another voice, and I think Judaism often encourages that. As far as historical challenges to the theology, as everyone here knows, you've had a lot of Jewish thinkers responding in a lot of different ways theologically to the Holocaust. From Rubenstein to Berkovits to Fackenheim. I would include Lévinas.

JP: Even to the ultra-Orthodox.

DP: Such as Bernard Maza. Within Judaism, I think we are dealing with the theological challenges. As I see it, Judaism is very explicitly and elaborately bound to history, so historical events are occasions to say, "Hey, wait a minute, what's happened here? What does it mean for our relation to God?" As for myth and history, Judaism is just as laden with myth as Christianity is. That is one thing we have in common, and in the book, we don't mean to suggest that myth means questionable or dubious or false. Myth is a way of articulating the ineffable and getting at a deeper and transcendent truth. So, a mythological aspect is necessary to any religious tradition.

JR: David, let me pick up on this, because I think we're on the same page. You and I know this about ourselves, I think. With regard to the point about how difference can enhance dialogue, there may be two points that I can add. Go back to my list of terms lifted out of your manuscript, about the abhorrent, the unintelligible, the foreign, and the inconceivable.

   I think, like David Gushee is saying, I think it's good for Christians to hear that there are concepts in our tradition that others would describe in terms like those. But it seems to me the discussion shouldn't end with that. Right here is a key place for dialogue, for the Christian to come back and say, "Yes, I understand that these ideas might, for historic reasons, have abhorrent, alien, foreign qualities, but let's talk about whether they really are unintelligible or inconceivable to Jews." One could put the ball in play that way, with regard to basic ideas such as the incarnation or the Trinity or things like that, where you're not trying to persuade one another of anything, but you're just trying to get to the next level of whether or not these ideas are intelligible in some way or another. That would be one way to advance the dialogue.

Another point would be that all religious traditions are less than the full truth. At least in my perspective, they are best understood as versions—some better, some worse—of something that they are trying to reach but haven't quite gotten to. I think dialogue would be helped if Jews and Christians would say to one another, "Look, we're trying the best we can to reach truth and reality, but we know that our ways of doing this are versions of them and not the full and complete story. End of story." Then there could be dialogue that would go to another level. It wouldn't erase either sameness or difference, but it would accept the notion that Jewish and Christian ways both have integrity and distinctiveness that are fallible.

DP: I agree with that a hundred percent. One point I would make is that in Judaism we have the teaching that we don't have the whole truth. We're taught, for example, that the Jewish people have nine parts of the truth out of ten, and the nations have one part, so we have to listen to the nations. That each of the seventy nations contains a spark of the divine that corresponds to one of the seventy faces of Torah. So in our own tradition we are taught that we don't have quite the whole picture and that we do well to listen to the stranger. When we hear that there is only one way to God and that's through Jesus, it looks to us like the Christians think they have the whole truth and nothing but the truth. So, you know, John, we know each other pretty well, and I would agree a hundred percent with your point that we need to adopt the position that none of us has the whole truth.

The Issue of Forgiveness

Alan Berger (AB):

I wonder if I could move the discussion in a somewhat different direction, perhaps away from truth, but more toward John Roth's issue about intelligibility, which I find completely on target. All of us know Simon Wiesenthal's *The Sunflower* and its emphasis on the issue of forgiveness. Furthermore, Pope John Paul II asked the Jewish people for forgiveness for past sins of anti-Judaism and the teaching of contempt committed in the Church's name. That might be possible in a corporate sense and in certain forms of Catholic Christianity, but it is just not the way forgiveness works in the Jewish tradition. So let's say that we come to this understanding that Catholic Christians do things in *x* way, and normative Jews, excluding fringes, do things in *y* way. Now what do we do then with the difference? It's a pragmatic question: How do we proceed from there? This is just me speaking, and not certainly for David, although he and I have discussed this issue in the past.

JP:

Well, first of all, I'd like to reinforce the emphasis on diversity as a positive. In fact, way back when I did the analysis of the St. Louis textbook studies on prejudice in Catholic teaching materials, it certainly had a significant impact on what eventually became *Nostra Aetate*. One of the points I criticized about the methodology of the study was that it was focused almost entirely on assessing the problematic nature of certain textbook passages as to whether they said Judaism and Christianity were similar. One of the things you really need to stress at the outset of your volume is the emphasis on diversity as a positive dialogical feature and something that in the end can produce more richness than can an emphasis on similarities.

I think forgiveness is one of the most intriguing issues. It does cause some tensions, particularly within the contexts of Holocaust discussions with Jews, because Christians, at least Catholic Christians, tend to say there ought to be forgiveness, maybe even of Hitler in the end, if there was repentance, I mean. But if we consider we are different in our perspectives on such a question of forgiveness, the conversation may not produce agreement or consensus, but it can produce and enhance understanding on both sides, which may not in the end coalesce. Nonetheless there is a certain value and profit in discussing the basis of differences, even if we don't find ourselves reaching agreement.

JR: Let me add one other thing on this. I think, also, the emphasis that does come through in the book from time to time in addition to the emphasis on diversity and difference is that dialogue is a long-haul process. That is important. My own thinking about forgiveness as a Christian has been deeply influenced by my encounters—through reading, through thinking about it, or with partners in dialogue who are Jewish. The fruit of dialogue comes through the process of working through these ideas. That takes time, and it isn't a case of conceding everything to the other point of view. The good results come as you bring your point of view into contact with a different one. You begin to assess the strengths and weaknesses of your position, and that leads to helpful change in your position.

So, Alan, when you used the word *pragmatic*, I resonate with that because philosophically I'm a pragmatist. So when you get to the point where you have differences, then what the pragmatist will say is, "Okay, what's at stake in the differences? What do the differences mean practically?" And once you get clarity about that, you can at least begin to assess and sift and maybe even make some decisions about things you'd want to reject in your tradition, or things you might want to incorporate into your own tradition.

JP: Let me just illustrate, because I think the discussion about forgiveness within the dialogue has certainly done that kind of thing for me. I come out of a Christian tradition which has had strong emphasis, certainly in the past, on the notion of confession, which ultimately is supposed to result in forgiveness. However, it's so easy to fall into a mind-set where that sort of practice becomes what I would call cheap forgiveness, similar to cheap grace. Where someone says three Our Fathers, three Hail Marys, and they're basically forgiven for something that might be fairly serious, without any additional commitment. I don't think, ideally, my colleagues in liturgy would say that the real notion behind the sacrament of penance entails something much more profound in terms of transformation than simply reciting a few prayers, but that's how the practice can go downhill.

There's been an attempt now to try to make that practice more meaningful; however, it's also encountered the fact that a lot of people have simply abandoned it. But in the dialogue, just reflecting on my own Catholic tradition, we are led to take the notion of forgiveness far more seriously and profoundly than oftentimes we've done in our tradition. Certainly when I was growing up there was a certain kind of catechesis around penance. It was always there in the background. It didn't need a deeper transformation, but you could get out of it fairly quickly.

DG: What I usually say about forgiveness is that the ultimate goal of forgiveness is restored relationships with God and neighbor. And so a process involving confession of sin, acknowledgment of wrongdoing, a request for forgiveness, granting of forgiveness, acknowledgment of healing in the relationship, and moving forward in reconciliation—that is the way the forgiveness process is supposed to happen, and it happens at the vertical and the horizontal level. That process is blocked profoundly when you don't have somebody willing to confess their wrongdoing. So, can you forgive Hitler or a death camp guard? Not in that sense, no. But forgiveness also involves a decision not to hold onto the grudge or the anger or the hurt and to keep it internal to the self, and, in a sense, give it to God and ask God to take it from you. That's pastorally what I say.

So it's possible, in that sense, to forgive someone who is dead. Someone who is not willing to be reconciled, someone who has not apologized or confessed. In that sense forgiveness is an act of self-cleansing, or divinely aided self-cleansing, leading to greater wholeness on the part of the person who has been offended. And so in that sense, forgiveness is for our own good, because it heals us. For those who are within the Christian theological tradition, our understanding of forgiveness is pretty well grounded, and I don't know that that's negotiable from my perspective. And yet, I am enriched by dialogue with the Jewish perspectives on this. But I don't think it is ultimately going to lead to a reconciliation of the two perspectives. We've put our cards on the table. Perhaps ultimately we're not going to agree on one perspective. We're going to say there may be some complementary, overlapping consensus, but not uniformity, and that's okay. In fact, it's more than okay. It's enriching that the human community includes these irreducible points of diversity.

JR: Alan and David, it seems to me that David Gushee has stated clearly and succinctly what I would take as the goal of your book. That if at the end of the day you asked what you hoped to accomplish here, it would be something close to what David Gushee just said, that there would be an enrichment and an enhanced respect between the two traditions, however many perspectives there are, Jewish and Christian.

AB: That's quite right. I was listening to David Gushee and thinking, "Yes, yes, that's what I want to do." It goes to your point about the fact that every religious tradition should recognize that it's not in sole possession of the truth. We're all traveling on a certain path. Sometimes our paths will intersect and sometimes not. Of course, dialogue doesn't occur in a vacuum. The culture in which we find ourselves seems to be very much fractured, and the orthodoxies of the various traditions are simply not interested in dialogue. We hear accusations of relativism, and finally if nothing really matters, what is the truth? And that's John Pawlikowski's slippery slope. There are many in the Jewish community who do dismiss the idea of dialogue. "You can't trust the Christians," they say. This is Eliezer Berkovits's notion: "All we want from Christians is that you keep your hands off our children." But that's a ridiculous and self-defeating position.

Another pragmatic question concerns what we are doing, both in this room and in our own lives: How does that translate? Does it translate into the culture at large? Are we perhaps engaging in the luxury of having a rarefied seminar? We say what we expect from our conversation, and certainly our conversation can result in what those engaged in this topic hope for. But what do we see from a broader perspective? That's one question I would like to have us address. The other is: What happens a decade from now, when the Church moves on, perhaps to Islam, perhaps to some other traditions in Africa and Asia—what will it matter? How can this dialogue in fact be fruitful on a larger stage? What do we have to contribute to the great world out there?

EUROPE AND THE REST OF THE WORLD

JP: Let me respond to that question, in the light of some of my experiences as president of the International Council of Christians and Jews, because that has brought me to a context wider than simply the North American context. The situation in Europe is significantly different because there's no question that in parts of Europe, religion is really a minority perspective. There may be a public veneer still out there, but folks will tell you, even from within the Church, that it's a pretty shallow veneer, and that deep down, the belief is that the future of belief in Europe is really a problematical issue. Now that naturally affects the dialogue.

First of all, why should you be interested in any kind of dialogue if you're not interested in belief? Secondly, for those who are still very interested in belief in Europe, the struggle now is to retain the impact of belief on the culture, and dialogue can seem to undercut that, because it tends to undercut identity. If you're going to resist the destruction of the public influence of religion, you've got to do that with a very strong self-identity. Anything that says, "Well, identity is not all that certain because we've either made mistakes in the past or we're not sure about certain things," may undercut the significance of religious belief and its potential for impact on the culture. So the issue of dealing with the emergence of secularism as the -ism of a large part of European society makes the dialogue in Europe significantly different than what it might be here in North America.

Now, moving to Asia, I think this is a very, very important issue. My colleague, Hans Ucko, of the World Council of Churches, has been really pushing this issue, and I think rightly so. For example, the noted Protestant theologian Wesley Ariarajah, who worked for many years at the World Council of Churches, would say, not in a harsh sense, that Judaism has little significance for a Christian in Asia. That in a sense Buddhism is far more significant in terms of dialogue. Yes, Jesus may have been a Jew; Ariarajah won't deny that. But whether it has any particular significance for thinking about what Jesus might mean as a focal point for Christian faith today, he would say it has no consequence at all. In fact, on the radical fringe, there are some voices within Asian Christianity that say we should get rid of the Old Testament and take, say, Buddhist literature or Hindu literature as our pre-text to the New Testament. We're going to have to deal with that, because—despite the attempt to stifle the thrust of Asian theology, which, when all is said and done, was the primary aim of the notorious document *Dominus Ieus*—it's going to have an impact. There's no question.

I teach a lot of Asian students. They are the future, in many ways, of Christianity, certainly on the Catholic side. Catholicism is moving to an Asian/African context, and sooner or later that's going to have a theological impact. There was an effort a couple of years ago, led by the World Council of Churches and the World Jewish Congress, to begin the dialogue in Africa. There was a major conference held in Cameroon for French-speaking Africa.

AB: What were some of the results?

JP: Well, on the African side, a strong, positive perspective on the value of the Old Testament. I think the Old Testament plays a role in African Christianity that it generally doesn't play in Western Christianity, so that's one thing. But the vast majority of Africans have never encountered a living Jew. You'll find a synagogue in Nairobi, but who's there? It's Western business people or diplomats or something, so it's not viewed as an integral thing, not real life. I think this is the cutting-edge thing.

DG: I think Christianity is an especially dangerous force when it is detached from its Jewish roots. Theologically we have no business even considering altering the canon. I think we have no freedom to do that whatsoever. And that a lot of what went wrong in Christianity was the de-Judaizing of Jesus, for example, and the loss of the Hebraic dimensions of Jesus and of the earliest Church. So Jewish-Christian dialogue like this is important for drawing Christians back to our origins, our Scriptures, both New Testament and Hebrew scriptures, and keeping us grounded in a faith that is much more likely to avoid an otherworldly, blood-sacrifice-only, gnosticized Christianity that happens when you lose the Hebraic roots of Christianity. And that's just fundamental, to me.

JR: It seems to me that David Gushee's comment, coupled with John's, would make possible in the manuscript an acknowledgment of the issue that we're on right now. It would appear that, as Christianity is evolving presently, it has a potential to get cut off from its Jewish roots, and one way to resist that unfortunate trend is to reemphasize the importance of Jewish-Christian dialogue. It is crucial to emphasize that one of the most important aspects of Jewish-Christian dialogue for Christians is that such dialogue takes Christianity back to its Jewish roots.

DP: One way to reconnect with Jewish roots is to reconnect with Jewish concepts and categories of thinking and understanding. For example, in David Gushee's opening remarks, he used the word "holy." The notion of the holy, the *kadosh*, as something that is set apart, not from other things in the world, but that is unlike anything in the landscape of being; it's not a *special thing*, it's unlike *anything*. It's the dimension of meaning. It's what sanctifies and give meaning to everything else. That is a notion that we share, and it's a notion that comes into the world through the Jewish people. That doesn't mean the Jewish people have a monopoly on it. In fact, the Jewish people are commanded to shine that light to the nations.

  In a Europe where you see religion in a state of collapse and a radical rise of culturalism and secularism, you see a loss of the notion of the holy and with it the very possibility of any authentic dialogue. It seems to me that dialogue, in principle, requires a way of thinking about a holiness or a truth in a third position and a vertical position, so that neither of us has a monopoly on it. Without that third position, dialogue becomes negotiation, power struggle, and, in the end, the one who is stronger is the one who is right. That's a danger in the world that Jewish and Christian traditions can confront together by listening to each other.

  What are the outcomes of dialogue? What do we hope to attain in this process? What is the pragmatic bottom line? Certainly as teachers we have an opportunity to have a huge impact on many young adults who are, in my experience, starving for a sense of meaning, and who do not have the capacity to respond to the secular nihilism in the world. They know it can't be the truth, because their souls are so troubled. And their being troubled is itself a sign of something *higher*.

The dialogue opens up that vertical dimension. It's not for nothing that, in both of our traditions, it is taught that where two come together there's a third presence of holiness. But that's possible only when the dialogue is grounded in a testimony that respects difference in a horizontal relation, precisely because it attests to a transcendent and ultimate truth in the vertical relation that each is trying to attain and can never quite reach. The bottom line I think is to make better listeners of one another.

THE MUSLIMS

DG: I would ask, apropos of the question of where the dialogue needs to go—and this came up a lot when I was reading the book—what do we do next in relation to the Muslims? Here's an anecdote.

I'm working on a declaration opposed to the use of torture by our government under any circumstances, and we've got a team working on it. In the current draft, someone has suggested that we name the people who attacked us on 9/11 as Islamist, radical Islamist terrorists. And most of the group felt that was both truthful and appropriate, but a significant minority thought that was unnecessarily offensive and would cut off the possibility of dialogue and partnership with Muslims in opposing torture by our government. And I'm genuinely uncertain as to what the right answer is here. Is it inappropriate to use "Islamist" or "Muslim" or "jihadist" or "Islamic" to describe al-Qaeda, or the people who attacked us on 9/11, or what Osama Bin Laden is, or whatever?

So when I think about the level of complexity of the Jewish-Christian dialogue, and then think about making it a trialogue in the light of every day's headlines on Iran, Ahmadinejad, and so on, I feel woefully unequipped and certainly think that my community is woefully unequipped to go there. It's much more complicated, as I was saying earlier, than a dialogue we have barely begun to have with the Jewish community.

JP: It's interesting with regard to some of the reactions I received from some Jewish colleagues relative to the Regensburg address of Benedict. They say that what he said was wonderful, but now they're really concerned that he's backing off. Some of us, however, didn't think that speech was necessarily wonderful and are much more pleased that he seems to have taken some advice from people who know something about the situation.

It raises a dilemma, because it's similar to what your book is doing. In a way, I suppose, you can argue that Benedict was bringing to the surface an issue that is certainly out there, namely, rights for Christians, but one could say for Jews or other religious minorities in Arab-dominated countries as well. By and large, they don't have equal rights, and so it's a very legitimate question. Unfortunately, I think the way he put it forth illustrates a continuing problem within the Vatican, which affects both Catholic-Islamic and Catholic-Jewish dialogue, and that is the total unwillingness to acknowledge any real major flaws in the Church as such, and that there are only a few wayward Catholics who deviate from what the Church was really teaching.

But there has to be an honest confrontation. There is also a need, both for political reasons and for theological reasons, to explore what sort of relationships might exist trilaterally. I've heard some Muslim scholars say, for example, anything that's in the New Testament or Old Testament which is not explicitly invalidated in the Koran remains binding on a Muslim. Now I'm not suggesting that all Muslim scholars, or even the majority of scholars, would hold with that, but if a significant minority would say that, that's an interesting proposal, in terms of some kinds of interrelationship. I've always said that for Christianity, Islam poses a challenge that the relationship with Judaism doesn't. But to some extent the reason it doesn't is not necessarily positive, since Islam clearly challenges the Christian assertion that all revelation came to an end in Jesus Christ. Some in the Christian community can deal with Judaism by seeing it as the precursor. But when you are told by a Muslim, "Hey, what you understand is good, but you missed the final revelation," it is really unsettling for a Christian.

DG: Which by the way is a nice experience of supersession-ism, right?

JP: When I was teaching at Tantur in the seventies, in a program on Judaism, Christianity, and Islam, we had a Muslim teacher, a member of the Muslim Brother-hood, who was part of the team. He was not much for dialogue, but he was very happy to talk about Islam to non-Muslims. One evening I was walking down the corridor, and he was involved in a very animated conversation with one of the Catholic sisters who was in the program. As I passed, I heard him say to her, "But, Sister, you must understand that while you have many good things in Christianity, you ultimately have missed the final revelation." And her eyes were sort of out there! Because Christians don't expect to be told they missed something. This is what they said to Jews for centuries, so this is a really profound challenge, I think, for Christianity, to come to grips with a tradition that claims that there's something beyond the revela-tion of Christ.

DP: Let me ask this, with regard to the Christian-Muslim dialogue: Do you think that it's incumbent upon the Christians to take up the issue of Muslim antisemitism?

JP: Well, I think it's incumbent. We have a Catholic-Muslim program at our institution parallel to our Catholic-Jewish program, and I've been very insistent that presentations of Christianity to Muslims must include the new understandings that have emerged from the Christian-Jewish dialogue, relative to the Jewishness of Jesus, and so on. In other words, in the dialogue with Islam, we cannot present Christianity in the way that predates the Christian-Jewish dialogue, which has significantly altered the way we understand the development of Christianity, its roots in Judaism, the Jewishness of Jesus, and that has to be part of the way we present Christianity in the Christian-Muslim dialogue.

DG: Absolutely. I agree.

JR: One of the things that all partners to religious dialogue ought to be concerned about is to deconstruct supersessionism of any kind, wherever it turns up. That may be difficult, because it may lead ultimately to the notion that no tradition can say that the revelation stopped with us. Which causes problems for everybody in a way, but they may be good problems to have.

THE STATE OF ISRAEL

AB: I wonder if I could use this as a springboard to talk about Israel, the idea of "the land," which at the Rome Conference of 2005, "*Nostra Aetate* Today: Reflections Forty Years after the Call for Interreligious Relationships," was prominently discussed, and to bring out the disturbing issue of the Sabeel Center, whose spokesman, Naim Ateek, invokes much of the supersessionist tradition. He calls Israel "the crucifixion machine" and Israelis are labeled the new Herods. Mainline Protestantism does not accept this at all. But there is a group in the Church willing not to speak up about this, and it's very troubling.

The long life of stereotypes for all traditions, and certainly the deicide issue, have become so ingrained in culture, even among people who aren't necessarily "religious," that I wonder if we could say something about stereotypes and their staying power and then talk about the issue of Israel. Because then we get the defenders of the state who say that anyone who criticizes Israel must be a secret antisemite, or not so secret, or an anti-Zionist, which is just a mask for antisemitism. Of course, that's absurd, I think. The prophets certainly had a lot to criticize ancient Israel about, but their motive was one of love. I don't think we can say that about the Sabeel Group.

Two things: How do we respond to this enduringness of stereotypes, and what about this issue of land in relationship to Jewish identity and the Jewish people? The irony here is that many Jews have no intention of ever going to the state of Israel, yet there is this primal connection, and I think that's worth our investigating a bit.

DP: In Judaism, the land is definitively tied to the people. Israel, the land, the Torah, they're all of a piece. In Judaism, the Holy Land isn't holy because certain things have happened there, but rather certain things have happened there because it's holy. So holiness is an antecedent notion to everything else. And nothing alters that in Judaism, and I'm talking about traditional, Orthodox Judaism.

JR: I think this is a place where Christians need to listen better than they have. And your manuscript picks up on this in an interesting way. You stress in the manuscript that while we can speak of the Jewish people, we don't speak of the Christian people. There's a reference that there can be courses that can be taught on the history of the Jewish people, but you don't get a comparable course on "the Christian people." That resonates a bit. Because of the way Christianity has unfolded historically, and maybe theologically, the religion works out, we Christians don't find ourselves tied specifically to a particular part of the earth in the way that Jews often do. I wrestle with this when I think about my own identity. I think of myself as a Christian and I think of myself as an American, but the two don't necessarily go together in the same way that a Jew might think of herself as a Jew and an Israeli.

Your book is correct that Christians are not geographically tied to history as much as Jews are. For Christians, I think, that fact has created a kind of inability, a tone-deafness, that impedes understanding the importance that the Holy Land has for Jews. David Gushee is absolutely right in saying that for many Christians, the names of towns and mountains and things in the Galilee is kind of a campy part of the Christian's mindscape. But still, I think my point is valid, too: Christians are a little less explicitly attached to parts of the earth's geography than would be the case for Jews, and that difference creates difficulties.

JP: I think it's perfectly correct that this has to be on the agenda. I think it did emerge in the conference in Rome. In fact the principal point that Ruth Langer made in response to my plenary presentation was certainly along these lines. It represents one of the more difficult issues to bring up in a dialogical context, for a whole variety of reasons.

First of all, I think you're quite right in the manuscript, that in large part people don't understand the more theological dimensions of the land. They may understand some of the practical, political dimensions, but not the theological dimensions. It's very difficult to discern this with accuracy because it's no longer explicit, but there's still a residue of the old theology, which basically argues that Jews were to be perpetual wanderers as a punishment for killing Christ. That was explicit theology for centuries. You'll find it even in twentieth century biblical scholars like Martin Noth.

Secondly, Orthodox Christianity, as well as evangelicals, would have somewhat different perspectives than, say, Catholics or maybe mainline Protestant Christians. Just looking internally at Christianity, various forms of spirituality have been quite strong at certain times and still have an impact even in contemporary Catholic spirituality, and that is what I would call a kind of disdain for the world. The world is considered the place of sin, and our spiritual home is really in heaven. And that spirituality is there, where some of the popular prayers call the world a "veil of tears." It's a very negative point of view.

Third, for many in the Christian community, Sao Paulo, Chicago, maybe even Memphis is as holy as Jerusalem.

So we need to raise the issue. But in raising the issue, there are some problems also on the Jewish side. I think this Christian committee within the Knesset, which has linked itself almost exclusively with John Hagee and his people, tends, in the minds of some Christians, and even in some Jews, to make the Hagee approach to this question the barometer that all other Christian groups have to measure up to, and if we don't quite measure up to that, which we never will, for various reasons, including theological reasons, we might be anti-Zionist. This is the way people react.

I think that some of the dynamics on the Jewish side have also hurt the ability of some of us who want to really make this a central point in the dialogue. But if we do put it on the agenda, we are going to have to have a genuine dialogue. Within the context of the recent war in Lebanon, for example, in the question of just war in Christianity, there is a decided turn against warfare; this certainly was true with John Paul, and I think it continues with Benedict. The real question is whether war is any kind of instrument that can be defended morally anymore, against the perceived Israeli security needs. The principle that came out of the '74 Vatican guidelines, which said that Christians must come to understand the Jews as they define themselves, is, I think, an operative principle here, and if Jews define themselves through the identification with Israel, that has to be part of the agenda. On the other hand, using the same principle, Jews may have to also deal with the fact that if Christians are identifying themselves more and more, if not as absolutely pacifist, but certainly moving toward an antiwar direction, and that's also going to have to be part of the dialogue. Jews will have to understand what's happening, perhaps, in the Christian tradition on this point.

DG: Within the Christian tradition, as in the Jewish tradition, there is an identification with people who are victims of injustice. So to the extent that we identify Palestinians as victims of injustice, and as, to some extent that portion of the population that is Christian, we have points of identification there, too. It seems to me morally inappropriate for us to identify solely with Israeli security concerns. We have to also pay attention to the daily experience of Palestinians.

JR: This is where I personally found myself in a bind in dealing with the recent Presbyterian divestment initiative with regard to Israel. That initiative, if you put the best face on it, was coming from a group of people who felt very strongly about the violation of human rights on the side of the Palestinians. So the Presbyterians who favored divestment went for some kind of a response that seemed concrete and practical, but to my mind was not wise or sound, and it led to initiatives that might result in divestment. The motive was ethical, but the policies and strategies were ill-conceived. Furthermore, there were problems about the way in which the emphasis on Palestinian rights was forged. The outlook, I believe, was amnesiac historically with regard to understanding the history of Christian-Jewish relationships and what that ought to mean for important elements of solidarity with Israel. There are fraught and vexed issues here, ones that go straight to the heart of a key area of commonality in the traditions, which would be their joint emphasis on the importance of justice. For Christians, the Hebrew prophets are crucial, over and over again. The way that they get referenced by Christians in relation to issues that have to do with justice is striking. I think of the two traditions' respect for the prophets and for justice as one of the chief ties between Christianity and Judaism.

AB: I quite agree with that. But I think that one of the things that makes this such an explosive issue for most Jews is that on the one hand there is a concern for justice, as the Deuteronomist puts it, "Justice, and only justice, you shall follow that you may live and inherit the land which the lord your God gives you." However, many Jews view the issue of Israel not solely in terms of justice. The overriding concern is for existence. This makes the issue so very complex.

The other thing is that I think in many ways the divestment issue is being manipulated. It's very one-sided. Israel alone is being singled out. Of course, Israel has made many mistakes, and they're still making mistakes. The Israeli government, for example, recently announced the opening of a new West Bank settlement. This, for me, just boggles the mind. What could they be thinking? But with the divestment issue there is never any acknowledgment of what many among the radical Palestinian leadership are encouraging. Take, for example, suicide bombers, vowing never to recognize the state of Israel and, moreover, exclaiming that the Jewish state has no right to exist. That is, to say the least, not the way to begin a dialogue. It is instead to declare an eternal jihad against the Jewish state. I think this will be a very difficult issue.

JP: I'm very strong on this, that whatever criticisms one wants to make about Israel, whether justified or unjustified, trying to put them in the context of historical categories related to antisemitism is simply a non-starter. I cannot accept that. I think we have to be very strong, saying that if Arab Christians want to critique the state of Israel, they are certainly able to do that, they have every right to do so. We have the right to engage with them as to whether those critiques are accurate, partially accurate, or totally inaccurate, but if they do it in the context of portraying Israel, the Israelis, and the Israeli government in terms of classical antisemitic categories, this is just not acceptable.

DP: But there's a critique that's leveled for the sake of Israel and then there's a critique that is part of an agenda to get rid of Israel. And we need to be able to tell the difference.

JR: Do you think for the sake of your book, we should come back to this, namely, how much do you want to try to bite off and chew? If you get into the current Palestinian-Israeli issue, and, at the same time, you want to deal with theological issues—those two things, of course, have relationships that meet at various points, but that's a lot to put on your plate, it seems to me.

JP: You know, one of the issues here concerns Bethlehem and what's happening in Bethlehem. I read three or four articles where, on the one hand, you're getting the thesis that the disappearance of Christians is due entirely to the Israeli occupation. On the other hand, you get just the opposite, that it's primarily due to the pressure on Christians internally within the Palestinian Authority. My sense is that it's probably a combination of both. Many of us are generally concerned about the disappearance of the vital Christian community. I would argue that Israel is bound to have a certain interest in preserving a living Christian community there. I could even argue for theological reasons, but that's probably not going to be very persuasive. But I think somehow we have to sort out this Bethlehem thing.

What you're getting from some of the Jewish side is a repeat of what we experienced during the Lebanese situation several years ago, where there was the strong charge by some elements of the Jewish community that Christians were ignoring their brothers and sisters in the Christian community in Lebanon. That simply didn't reflect an accurate enough understanding of the dynamics in Lebanon. First of all, the Maronites have never been highly appreciated in many segments of the Christian community. I won't say they've been viewed as sleazy, but frankly that's how they have been viewed by a lot of folks. But the dynamics in Lebanon are more complicated because what you really have is wealthy Christians and wealthy Muslims lined up against the poor Muslims. And I think Hezbollah has proved to some extent to be a phenomenon that reflects that dynamic.

Now I see the same thing with Bethlehem, with people like Melanie Phillips saying to the Christian community, "You're failing, you're not protecting your brothers and sisters in Bethlehem," and that may be true. But I suspect it's more complicated. In the meantime, you've got Tony Blair, the archbishop of Canterbury, and Cormac Murphy-O'Connor, the cardinal of Westminster, going over there and putting the blame almost exclusively on Israel, whereas the evangelical community has been very strong in saying the problem is primarily on the Palestinian side. I don't know how we sort through this.

DP: I'm sure that most Israelis would rather see a Christian Bethlehem than a Muslim Bethlehem.

JP: There's no question.

Mel Gibson's *Passion of the Christ*

JP: I think you should probably tone down the thing on Mel Gibson. Because there's a way, I think, he screwed himself. The reality is what you identify as the main, continuing problem, the DVD and its possible use in educational circles; at least on the Catholic side, that, fortunately, is no longer a big issue.

DP: Is that because Gibson discredited himself or...?

JP: Yes.

DP: Or because there's no longer a latent antisemitism...?

JP: No, you're right. It's still there. I'm not suggesting that you drop the reference to Gibson entirely. I think the point should be made, clearly, and I've made it. I think it did represent a real failure to understand anti-semitism. Now, some will say that people didn't see the antisemitism.

DG: They didn't see it in my community.

JP: Is that a good or bad thing? Some would say that's a good thing, but it was there, and I think so long as the seeds are there, it remains a danger.

DG: Evangelicals that I know saw it as a powerful depiction of the suffering of Christ, and it fed their piety in that sense; that's what they saw.

JP: To some extent, if our group made one mistake, it was probably allowing the publication of that article in the *New Republic* by Paula Frederickson. That article was written in the name of all of us, and we did see it before it went to press. She had a line in there saying that Gibson may be responsible for Jewish blood on the street. That probably was over the top. I don't think any of us expected that, as a result of seeing this film, Christians were going to rush out and attack synagogues and Jewish community centers and things like that. The problem is that, since that didn't happen, even some in the Jewish community said, "See, the ADL overreacted." The danger is that it misplaced the real threat of the film, which was to bring back these seeds. Even if one didn't act on them in the way that some people tend to.

DG: Did it get wide distribution in the Arab world?

JP: Wide? I don't know. It got some. It got some. I think the problem was, in the Arab world, there was a hesitation to promote it too much, because they didn't want to promote Christianity. While they may have liked the anti-Jewish dimension, they may not have liked that they would be exposing the Christian message.

DG: In retrospect, what do you think are the main ways in which that movie is clearly antisemitic?

JP: I think it has every classical stereotype of the Jews as connected with evil and the devil—the portrayal of the high priest, the portrayal of Pilate as almost a sensitive human being, where all the history would say otherwise.

DP: There is the reversal of the scriptural account of the Barabbas scene, the collapse of the Temple, as Alan and I have mentioned.

JP: Yes, it is not even biblical!

DP: There are several things that are not biblical, which I would think Christians would have an issue with, the departure from Scripture.

DG: I refuse to see the movie, so I've never seen it.

JP: Well, I actually sat through it at a showing sponsored by the American Jewish Committee, so the crowd that was there was generally not favorable. The hardest thing for me, I think, was the violence. Having the script did not expose you to the profound violence of the film.

DP: It's graphic. Probably unnecessarily graphic.

JP: Oh, way over the top.

DP: But the horrific suffering of Jesus as part of the Passion is essential to the way the whole thing plays out, isn't it? Suffering for our sin.

DG: In that sense, the more suffering the better.

DP: So, theologically, he has to suffer horrifically, for the horrific sins of *all* humanity.

JP: Yes, but that's one theological tradition of the atonement. One of the criticisms that I would make of the film and that others have made of the film is, from the strictly Christian point of view, the separation from the Passion and the death of Jesus and his active ministry. My argument will always be that he died because of what he preached and said. So there's an intimate connection between the two. But then you get into this theology where my sins are essentially wiped away by the blood of Christ, and it doesn't make all that much difference what I do. There a sense in which I'm more activist. I don't want to say that you simply are saved exclusively through your works, but certainly that's an integral part of it.

Theological Stumbling Blocks

DG: My gut tells me that the core issues raised by this book are the theological issues at the intersection between Judaism and Christianity; I'd like to put those on the table, and shift directions a little bit. I teach Old Testament Survey, which all of our students have to take at Union. I taught it again this fall. I do that every other year.

I was struck by the difficulty of communicating to these students what we understand the Old Testament Scriptures to be and to do. The sense in which a Christian understanding is really quite at variance with what the Jewish community understands the Hebrew Scriptures to be and to do; it's a profound difference, and most Christians have no idea. In fact, most Christians believe that the Old Testament functions for the Jewish community in exactly the same way as it functions for the Christian community, except for belief that the prophecies are fulfilled in Jesus. Most have no idea that there is a whole two thousand years of literature that followed the Talmudic tradition. All of that is completely lost to us. We don't study it, we're not taught it. So one of the things that we need to do in getting back to the roots of the split and of the origins of Christianity is reconnecting and reclaiming a more historically accurate understanding of what was going on in the period, say, from the fourth century BCE to the first century CE and the background in which Jesus conducted his ministry.

I'd like to just make a couple of comments, theologically. I think that Christian messianism is susceptible to the critique that you made, where it has become essentially a fully realized eschatology: Jesus came, he died on the cross, he rose again, and everything is done. Which is kind of how you presented it. I teach what I call an inaugurated eschatology, in which Jesus came to reclaim the world for God. The language I use for that is the kingdom of God, or the reign of God. In our book *Kingdom Ethics,* Glen Stassen and I claim that Jesus came proclaiming the reign of God and that the reign of God had specific marks drawn from biblical teaching, especially in the prophets; then what had developed in the intertestamental period, among those marks, were justice, peace, reconciliation, inclusion of outcasts, return from exile, things like this, which are very this-worldly, very Hebraic.

We argued further that Jesus stood in the line of the prophets of Israel in proclaiming justice and peace in the midst of injustice and violence, and the reason he was nailed to a cross was that he was a prophetic challenge to the established order, fundamentally, Rome, but also the social order that Rome had established in all the lands that it occupied. And so it's an inaugurated eschatology. He came to reclaim the world for God.

Tikkun olam is a very congenial concept for me, too; it's very similar, the healing of the world. The only sense in which eschatology is fulfilled in him lies in those people who join him in the commitment to the advance of God's reign, understood concretely as justice and peace, and reconciliation, and so on. Those people are the continuing incarnation of the kingdom of God. Now, as they live the deeds of the kingdom, then you might say eschatology is realized, but only in a fragmentary sense, very partial, and we await the consummation of the reign of God at the end of history. But we don't just wait passively; we work as we wait. As we do the practices of the kingdom of God now, we participate in the reign of God in its advance, and it's a great privilege. Every advance of justice, peace, inclusion of outcasts, reconciliation, the spread of the knowledge of God, the treatment of people according to their image, the image of God—every time that happens, the reign of God wins some victories. But the world is sufficiently broken, and those victories are sufficiently partial, so that there's no way we can say that everything has been done, and we're just waiting for the end.

This affects my understanding of the whole law and grace thing. I understand that all biblical commandments are given to enable us to do God's will, and that what Jesus offered was commentary on Hebrew scriptural commands that do not abrogate those commands, and in many ways they elucidate them, they articulate them, they help us to understand ways to live them out. And so Christian existence, understood as the pursuit of the reign of God, is very activist; it's very much about living, creating a reality through your living that one day will be fulfilled by God's decision at the end of time. And so the law/grace thing, I acknowledge is a major problem in historic Christian theology, but I try to get past it by saying that the giving of the law is an act of grace. It shows us how to live. God empowers us to live out His will, and as we do so, God's grace is, you might say, multiplied and spread and shown in the world.

JP: Just on that point, if I could interrupt, one of the most powerful statements I have ever read is Luther's "The Freedom of the Christian Man," where he argues that unless the Christian becomes a slave in service of his neighbor, he really doesn't know Christ. So this sort of separation between faith and works, which is so often attributed to Luther, doesn't even stand up, if you take the fullness of his own writings. And so I think an emphasis of God's grace tends to be a stereotype of Christianity.

DP: What you describe as the messianic time is very much the way Jews think of messianic time. Peace, justice, in concrete ways, the inclusion of the outcasts. Being able to answer the questions that God puts to Cain: "Where is your brother?" and "What have you done?" And that's what it means, from a Jewish understanding, for God's word to be engraved on the heart, as the prophets said. I was waiting, and I know you weren't going to say this, but I was almost waiting to hear you way, "And everyone will accept Jesus as their savior."

DG: What we say in *Kingdom Ethics* is that one of the seven marks of the kingdom is that God is honored, praised, and glorified. As God's will is done on earth as it is in heaven, the response of human beings is a response of great joy and a response of gratitude to God and honoring God. I know that there are New Testament materials that emphasize the acknowledgment of Jesus Christ, as that's the culmination of the experience of the historical journey. I think the kingdom emphasis that we suggest offers a way to put the focus on God—God the Creator, God the sustainer, and God the redeemer.

        The way I would say it is: Everybody who is participating in the healing of the world is doing the work of God in the world. And they generally are at their best

when that is joined to a covenantal religious understanding that provides depth and helps to avoid errors
on various sides. When you have a messianic vision or
a redemptive vision without theological grounding, it
is very dangerous. But there are enough striking suggestions in the teachings of Jesus himself, like when he
says, "Not everyone who calls me, 'Lord, Lord,' will
enter the Kingdom of Heaven, but he who does the
will of my Father in heaven." Or when he makes reference to the resurrection of the just, of the righteous.
And so we should be agnostic in passing judgment on
the eternal destiny of anybody, including ourselves; I
think Paul says that. My suspicion is that God is most
interested in those who are doing *tikkun olam* in the
world. And those people are partners in the salvific
process on the planet.

DP: That sounds like the salvation or redemption at issue is
a communal, not just a personal affair, is communal to
the extent that it undercuts the personal.

DG: The personal is part of it.

DP: To my Jewish ears, it sounds like you can't understand
individual salvation apart from communal salvation.

DG: That's what I would say, and Christian theology is moving in that direction, for sure.

JP: I think so. There's no question. I think what David
Gushee just articulated is really becoming mainstream
Christian thinking. Certainly within the scholarly community, but even at the more popular level. There is,
I think, a clear communal orientation, but not to the
exclusion of the individual; I got from your manuscript
the sense that Christians really are first and foremost
concerned about personal salvation, and I think that's
really inaccurate. It's not that we're *not* concerned about
personal salvation, but there is a strong communal

dimension. It depends on the particular Christian denomination. In the Catholic community, for example, but even in much of the Protestant community, the principal worship service is the high point of the Christian week, and it is communal. It is not individual. We don't gather in one building and all just do our thing individually. This is exactly what the whole liturgical reform in Catholicism was countering, the kind of deviation where there's something's happening up there on the altar and the individual is reading his own prayer book. That was viewed as inauthentic.

DP: So is the monastic cloister becoming more and more a thing of the past?

JP: Oh, I think so. Not to say that there isn't a function for that, but it's not viewed, even by those who practice it, in the same way as it was some years ago, where it's just a kind of withdrawal from the world in the sense that the world is really a bad and dangerous place for anyone who is to be spiritual. But it's not withdrawal simply because you're saying, "Pox on that whole world, it's an awful place." It is a part of God's reign.

DG: Withdrawal in preparation for service, or as an aspect of service.

JP: And someone like Merton was really struggling with that. Can I really be concerned about racism and war and so on if I'm isolated from what's actually happening out there?

DP: This almost sounds like heresy to me, if I'm trying to listen as a Christian. It almost sounds as if, in some quarters of Christianity, there is a question, "Are you saved?" And the answer is "Yes, I'm saved." But it sounds like you're saying, "Not yet. I'm not yet saved." It sounds almost heretical; I know it does to some Christian ears.

DG: Here's the way I would say it within my community. The personal experience of a commitment to Christ, and coming into a relationship with him, is the first step, for us. And then the question is what do you do? How do you live? Of course, the way it ought to be taught is that you make the commitment in light of the expectations of what will follow from that commitment, and the expectations include a life devoted to the reign of God, in whatever aspect that God asks you to do, in addition to the overall work of charity and justice and mercy that we're all called to do. And so now you're enlisted as foot soldiers in the worldwide work of advancing God's reign. And that life is nourished by Bible study and prayer and worship and all the things that you do to keep yourself spiritually strong and ready to go. But it's an activist vision of serving the neighbor and advancing God's reign.

I find that with young people in my community, they are increasingly attracted to that vision as opposed to relentless sermons that week after week talk about how everybody needs to come to a personal relationship with Christ. And that's all that we've got. In many thousands of churches that is the only thing that is preached. Believe in Jesus. Attain personal salvation. Go to heaven. And then if there's work to be done, it's probably primarily evangelism—tell other people, so they also can come into a personal relationship with Jesus and they also can go to heaven. So, yes, it is out there, but it is increasingly unsatisfying to large sectors of the Christian community, even in the evangelical community, to young people who know that that can't be all that Christianity is all about. Especially if they are led to read the Scriptures, to see what they actually say. Read the Old Testament, and read what Jesus actually taught, and read the relevant material in the rest of the New Testament, and you find a different kind of vision. We have to be careful, and there is some point of tension here. This is a Jesus and reign-of-God theology in some tension with the popular construal of a more Pauline soteriology or cross-focused theology.

JP: Or the blood. The Gibson blood.

DG: But there is creative work that can be done to keep these together. And one way you keep this together is to talk concretely about why Jesus went to the cross as the latest martyr for the cause of God's reign.

JR: I want to interject something here because I'm very sympathetic to the theme about the kingdom; I really like the *Kingdom Ethics* approach, and I'm not carrying such a big brief for what you call the Pauline soteriology in the cross. But there's a problem that both traditions have to face here. In addition, I think it's one of the key links back to the Holocaust. I could put the issue this way: History is an arena that is so immensely destructive, just empirically, that it's very hard to settle, if you have any kind of messianism at all, for one who never seems to arrive, or never even seems to really make very much progress. And I was struck in the manuscript where the book comes very close to saying something like the "Messiah *is* history." That I find strange, because my own reading of history is that the kingdom of God is never going to be complete in history. I just don't see how that's happening. What about all the dead at Auschwitz? What about them? This is where, either on the Christian or Jewish side, there begins to be too much of an emphasis on the community of the people over and against individual people. I don't know what to make of all the dead. And it seems to me without some kind of emphasis on the individual particularity, the preciousness of the dead, you're going to have a messianic view that isn't going to be credible.

DP: I agree, but just one thing: We don't exactly say that the Messiah is history; what we say is that the *persistent wait* for the Messiah is history, and that waiting is a doing, a going toward God.

JR: But where is the redemption, if it's to be in history only?

DG: Well, you have to say there are at least as many defeats as there are victories. But Christians have to be pushed to return back to history to fight for kingdom victories concretely, in Sudan and in family life and in every other aspect where the values of God's reign are under-cut or violently attacked. And so you're right that if you drive people back to history and you say, "Fight here for God's reign," and what they mainly see is bloodshed and disaster, then it can be deeply discouraging. But the alternative is an otherworldly faith, that says, "Well, in light of this, just withdraw, wait for personal salvation, wait for heaven," and I think that's often what Christians have done.

JR: I would think of a third way, which goes back to David Patterson's sense of the vertical. A Christian trusts that there is a reality that makes the last word belong to love, reconciliation, healing. You don't see those things happening completely in history, but because you have faith, that truth extends beyond history: That's what drives you back to work in the historical order. It's not that you see progress in the historical order that says, "Oh, we're really winning, let's get with it, and make it all right." My sense of the historical is that we're losing it, historically, but that we still, in spite of that, oper-ate with a conviction and a trust that ultimately the his-torical will not be the last thing. But whether it will get worked out historically, I'm very dubious of that.

DP: That resonates in the Twelfth Principle of Faith of Mai-monides concerning the wait for the Messiah: "No mat-ter how long he may tarry." No matter how long it takes or how impossible it seems.

DG: I think Jesus had that. That's why I think it's appropriate to talk about not just faith *in* Jesus Christ, but the faith *of* Christ, as Richard Niebuhr did. Christ's teachings and his carriage of himself in ministry had this immense trust in God. And determination to live accordingly. And that's what makes his story so compelling. He taught that trust; he had that determination. He gets nailed to a cross, but then, of course, the resurrection, we believe, vindicated his trust, and then helps us to vindicate our trust, despite all the murders that don't result in resurrection, yet.

JR: Now you've stated why I said earlier, that for me, in the light of the Holocaust, the doctrine of the resurrection is immensely important. Because absent that, I think you're left with history.

JP: I think we have to avoid two extremes here, and in the end admit that there's considerable ambiguity that we can't penetrate. Number one, I think to advocate a view that somehow the kingdom will simplistically emerge out of the historical process is naïve and certainly goes contrary to the data of history.

DG: And I'm not saying that.

JP: I know you're not, and I wouldn't either. On the other hand, the equal danger is to say it's all going to end in fire and brimstone, and so maybe we should just enhance the process of the fire and brimstone arising. That's equally dangerous and irresponsible. Now what I've always argued is that somehow the kingdom is emerging in and through what we call history, but its final form will be post-historical and exactly what that will entail, I don't know. I'm not sure anybody knows. But I think we have to have some sense, as Christians, that we are actively contributing to the emergence of that kingdom. Not that the institutions, the structures, we develop are going to endure into the final kingdom, but that somehow they're related. Now there's ambiguity there, and I can't penetrate that.

I would just say, though, John, that your stress on the individual certainly remains a center point, if you want to call it "kingdom ethics," or that kind of ethical approach. It would certainly put the dignity of each individual person as a core value. So, I wouldn't think it's either/or. It's not, I think, a stress on the individual over against the communal, nor a stress on the communal to the detriment of the individual.

JR: I think that's where I would come out, too.

DG: There's one thing I would add. When you end up working for concrete justice, peace, reconciliation, inclusion, and so on, you discover something—and Bonhoeffer has taught us this—you discover that alliances cut across religious community lines rather than being confined within them. If you were to convert the entire world to Christianity, but to teach them the same kind of miserable version of Christianity that is so widely prevalent, you would not necessarily make the world a better place. You would just reproduce mediocrity.

Alliances are with like-minded people who are committed to the reclamation of the world, or the preservation of the world, or whatever the cause is, the prevention of injustice or victimization, and I often find a deeper sense of community with nonbelievers, or people who believe in all kinds of other things, or people who are unsure of what they believe, but they do share this particular justice vision, and they are happy to work alongside you. I find sometimes a deeper sense of community there than with morally complacent fellow Christians. And so what does community look like? At its best, for me, it's probably morally committed fellow Christians—that's probably the pinnacle where I experience community. But when I got together with Rabbis for Human Rights, or when I was at a meeting in December with mainly secular scientists and Evangelicals talking about environmental issues—there is a deep sense of community there. Wasn't it Bonhoeffer who discovered his community was found in the resistors, not in the complacent, or even in the collaborationist church? And somehow if I'm able to experience a sense that God is at work in those communities of justice and peace that cross religious lines, then surely God is far more engaged in such efforts than I can even imagine. And so, as the only parameter, religious credo confession ends up receding somewhat in significance.

SEEKING THE MESSIAH

AB: I think that's very true. Furthermore, I think one of the issues here concerns referring to God and religion after the Holocaust as if nothing had changed. I think John Roth is right: "What do you do with the dead?" Irving Greenberg once said, memorably, "No statement, theological or otherwise, should be made that would not be credible in the presence of the burning children." I think that this should lead us to a great measure of humility. The whole issue of history, as I listen to the discussion, reminding myself of Wiesel's many works whose message is, "To be a Jew is to have all the reasons in the world not to have faith in language, in singing, in prayers, and in God, but to go on telling the tale, to go on carrying on the dialogue, and to have my own silent prayers and quarrels with God" *(af al pe chen)*. The alternative is simply unacceptable.

I wonder if it would be helpful to reflect briefly on Yitz Greenberg's statement concerning Jesus as not a false Messiah, but as a failed Messiah. I think that does address the issue of history as we're trying to grapple with it. What does history mean? It can't be the definitive answer because history's countercovenantal claims are too overwhelming. Everything can't depend on history, and yet we measure the credibility of theological proclamations against the events of history.

JR: I think that Christians ought to understand Jesus messianically in a way that's like what David Gushee said: Jesus reveals the ultimacy of God's commitment and love for the world. That comes through the resurrection. But clearly, as things have worked out, his coming does not fully redeem the historical order. Given that this is the case, it makes sense that Jews would not want to identify Jesus as a messianic figure.

JP: This is where Greenberg's thesis moves in a new direction from the Jewish side. Because while he calls him a failed Messiah, there is in that an explicit acknowledgment that what he was trying to do was positive.

AB: No question about that.

JP: And I suppose one could say it was within the context of Jewish teaching.

DP: Well, we have other failed Messiahs. Bar Kochba was a failed Messiah. But the Talmudic teaching is that he failed because we had not done enough to prepare a way for him. Rabbi Akiva correctly recognized him as Messiah, but he's not like Shabbtai Zvi or Jacob Frank, a false Messiah.

DG: I guess I might say that for evangelicals, that would be a scandalous notion, of Jesus as a failed Messiah. But I might say that you could have biblical warrant, a New Testament warrant, for saying that in a sense our actions will determine whether Jesus will be perceived as a failed Messiah.

JP: I did a lot of writing for Cardinal Bernardin, who spoke a lot about Jewish-Catholic relations. One day he was supposed to respond to a paper by Byron Sherwin, and Byron had more or less taken this image of Jesus as the failed Messiah. I got this panicked call from Bernardin: "What can I say about this? It sounds like an insult to Jesus." I tried to explain, but you're right, the immediate reaction of Christians will tend to be that it's almost an insult to Jesus, an insult to the tradition. But when you try to understand it, I think it's actually an effort at a positive attempt. Maybe it's not the way to do it because the reaction, if it's not understood, could be more negative.

DP: This is tied to how we understand history. Christians and Jews, at least in some sense, believe that God is connected to history, involved with history, present in history, whatever those terms might mean, specifically. God's involvement in history presumably lies in our traditions, and that involvement has a messianic dimension. That history has a point, has a certain teleology, is about something. So I don't want to say the Messiah is *the same as* history, but certainly, in some sense, working for the Messiah is a defining aspect of history, inasmuch as history is about something, and not just a register of one tragedy after another.

THE CONCEPT OF CONVERSION

JP: I want to go back to something, because I think it is critical, and we kind of skirted it, although we did raise it, and that is the concept of conversion. You rightly identify it in the book, and I think it should be identified as an important, unresolved, and even avoided question in the dialogue. A talk at a conference we had in 2002 in Cambridge raised this, saying we're in a "don't ask, don't tell" mode right now. When I did raise it, Eugene Fisher said, "Oh, well, it's a false question. We're not doing it." It is true that historically Catholicism, in contrast to many parts of Protestantism, did not have organized efforts to convert Jews. The Sisters of Zion and the Fathers of Zion were founded ostensibly for this purpose, but if you know anything about their history, they mostly confined themselves to praying for Jews and did all sorts of other work, like educating Muslims in Turkey and things like that.

So there really was no organized effort, whereas in the Protestant community, including in the mainline Protestant community, there are, particularly in

Europe, offices for the conversion of Jews. In the Anglican Church there is one such office. I think it has got to be confronted much more directly.

When I was growing up, we had to put coins in containers with a bobbing black head. Every time you put a coin in, the head would bob. But there was a sense that if we could only raise enough money and get enough missionaries, the world would convert to Christianity. So that was the challenge. Get enough missionaries and you'll get the whole world. I think the realization now is that this ain't gonna happen, that large parts of the world are not going to become Christian; it represents a real trauma for Christians. And I see it being played out.

We have a lot of students at our school who are connected with historic Catholic missionary orders. Many of them, if not most of them, after Vatican II, redefined themselves in very significant ways in terms of saying our emphasis now is on what's sometimes called social promotion and being present, making God's love visible through helping people. Yes, there still is the idea of bringing people in if they so choose. They've run into a tremendous amount of flak within the Vatican in the last few years, with the Vatican saying you have to go back to your more traditional emphasis on outright evangelization and conversion and so on. So the issue is not resolved by any means, and it's not resolved with respect to Judaism, because what we're finding now even in the Catholic community is the increased emphasis in certain circles on evangelizing Jews and a campaign to do that. One of the strongest critiques of *Reflections on Covenant and Mission* was on this issue. It was Jewish Catholics who just inundated Cardinal Keeler on this point, and it was one of the reasons why the statement was withdrawn from the bishop's website, even though it was an official study document. One of the strongest objections was that we should not engage in proselytizing the Jews, and while there's no organized effort as such to do that, there is a reluctance theologically to withdraw from it.

DP: I've had conversations with some Catholic theologians, whom, I think, you know: Didier Pollefeyt and Jürgen Manemann, who are Belgian and German Catholic theologians respectively and who maintain, theologically, that Jesus is unnecessary to the salvation of the Jews, that the Torah is sufficient. That the Covenant of Abraham is where their redemption lies. And when I heard that, I was looking for people to come and burn them at the stake or something. But I thought, well, this could open some doors for conversations between Christians and Jews. Part of what makes Jews uncomfortable about sitting down and talking with Christians is that in your mind you're thinking, "Am I talking to someone who thinks I'm damned because I reject his teaching?" And so when I heard Pollefeyt and Manemann say that their thinking on this is that the Covenant of Torah is enough for the Jews, that it's the nations who find their salvation in Jesus, and so on, it sounded pretty controversial to me from a Christian standpoint, but refreshing from a Jewish standpoint.

JP: Well, Manemann, of course, is a student of Metz's. And Metz's students right now are finding it extremely difficult to get appointments in a university where you have the Catholic chair and the Protestant chair. A lot of this is due to the influence of Ratzinger when he was in Munich, who really clamped down on Metz. There is that reality.

JR: Personally, David, I would be comfortable with the position that Didier Pollefeyt and Jürgen Manemann have taken. As a Christian, I think the case can be made that the Covenant of Abraham is sufficient, and that there would be no need—in fact, it would be undesirable—for Christians to proselytize Jews. This leads me to comment on another feature of your book that interested me. Toward the end, you seem worried that Christians might not be able to say certain things because they would be engaging in blasphemy or rejection of their tradition. I actually found myself very comfortable with the contrarian versions of Christianity that you are pointing to there. For instance, when you say that Jesus is superfluous to salvation for the Jews, I think some version of that position is one I gladly embrace. I don't know if I'd use the word *superfluous* there, but "not necessary for," or something like that. Likewise, when you say, "Could a Christian truly say to a Jew, 'Do not convert to Christianity, it's no good for you. You're better off with your teaching and tradition.'" Again, I might not word the point exactly that way, and David Gushee and I might differ here, but in fact I have said to my Jewish students that I think you're better off with your tradition. Be a good Jew. That's what you should be. That's your identity. That's what you should do and that would be sufficient and fine. I think it's possible for a Christian to take those positions.

JP: Well, Walter Kasper has made some statements along these lines, but he's also made the statement that Christology must have a universal dimension to it, and we have pressed him to say that you've got to put those two things together. But he hasn't. Kasper made some of these statements when he first came into the position of head of the Vatican commission for relations with Jews. In recent years, however, he's been extremely cautious and said virtually nothing more on these issues, so we're not sure. Actually, the 2001 Pontifical Biblical Commission document tends to move in that direction without being as explicit as Kasper, saying that Jewish messianic interpretations are not in vain. Now that's a very indirect way, but there are seeds there. And even Ratzinger, in some of his writings prior to becoming pope, made some statements not all that different from Kasper. However, he has not said anything along these lines since assuming the papacy. I'm rather skeptical that he's going to say anything. So I don't know. This is where you're perfectly right.

We move to a certain level, but there's been a halt to creative thinking. I see that exemplified in Walter Kasper, who really started out offering some really creative seeds, but has never pursued them. In fact, we did *Reflections on Covenant and Mission* as a document precisely because when he was speaking at Boston College and at Sacred Heart University, he said, "While it can't be done at the Vatican level now, it's got to be done at the National Bishops' Conferences." And *Reflections on Covenant and Mission* was trying to take him seriously. But it encountered the ire of Cardinal Dulles, and we know now that Ratzinger himself—perhaps because of the influence of Dulles—wrote a letter to the American Bishops Conference castigating the document.

JR: I think the issue of conversion also leads back to a question that David Gushee put on the table early on: How do we think of Jesus? But it also goes back to the question that David Patterson and Alan raise in the book, which is: Do Christians and Jews worship or relate to the same God? I'd be interested in learning what we think about that.

DG: Before we go there, I'd like to jump in and not duck this very difficult issue for me, for my community.

JP: You mean the conversion issue?

DG: The conversion issue. The default position of all evangelical Christians is that we are called to go into the world and preach the Gospel, which of course is normally understood to mean "come to belief in Jesus Christ and be saved." I think that given the evangelical structure of thought, the only way to challenge that is from within Scripture. There are passages that are suggestive here, that provide a way forward. If you focus on *Kingdom Ethics* and on the teachings of Jesus, there are some ways forward.

For example, again, in Matthew 7: "Not everyone who calls me 'Lord, Lord' will enter the Kingdom of Heaven, but he who does the will of my Father in Heaven." "Enter the kingdom of heaven" is a cognate for salvation. Who gets in? He who does the will of my Father in Heaven. That's what Jesus said. So I am working with the possibility that the best way forward is to say that humility related to the eternal salvation of other people is the first and nonnegotiable point. I would never presume to stand in the shoes of God in judging a human being and say what's going to happen to somebody else eternally. I think that's hugely presumptuous.

Second, what Jesus focused on was doing God's will. Who is my mother? Who are my brothers? Those who do God's will are my mother and father and sisters and brothers. He was radical on that. He didn't divert from that. So if I were pushed up against a wall and asked who then shall be saved, those who obey Christ by doing the will of God are the saved. And then when you explore Jesus' teaching, as to who does the will of God, it's the things we've been talking about.

DOING GOD'S WILL: THE RIGHTEOUS

DP: Isn't the will of God something that is revealed in Torah?

DG: Yes, and then elucidated and articulated by Jesus, yes, and it's those who heal the broken, who include the excluded, who serve and feed the poor, who prevent violence, who stand up for justice, who rescue those who need to be rescued.

DP: A. J. Heschel says we may not be able to fathom God's essence, but we know perfectly well God's will. It's spelled out: Don't murder; don't steal; help the poor; seek justice.

DG: The rich young ruler comes to Jesus and says, "What do I need to do to be saved?" Jesus answers, "Love God with everything; love your neighbor as yourself." He asks, "And who is my neighbor?" And Jesus goes into the story of the Good Samaritan. Both of those are action steps: service to the poor and radically following Jesus. So that's the direction that my thinking is going. I think it's biblical, but it doesn't fit with the tradition of my people right now. What do you think about that, John Roth?

JR: That sounds good to me. It would fit with what I was saying a moment ago, too. If what you are saying were the case, then you'd have a version of David Gushee's cutting across traditions. You'd look to see, as best you can, who are the people who are following the will of God, and whoever those people may be, the fact that they're doing that is the key thing. I like also the way the preaching of the Gospel now becomes a call to participate in the kingdom. It doesn't have the emphasis that would say, "Oh, you must confess Jesus as Lord," so much. It suggests that "preaching the Good News of the Gospel" means extending an invitation and taking on a responsibility to participate in the effort to try to follow the will of God.

DG: I would not juxtapose those negatively, but I would say that God is acting to reclaim the world. For me, to acknowledge Christ as Lord is to believe in him, and to make a commitment to doing God's will, and to invite others to do the same. Come to Jesus as your entry point for that commitment, if you are not involved in another covenantal tradition that is already doing God's will as revealed in the Scriptures. It means submitting your will to His, which involves living this kind of life.

DP: Then you're making room for a Christian notion of something like the righteous among non-Christians, similar to the Jewish notion of the righteous among the nations?

DG: I first discovered the "righteous among the nations" concept when I was working on *Righteous Gentiles*; I was very struck by it. It was an expansive understanding. It welcomes to the eternal table all who are just and righteous.

DP: Based on what they *do*.

DG: Yes. The fact that Israel acknowledges the righteous among the nations so profoundly, theologically, and at Yad Vashem and in the tradition after the Holocaust, struck me as very gracious and very wise, and it struck me that there is an asymmetry here, because we have had trouble doing the same thing on our side. I would like to see our tradition do more to explore this idea.

JP: I should mention, as just an aside, that there's been an interesting debate at the Holocaust Museum in Washington, as to whether the term should be *rescuers* or *righteous*. There is a reluctance in certain quarters to use the term *righteous* because in some cases, though people saved people in the end, some of their other actions were not deemed morally righteous.

AB: Oskar Schindler is an example. I interviewed some of the Schindler *Juden*, who said that he was a moral man; no matter what he did before or after the war. He saved lives.

JP: I wanted to just add two dimensions to the conversion issue in this connection. One is that if we take the Holocaust seriously, then it has altered, perhaps significantly, our understanding of God. And if we make the claim in Christianity, which we have, that there is an intimate relationship between Christ and God, doesn't that mean, then, that the Holocaust also impacts our understanding of Christology or our understanding of

Christ? That issue has been pursued very little, and I think it's one that has to be pursued.

The second thing is this question of whether from the Christian point of view we can eliminate Jews from the proselytizing mission of the Church, perhaps on the grounds that someone like Kasper uses, namely, that they are the only group that has authentic revelation from the Christian point of view. There is an attempt certainly within the Catholic tradition at the moment, to really make the relationship with Judaism *sui generis*. Absolutely special. And even someone like Michael Fitzgerald, who is in charge of Catholic-Muslim relations, would actually validate that, and say, "Well the Muslims perhaps are the first among the others," but there's a real gap there. If we are going to pursue the kind of track that, David Gushee, you've been laying out, which I'm very sympathetic to, do we then need to expand the notion to the point where it isn't only Jews who are not objects of proselytizing, but almost any other person of faith?

HEBREW SCRIPTURES

DG: The goal is the same as Jesus' goal: to see every human being in the world be committed to doing God's will and advancing the reign of God. I don't want anybody not to do that. Is that proselytizing? It is a mission-based stance. It is a world-transformative stance. It is not happy with the status quo. It wants change. It is not so much demanding that everybody come to believe the exact creedal declarations that we believe, but to come to the moral commitments that God has revealed in Scripture and in Christ and that are written on the human heart. I think that stance is applicable to all human beings. Christians learned these principles and these priorities through the Hebrew Scriptures and through Jesus, the Son of Israel. And so the humble recognition that we got grafted onto this tree does make the relationship with Judaism unique, I think.

JP: One of my problems with the argumentation of people like Kasper, and I've said this to him, is that it seems to identify Judaism almost exclusively with the Hebrew Scriptures, but this is not all of Judaism. A Jew would not want to argue that his or her identity is based solely and exclusively on the Hebrew Scriptures.

AB: Isaac Bashevis Singer, in *Enemies: A Love Story*, describes the Bible as "the Book that has hypnotized them (the Jewish people) forever." Most Jews know nothing about the Christian Scriptures, and that's taken for granted. But most don't know anything about the Jewish Scriptures, either. David Patterson has mentioned the Jews' lack of familiarity with the rabbinic tradition, the tradition of Talmud, the tradition of medieval poetry and mysticism—it's as if there were an unconscious decision to accept David Ben Gurion's patronizing and dismissive definition of the diaspora as a two-thousand-year parenthesis in Jewish history. But I don't know whether I could accept such a statement about the Bible.

DP: The Hebrew Scriptures are not the only thing that Jewish identity is based upon, but they are the most essential and fundamental. The streets of Tel Aviv are named after prophets and mystics and Talmudic sages, and on Independence Hall we have a quote from Jeremiah that Ben Gurion put there, so you can't have Jews without the Bible, even secular Jews.

JP: You can't have Jews without the Talmud.

DP: Yes.

JR: I wanted to weigh in on the issue concerning the relation between Judaism and Christianity, Jews and Christians. I think it is a distinctive relationship. A relationship between a Christian and a Jew is different from the relationship a Christian may have to a Muslim or to a Hindu. Not absolutely different, of course, for ethical obligations, but religiously, I think there's something approaching a *sui generis* kind of relationship there that is really important to keep in mind. Now, regarding the Christian's responsibility to testify in the world as a Christian, with the idea of influencing other people, I think this becomes an ongoing issue that doesn't have a one-size-fits-all kind of answer.

I often think about this in my teaching. I think of myself as a Christian teacher. But I ask myself in the setting where I work: "What does that mean? What words do I use?" And very often it seems to me that the thing I'm most interested in trying to communicate and share with other people is very close to the kind of ethical outlook that David Gushee was articulating, so I have to pick and choose when I use a vocabulary that is explicitly Christian, and when I use one that isn't. But in the latter case my vocation is still that of a Christian teacher. So there is ambiguity and grayness in this, but the ultimate goal is very close to what David Gushee was articulating, that you're looking to do what you can to encourage people, whatever their traditions may be, to work in a way that would attempt to fulfill the will of God.

Do We Worship the Same God?

DP: John Roth, you mentioned the question of whether we in fact worship the same God. We say in the book that on a certain level, a mystical, transcendent level, yes. But we dress our God in different clothing. And in Judaism we have this concept of the *Livushim Hashem*, the clothing of God. It entails things like the discourse surrounding God. What is the nature of the testimony to God that we engage in? Clearly, it is quite different in the two traditions, but I think this is one of those differences that can be a good thing—the different ways in which we talk about God.

I think dialogue is very similar to the story of the seven blind men trying to describe an elephant. Each one of the blind men is feeling a different part of the elephant. One says the elephant is like a snake, another says the elephant is like a tree, the elephant is like a wall, and in the fable, they start fighting with each another, when, in fact, if they would speak to one another and listen to one another, they could start to get a better picture of the elephant. So God is the elephant that we blind men and women are trying to describe, dressing or articulating one aspect according to how we see it, the best we can. So we're not done. Dialogue, by definition, is open-ended, and never done.

Before we part, I just wanted to get that out there, in case someone might be a little uneasy about our assertion that we don't talk about God in the same way. We talk about Creator, we talk about Holy One, but in Judaism we never speak of God as becoming a man. That's just not part of the thinking.

JP: I know that was an assertion in *Dabru Emet* that received considerable discussion, and even strong criticism. And it's interesting because that assertion was forged by four Jewish scholars who are quite divergent in their understanding of the Jewish tradition. This is a difficult thing. You can be too absolutist in saying it's a different God, because ultimately, I think, underlying the Christian conception is a God who was, yes, revealed in and through Jesus Christ, whose presence is continuing to be manifested through the Spirit, but it's more complex than that. Many years ago, probably twenty to twenty-five years ago now, the late Raymond Brown wrote a piece I think originally published in *Catholic Biblical Quarterly* and included in a collection of essays that became a book, *Does the New Testament Call Jesus God?* His conclusion was that many of the passages are ambiguous. He outlines all the passages where there seems to be an absolute connection, and then he outlines passages where there seems to be a clear distinction. And in between, a lot of ambiguous ones. So the relationship between the man, Jesus, and God is not as clear, I think, in the Christian tradition, or even perhaps in the biblical tradition. For example, there's always been a reluctance, at least in Catholic hymns, to honor Jesus in song. It's happened, but in a sense we don't worship Jesus. We worship Christ.

The third point I would make is that if the Holocaust has altered our understanding of God, then both of us need to go back and reflect further on what, in God's name, God means today.

DG: I want to say, in honor of my teacher Irving Greenberg, that everything that I say theologically has been affected by that "burning children" test. And I hope that what I have said today fits that, because it has had a huge impact on me. It has almost a revelatory power to it, that statement. Of course, when you hear that statement in the light of close study of what actually happened at Auschwitz and places like that—I've been transformed by that.

I think that there is only one God, and so we worship the same God. I think that the Christian theological tradition introduced new elements in understanding God that have been fruitful in their own way. I'm thinking of the way the trinitarian theology has been richly fertile in developing a theological relationship and relationality, and that human beings are ontologically relational. If we are made in the image of God and God is one in three and three in one, then we are in a sense one in three and three in one. We are relational: We need others, relationship is at the core of our identity. There may not be a reconciliation between the perspectives, but there is richness in the diversity, and there is only one God.

DP: That's what Jews teach: The Lord our God, the Lord is One.

DG: There is one God whom we struggle to understand, based on God's revelation to us, and there are our feeble efforts to then elaborate and reflect and develop our understanding. It goes from there. And so, we worship the same God. We may have different understandings of that God. But I can't ever assent to a statement, you know…

JP: Christ and the Spirit really represent manifestations of God rather than somehow new gods.

JR: Coming to a trinitarian understanding of God, as a Christian, I have a low-level metaphysical understanding of this teaching. Trinitarian language, I believe, refers to aspects or manifestations of the oneness of God. The ultimacy falls on God's unity. But it's a unity that has dimensions to it, aspects to it, which I don't think is completely antithetical to the notion of the oneness of God in Judaism. In Jewish tradition, God speaks, God is in relationship. Whatever it means to say God is One in Judaism, this is not a oneness that precludes relationships, and relationships always involve dimensions and aspects.

DP: That's correct.

JR: Or the oneness of the Unmoved Mover, as you point out. This is a rich dialogical oneness of some kind, I think.

DP: I'm so happy to hear you say that. Often, especially in studies of Kabbalah, you do get manifestations of God by different names, showing different aspects, different faces; Shekhinah, Hashem, Elokim, all of that.

JR: Yes. I think there are clear differences in the two traditions, but the differences are not, or shouldn't be, ultimately at odds. They're not differences necessarily at odds, they're differences that can be looked at, at least in part, as complementary.

DP: Yes. There's just one elephant, but each of us has a different avenue of approach and understanding, and that's, as I said, an example of a positive difference that contributes to the dialogue, the depth of the dialogue, the understanding to be attained in dialogue.

JP: Well, it seemed in the manuscript, though, that the two of you had expressed sympathy for the kind of Jon Levenson attack on that statement in *Dabru Emet*, and I think Jon is a little over the top on that.

DP: I'm a little leery of having too many fuzzy feelings about how wonderful it is that we all embrace the same thing, and that basically we have nothing much to talk about except how we might fix the rest of the world, or something like that. I'm the last one that would say there's more than one God, but I do say we have significantly different ways of talking about God.

DG: With regard to your manuscript, David and Alan, there are places where there is not a real good feel for Christian theology, but I think we've talked about most of those things today.

JP: Well, the tone of the manuscript is one that I think stresses that this is an effort at a positive discussion and not just a critique of Christianity. You're critiquing for the sake of dialogue, not to destroy dialogue.

DP: That's correct. If you sit down together in trust and friendship, then it's in the interest of helping one another, not to get you to think what I think, but for each to help the other to take his or her thinking to deeper levels.

Here, after farewells at the end of our gathering, ended our first attempt at a renewed direction for Jewish-Christian dialogue. The constraints of time made it necessary for each of us to go his own way for the time being, despite our sense that we had only scratched a surface or two. Alan Berger and David Patterson are deeply indebted to John Pawlikowski, John Roth, and David Gushee, who agreed to gather for this encounter on their own precious time, with true courage and commitment.

SEVEN

CONCLUSION

WHAT HAVE WE LEARNED

Our exploration of post-Shoah Christian-Jewish dialogue has been personally and theologically enriching. Facing the daunting task of seeking to draw honey from the ashes of the crematoria that consumed two-thirds of European Jewry, our study evokes in us both humility and some measure of hope; those ashes may contain embers of possibility for a genuine dialogue. Much depends on trust, the willingness to persevere, and a recognition that theological differences will remain. Concerning the role of trust in the post-Auschwitz dialogue, it is significant to remember Emil Fackenheim's observation. He writes that "a Tikkun of Jewish-Gentile trust, genuine even if fragmentary, is possible from the Jewish side, here and now, because a corresponding Tikkun was already begun from the Gentile side then and there." He refers to the public prayers of Prior Bernhard Lichtenberg "on behalf of the Jews and the poor concentration camp prisoners," an act, notes Fackenheim, "not done even once by the Vicar of Christ in the safety of the Vatican."[1] Fackenheim also notes what he terms the "Tikkun of ordinary decency"[2] by which he refers to the "moral minority" of Christian helpers.

Jews, for their part, need to recognize and respond to efforts on the part of Christians to "repair the great rupture of trust."[3] Extending his well-known 614th commandment that after Auschwitz Jews must remain Jewish in order not to grant Hitler a posthumous victory, Fackenheim attests that to refrain from sharing in the mending of post-Holocaust Jewish-Gentile relations would yield the same unhappy result. Consequently, contemporary Christian-Jewish dialogue emerges as both a moral and ontological necessity. The fact that there were some "righteous among the nations" who, acting against all self-interest under a regime dedicated to death, helped hide Jews during the kingdom of night, means that there is reason for hope now.

But mending will come neither easily nor evenly. The rupture caused by the Holocaust to both the Christian and Jewish traditions is, as we have argued, staggering. Further, the fact is that Vatican II and subsequent Vatican implementing documents recognize that the Holocaust is an enormous theological scandal in the heart of Christianity. To acknowledge and address this scandal requires a theological and historical honesty that was not possible prior to the Holocaust. The Shoah reveals with absolute clarity what happens when the malignancy of antisemitism spreads and goes untreated. Post-Auschwitz Christian-Jewish dialogue is the principal vehicle for the attempted mending of the world. However, the dialogue, like a garden of hybrid orchids, requires constant tending.

Looking back as well as ahead provides a sense of perspective that is simultaneously hopeful and cautionary. Like Walter Benjamin's Angel of History, we suggest that all who participate in the post-Holocaust dialogue need to look back as well as toward the future. The face of Benjamin's angel looks toward the past. The angel's back faces the future toward which he is being swept by a storm from paradise. Looking back is, however, not the same as being paralyzed by the past. Quite the contrary is the case. This view enables us to appreciate even more the revolutionary nature of post-Auschwitz Christian thought. Vatican II ushered in a new era of theological self-critique on the part of the Church as well as a rethinking of its centuries-old teaching of contempt for the Jews. The contemporary dialogue *is something new under the sun*.

One of the most significant developments in the dialogue is Christianity's rediscovery of its Jewish roots. Exploration of these roots yields a greater understanding of both Judaism and Christianity at a time when the two communities had more in common than is generally assumed. This research has helped clarify the historical and theological issues that emerge as both bond and barrier between Judaism and Christianity. The parting of the ways did not occur until at least the fourth century CE. Furthermore, scholarly analysis aids in dispelling hurtful and distorted stereotypes of each tradition that fan the fires of hatred and mistrust. Concomitantly, Jewish scholars such as Martin Buber, David Flusser, and Pincus Lapide have begun to "rediscover" Jesus. On the other hand, there is the constant danger of divorcing Christianity from its Jewish roots. *The Passion of the Christ* is the most recent example of how seamlessly antisemitism emerges when Christianity first ignores then denies its Jewish origin. Jesus was not a Christian in the sense that fundamentalists understand the term.

The emergence of knowledgeable and sincere post-Holocaust dialogue partners augurs well for the continuing efforts of Christians and Jews to deepen their understanding both of their own and of the others' faith community. This can aid in overcoming prejudice and thereby become exemplary for relations between other world religions. Wrestling, like Jacob of old, with images of the Christian-Jewish relationship is a positive development, one that decreases the danger of triumphalism while expanding the possibilities of enriching understanding between the two communities. Various relationship models have been put forth, e.g., 'siblings' by Jewish scholars such as (Alan Segal and the late Hayim Perelmuter); 'fraternal twins' (Mary C. Boys); 'partners in waiting' (Clark Williamson); and 'coemergent religious communities' (Daniel Boyarin).[4] Yet even here there are difficulties. When Pope John Paul II spoke at the Great Synagogue of Rome in April 1986, he called Judaism the elder brother of Christianity. But we note that in the Hebrew Scriptures, the younger brother triumphs over the elder as in the examples of Jacob and Esau or Joseph and his brothers.[5]

Real theological differences exist and will remain. But this is a situation that does not call for despair. Rather it is one that demands to be acknowledged. Clarifying the nature of the differences is one mark of the dialogue's maturity. Difference within the context of religious pluralism is not only possible, it is highly desirable. We recall here an instructive episode from

American political history. Thomas Jefferson, although not using these precise terms, recognized that America saw no conflict between religious and cultural diversity, on the one hand, and civil unity on the other. He wrote that the maxim of civil government is "reversed in that of religion, where its true form is 'divided we stand, united we fall.'"[6] Judaism and Christianity *are* divided on key theological concepts, such as messianism, the meaning of the cross, and the trinity. Yet we continue the dialogue as part of the mending process and in the hope that understanding will replace contempt.

CONTEMPORARY IMPLICATIONS

Academic centers, university courses, and scholarly conferences on interfaith issues have grown enormously in the wake of the emergence of genuine post-Holocaust Jewish-Christian dialogue. There is, however, a certain irony in the fact that universities are leading the way in contemporary post-Holocaust Christian-Jewish dialogue. For centuries European universities had been bastions of antisemitism. In America the situation was hardly better. Many institutions of higher learning imposed severe restrictions *(numerus clausus)* on the number of Jews admitted to study. Today, as a result of the dialogue, there are chairs of Jewish studies at Catholic universities. Furthermore, many institutes of Catholic-Jewish relations exist within an academic setting. We think here especially of the Sister Rose Thering Endowment for the Department of Jewish-Christian Studies at Seton Hall University.

Fraternal reading of sacred scriptures, led by informed individuals, has done much to help in listening to the other's narrative. Furthermore, there is a growing awareness of the distinction between history in the Western sense of the word and biblical narrative, which is put forth to argue the "infallibility" of a certain mythic perspective. Academic conferences dealing with antisemitism, the Holocaust, and the history of interfaith dialogue have done a great deal to help advance understanding of crucial issues by sharing the results of contemporary academic research. Scholarly working groups such as the one that examined and critiqued the script of the Gibson film reveal the extent of the contribution that informed scholarship can make, although in this particular case the scholarship was ignored and the scholars subsequently ridiculed in a smear campaign inaugurated by Icon Productions and joined by right-wing and fundamentalist groups. Nevertheless, joint statements and declarations on issues of social justice, opposition to genocide, and environmental concerns are no longer viewed as rare occurrences, but have become the norm.

But serious, and still unresolved, tensions between Jews and Christians remain. We think of issues such as the role of the Vatican during the Holocaust and efforts to canonize Pius XII before his wartime record is fully and publicly known. Revelations of Christian complicity in the Holocaust such as at Jedwabne in Poland, and the ugly dispute over crosses at Auschwitz underscore the complexity of issues confronting the dialogue. Furthermore, confusion exists over the discrepancy between Vatican pronouncements endorsing the need for better relations with the Jewish people on the one hand, and official silence in the face of rabidly antisemitic statements made by Arab officials and the acquiescence of the United States bishops—acting contrary to their own stated principles for how to present the Passion—in the wake of the mass enthusiasm that greeted Mel Gibson's patently antisemitic film on the other. We also note the conservative "push back" against the liberalism advanced by the Second Vatican Council and wonder if this will lead to a backsliding in which the dialogue is placed on a theological back burner.

On the Jewish side, there is a twofold need. On the one hand, it is important to remember—indeed, what Jew with any sense of history could forget—the church's bimillennial teaching of contempt for Jews and Judaism. No less important, however, is the need on the part of far more in the Jewish community to acknowledge that a *fundamental change* has occurred in Catholicism's theology of the Jewish people. Focusing on the former dooms the dialogue to an unending series of accusations that may well result in the Church wondering why Jews cannot take yes for an answer. It may also lead those on the Catholic side to resentment. Attention paid strictly to the new situation runs the risk of obliterating memory of the

Shoah's victims. It is their deaths that cry out as a reminder of where the cancer of antisemitism leads.

Christian-Jewish dialogue after the Holocaust can serve as a model for civil discourse about theological issues over which the parties disagree but nevertheless continue to share their respective narratives. Dialogue is after all as much, if not more than, about differences as well as similarities. Furthermore, neither Jews nor Christians can say with certainty what God's plan is for humanity. This should evoke a shared sense of humility concerning eschatological speculation. Moreover, this recognition can be the stepping-stone toward a respect for religious pluralism in the Jeffersonian sense cited above. Taking its cue from note four of *Nostra Aetate,* the contemporary dialogue between Jews and Christians can speak to the global village of religious beliefs, oriental and occidental. Adherents of Hinduism, Buddhism, and Islam, no less than those of Judaism and Christianity, each seek a salvific path. Although it is manifestly clear that Judaism and Christianity share a unique and unparalleled relationship—the Christian savior is a Jew—the Christian-Jewish dialogue may, with certain necessary modifications, serve as a paradigm for interfaith relations among the nations of the world.

THE CURRENT STATE OF THE DIALOGUE

Contemporary Jewish-Christian dialogue is at a crossroads. On the one hand, enormous progress has been achieved over the past forty years. As we have noted, relations between mainstream Christians and Jews have never been better. We note three areas where this improvement is especially noticeable. Local interfaith dialogue groups have emerged across the country. These groups engage in Bible study, religious leaders exchange pulpits, and holiday observances are shared and explained. In addition, there has been a continual movement toward improving educational materials, given impetus originally by the incorporation into *Nostra Aetate* of the pioneering work of Sister Rose Thering. Sister Rose's work has been advanced by subsequent Vatican implementing statements, on the one hand, and, by the work of leading scholars and educators such as Mary C.

Boys, Eugene Fisher, Edward Flannery, David Gushee, John T. Pawlikowski, and John K. Roth on the other. Third, joint action on areas of common concern continues. None of these activities would have occurred prior to Auschwitz. Furthermore, the stress on civil discourse is a radical departure from pre-Holocaust encounters, which had no interest in dialogue.

Moreover, both Judaism and Christianity find themselves in a global village. Each tradition has a shared existential situation of being under terrorist threat from without and fundamentalist assault from within. Furthermore, both faith communities need to deal with the fact that secularism has become an increasingly attractive option in postmodernity. Each faith community grapples with the challenge of making its message meaningful to contemporary adherents at a time when religious authority is no longer the sole arbiter on matters of faith, morality, and meaning in the world.

The dialogue today does, however, face increasing difficulty. The difficulties are threefold: political, cultural, and theological. Politically, the ill-advised effort to divest from Israel on the part of the Presbyterian Church, influenced by the "Christ-killer" imagery of Naim Ateek of the Sabeel Institute, led initially to great confusion. If the Presbyterian leadership wished to take a position on the Israel-Palestinian conflict, why was it so one-sided? Why did certain members of the governing body of the church not protest the blatant Jew-hatred of Ateek? Divestment emerged as a theologically motivated weapon. However, after considerable dialogue with the Presbyterian Church initiated by Jewish groups such as the American Jewish Committee and the Anti-Defamation League, the language has changed from divestment to "investment "for peace. The Presbyterians have moved to an understanding that one-sided actions will bring neither justice nor peace.

The role of Israel in relationship to the Jewish people remains an area of concern. On the one hand, as we noted, the Vatican has granted diplomatic recognition to the Jewish state. Moreover, Pope John Paul II's visit to Israel emphasized that more than diplomacy was at stake. His pilgrimage to Yad Vashem and to the Western Wall were laden with theological implications. However, Israel also has a profound impact on Jewish life and identity that transcends the purely political. This impact is seen both in positive and negative ways. Israel is inseparable from Jewish identity and consciousness. It is an irreducible part of the central drama of death and rebirth experienced by the Jewish people during the twentieth century. Moreover, antisemitic acts against both people and institutions increase when there are tensions between Israelis and Palestinians; this is especially the case in Europe, where large numbers of Muslim immigrants reside. Consequently, what Michael Kotzkin calls the Vatican's "two-track approach," relating to Jews religiously through dialogue but viewing its relations with Israel solely in political terms is, from the Jewish perspective, flawed.[7] Furthermore, the very existence of the Jewish state continues to incite threats of annihilation. This existential threat needs to be acknowledged.

Culturally, group memory of the significance of Vatican II grows dimmer with each passing generation. Father John W. O'Malley, S.J., notes that "even the basic contours of what happened [at Vatican II] are fading from the collective memory of Catholics around the world. For younger generations [the council] can sound as remote as Trent and just as unfamiliar."[8] When this phenomenon is linked with widespread religious illiteracy, the situation is ripe for fundamentalist beliefs. This is a combination that has historically fueled antisemitism. Moreover, the pervasiveness of antisemitic stereotypes in culture ranging from classical literature to popular film is worrisome and unlikely to abate anytime soon.

On the theological level, we note that immediately following the Holocaust, antisemitism was for a brief historical moment, with the exception of certain fringe groups in America and tyrannical European governments, unfashionable, although it was never absent. Today the rise of Holocaust deniers, and minimizers, on the one hand, and the attempts to boycott Israeli academics on the other, reveal that antisemitism is very much with us. Albert Camus wrote his allegorical novel *The Plague*, near the end of World War II, in a farmhouse not far from the village of Le Chambon, where five thousand Chambonais saved the lives of five thousand Jews. The novel concerns an invasion of rats carrying the bubonic plague. In a ten-month period the pestilence kills many of the town's residents. Smoke from a crematorium where the corpses of the victims are burned, casts a pall over the city. Normal life has ceased. Dr. Rieux finally succeeds in bringing the plague under control. The citizens rejoice. But the doctor knows that "the plague bacillus [Jew hatred] never dies or disappears for good"; it can lie dormant for years and years, and "perhaps the day would come when, for the bane and the enlightening of men, it would rouse up its rats again, and send them forth to die in a happy city."[9]

THE PERSISTENCE OF ANTISEMITISM

From the Holocaust denial debacle held in Tehran in December 2006 to the antisemitic diatribes voiced daily from Islamic pulpits throughout the world, to intellectuals who insist that their anti-Zionism is not antisemitism, Jew hatred is alive and well. What feeds it? Why does it cover such an unlikely range of outlooks, from postmodern liberalism to Islamic fundamentalism? And what role does Jewish-Christian dialogue play in the response to it? When we consider the millennial reasons for antisemitism, we find reasons that span the spectrum of human consciousness; they are theological, philosophical, psychological, historical, cultural, social, racial, economic, and on and on. Each perspective on the Jews has its hatred of the Jews. But, we ask again, why? Why does it persist?

All of us know very well the stock answers invoked to explain and often to justify antisemitism: scapegoating, envy (of whatever kind), suspicion of the "other," Jewish conspiracies, Jewish isolationism, Jewish elitism, Zionism, etc. But, just as none of these answers could explain away the phenomenon of Nazi Jew hatred, so they all fail to account for the persistence of antisemitism in the twenty-first century. Indeed, Jew hatred is older and more pervasive than any of these facile explanations; it is as old as the messianism that, among other things, distinguishes the Jewish religion from other traditions. In fact, one answer to consider is this: Antisemitism persists as a form of anti-messianism. Let us explain.

In Judaism, messianism is an endless wait for an impossible resolution, namely that one day swords will be beaten into plowshares, the divine wisdom will be engraved in every heart, and peace will reign on this earth—not just through divine intervention but, above all, through human effort, for which each of has an infinite responsibility. There's the rub: It is the infinite responsibility—for God, world, and humanity—that the Jew insists upon. Who can tolerate such a burden? Who can endure such a wait? And if anything defines the Jew, it is this teaching concerning an indeterminable wait for redemption, for which each of us is infinitely responsible. As a terror of the infinite responsibility, antisemitism breeds terrorism among those who insist that matters have been settled, that the fixed formulas and ready answers are in, and that salvation has been decided: Either you are among the saved or you are among the damned. Whereas Judaism insists that the verdict remains to be decided for anyone, the antisemite—whether Nazi or Communist, whether Christian or Muslim—insists, vehemently and violently, that the matter has been decided. In short: Rooted in a longing for resolution, antisemitism is a longing to be relieved of the endless waiting and the endless doing, of the infinite responsibility that devolves on the ego.

That's it: The antisemite hates the Jew because the very presence of the Jew robs him of his ego. It robs him of his ego because it signifies the infinite responsibility that makes the waiting and the working for the messianic redemption infinite and without respite. In a word, it robs him of his ego because it disturbs his sleep. And no one is more hated than one who disturbs our sleep. The presence of the Jew forces him into an "awakening," as Emmanuel Lévinas puts it, that is "a demand that no obedience equals."[10] In traditions that insist more on obedience than on questioning—whether it is radical Islam or left-wing fanaticism—such a demand is as unacceptable as it is undermining. Thus the presence of the Jew is a constant reminder that we are forever in debt and that redemption is a matter always yet to be settled. There is no settling the accounts: No payment will do, because payment is always due. It is no wonder that among the antisemites it is a truism that the Jews control the banks and ledgers of the world.

In the ontological tradition, antisemitism shows itself in the impetus—whether philosophical, political, or nationalistic—toward the last line in the syllogism, toward a truth that is rational, resolved, and self-legislated. In religious traditions that preach personal salvation through a specific belief in a specific doctrine, and not a never-ending responsibility to and for the other human being, antisemitism arises when the fixed formulas and ready answers of the creed are challenged by the prospect that the creed is not enough. For this reason, what Franz Rosenzweig says of Christianity may also be said of Islam: "The existence of the Jew constantly subjects Christianity to the idea that it is not attaining the goal, the truth."[11] To be sure, it may be said that the existence of Christianity subjects Islam to the idea that it is not attaining its goal; hence the rising Muslim presence in formerly Christian areas. Here, in the face of radical Islam, the Christians assume the Jewish condition of insisting to a murderous faction that their covenant has not been superseded.

The hatred of the Jews is the oldest hatred, because the challenge from the Jews is the oldest challenge to the personal autonomy and the personal salvation that would curl up in the comfort of looking out for Number One: Historically speaking, for Christianity, as for Islam, salvation is about *me*. And my ego insists that everyone be like *me* in his or her belief. And so I set out to appropriate all others and either draw them into my circle of control or eliminate them. Looking to the examples set by Gushee, Pawlikowski, and Roth, we find that at least some leading Christian thinkers are rethinking the matter of whether salvation is settled, whether it is just a personal affair after all, and whether Christians should set out to Christianize others. One finds very little of this kind of rethinking in the Muslim world. If one may speak of any rethinking—or reforming—in the Muslim world, it is among the Muslim radicals, with more and more Muslim clerics[12] rereading the texts and the traditions of Islam to transform murder into a sacred duty. How to understand this move? Viewed as a reform movement, it is not an effort to deepen a connection with God through a return to tradition or Scripture. Rather, it is a turning against God in an appropriation of God by setting oneself up, like Cain, as the one who determines who shall live and who shall die. Radical

Islam's radical hatred of all who are not Muslims is, in the end, a radical hatred of God. It persists as the most current, most insidious form of the most ancient of temptations: to be as God in a usurpation of God.

How, then, might a Jewish-Christian dialogue become part of a response to left-wing intellectual and radical Islamic Jew hatred?

In chapter 3 we noted two parallel teachings from Judaism and Christianity. It is written in the Talmud that "if two are sitting and studying the Torah together, the Divine Presence is with them" (*Berakhot* 6a). Similarly, in the Christian Scriptures we read, "Where two or three are gathered in my name, there I am in the midst of them" (Matthew 18:20). If it is truly dialogue that Jews and Christians are engaged in, then it is, as it were, "for the sake of heaven." It is not about getting along, coming to a mutual agreement, or even attaining a deeper understanding of one another—all of which may fall under the category not of dialogue but of negotiation. In *Jewish-Christian* dialogue the aim of attaining a deeper understanding of one another is to attain a deeper relation to Another, to the Most High. It is to draw the divine presence into this realm, not only for the sake of heaven but also for the sake of earth, for God and humanity—that is what is at stake. And that is the aim of creation itself. The Torah begins with the letter *beit*, which means "home" or "dwelling," to teach us that the purpose of creation is to create a dwelling place for the Creator. The Holy One is able to dwell in this world to the extent that we enable the other human being to dwell in this world. Jewish-Christian dialogue—if it is indeed *dialogue*—is about dwelling.

Antisemitism, whether from the left-wing intellectual or the religious radical, is precisely the opposite of this dwelling. Recall the insight from Lévinas: "Antisemitism is the archetype of internment."[13] Antisemitism refuses a dwelling place for the Jew—and in its left-wing and Muslim modes, for the Christian—and thus drives the divine presence from the world. Notice how the world goes into an uproar if a Jew should attempt to live in the West Bank or Gaza; indeed, the world applauded when Gaza was made *Judenrein*. There is no tolerance for Jews who wish to dwell in either area and very little tolerance for Christians. Remember the desecration of the Church of the Nativity in 2002, the pogroms against the Christians of Ramallah in 2002 and against the Christians of Taibe in 2005, and the burning of churches after the pope's remark about Muslim violence in 2006? To be sure, since the Palestinian takeover of Bethlehem after Oslo (1993), the city has gone from about 75 percent Christian to about 15 percent Christian. But imagine the outrage if one were to suggest that Muslims should not be allowed to live in Israel.

Thus understood, Jewish-Christian dialogue can serve as a model for overcoming the persistence of antisemitism by affirming the aim of enabling the Holy One to dwell in this world—for the sake of God and humanity.

QUESTIONS FOR THE FUTURE

Jewish-Christian dialogue after the Holocaust raises many possibilities and questions. The possibilities have global potential. The dialogue between the two faith communities addresses not only issues of mutual concern, but implicitly involves speculation about the relationship of Christianity and Judaism to the global village. Neither tradition, especially not Judaism, can claim a majority of the world's population among its adherents. Moreover, European theological categories are not the same as Asian concepts of salvation, redemption, and repentance. Yet people in the global village do share common concerns. Humans created in God's image seek, at their best, to emulate their Creator. The post-Auschwitz Christian-Jewish dialogue can offer a model of how to appreciate the shared holiness of all humanity even while recognizing significant theological differences.

We think of two examples of dialogue in action that reveal precisely what is at stake for the future. Both occurred during World War II, each exemplifies that faith without works is meaningless, and both are steps on the path to achieving a *tikkun*. In February 1943 four army chaplains, all lieutenants, George L. Fox (Methodist), Rabbi Alexander D. Goode, John P. Washington (Roman Catholic), and Clark V. Poling (Reformed Church of America), were aboard the *Dorchester* when the ship was struck by torpedoes fired from a German submarine.

Amidst the chaos that ensued on the sinking vessel, the four chaplains ministered to the confused and wounded on board. They also distributed life jackets. When the supply of jackets was exhausted, the chaplains removed their own jackets and gave them to four servicemen, irrespective of religious faith. On board the rapidly sinking vessel, the chaplains linked their arms and joined in prayer. The four were posthumously awarded a Distinguished Service Cross and a Purple Heart. In 1948 the United States Postal Service issued a commemorative stamp in their honor. Nearly three decades later the Immortal Chaplains Foundation was established. Its mission was to present an annual Prize for Humanity in honor of those who "risked all to protect others of a different faith or race."[14]

The villagers of Le Chambon sur Lignon, led by Pastor André Trocmé, a Protestant pacifist, fought the Nazis with "weapons of the spirit." As noted earlier, the five thousand mostly fundamentalist Protestant villagers saved the lives of an equal number of Jews. Pierre Sauvage, one of those whose lives was saved, made a documentary film, *Weapons of the Spirit,* honoring the deeds of the villagers.[15] The film was shown in Japan, where there are substantial numbers of neither Christians nor Jews, and where the audiences were captivated by what they saw. Sauvage believes the film's impact resides in the fact that people everywhere are fascinated by goodness. Post-Holocaust Christian-Jewish dialogue may cause people to reflect on the possibility of helping the process of *tikkun olam* by acting in a manner that helps further the desperate need for peace, justice, and tranquility.

Foremost among the questions raised by the dialogue is its staying power. Will either or each side tire of the effort? Furthermore, in a global context, will the relationship between Judaism and Christianity, which has played a key role in Western culture, be of interest as the Church seeks to renew its influence in South America and extend its contacts with peoples in Africa and Asia? How will the fact of the deep-seated nature of antisemitism in Church teachings be dealt with? According to the sixteenth-century Kabbalah of Isaac Luria, the task of mending *(tikkun)* may take centuries, or longer. How likely is it that both Jews and Christians will believe that living in a religiously plural global village means that no religion can have purchase on absolute truth? Theological language is by its nature not one of accommodation. Rather it tends toward triumphalism and away from any impetus toward theological self-critique.

The theological ferment and intellectual excitement wrought by the emergence of the post-Holocaust Christian-Jewish dialogue is, nonetheless, something palpable. So too is the growing contact between individual Christians and Jews, as well as that between interfaith congregations and institutions. The future of the dialogue, and its potential success in contributing to the task of *tikkun olam*, is bound to education. But religious education is itself uneven. Much depends on local leadership, both lay and clergy. We wonder about their training, their willingness to engage the other, and their readiness to accept the other's self-definition. Further, the ability to accept, learn from, and appreciate theologically divergent points of view will determine the maturity of the dialogue and its ability to influence a global audience.

We have suggested a Jewish response to the post-Holocaust Christian-Jewish dialogue. Our response is that of two Jewish scholars whose reflections have been shaped primarily, but not exclusively, by the perspectives of Holocaust studies, literature, philosophy, and religious studies. We make no pretense at inclusiveness. Indeed, we recognize a plurality of viewpoints both within the Jewish and Christian communities. Moreover, we appreciate the fact that the post-Holocaust dialogue is still in its infancy; sixty post-Holocaust years is not a long time span when measured against the preceding nineteen hundred of the pre-Shoah era. Our hope is that we have made some contribution to the furtherance of the dialogue, at the very least by highlighting its thorny theological dimensions. Bearing this hope in mind, and seeking to continue the dialogue by opening it to as broad an audience as possible, we invite interfaith reader response to this book.

ENDNOTES

CHAPTER ONE

1. John K. Roth, *Holocaust Politics* (Louisville: Westminster John Knox Press, 2001), 191.

2. Alexander Donat, *The Holocaust Kingdom* (New York: Holocaust Library, 1978), 101.

3. Franklin H. Littell, *The Crucifixion of the Jews* (Macon, GA: Mercer University Press, 1986), 129.

4. Elie Wiesel, *A Beggar in Jerusalem*, trans. Elie Wiesel and Lily Edelman (New York: Random House, 1970), 56. We hasten to add, however, that Wiesel is much more optimistic than before about interfaith relations; there is a distinction between his stance prior to Vatican II and after *Nostra Aetate*. See Alan Berger, "Interview with Elie Wiesel," *Literature and Belief* 26.1 (March 2007): 13–14.

5. Roth, *Holocaust Politics*, 192.

6. Susannah Heschel and Sander Gilman, "Reflections on the Long History of European Antisemitism," in Marianne Hirsch and Irene Kacandes, eds., *Teaching the Representation of the Holocaust* (New York: Modern Language Association of America, 2004), 88.

7. Jacob Neusner, *Telling Tales: The Urgency and Basis for Judeo-Christian Dialog* (Louisville: Westminster John Knox Press, 1993), 9–10.

8. See Jon D. Levenson, *Resurrection and the Restoration of Israel: The Ultimate Victory of the God of Life* (New Haven: Yale University Press, 2006).

9. James Carroll cites Kung in "Christian-Muslim-Jew: The Necessary Trialogue," May Smith Lecture Series on Post-Holocaust Christian-Jewish Dialogue. Florida Atlantic University, January 27, 2004, 8.

10. James Rudin, *The Baptizing of America: The Religious Right's Plans for the Rest of Us* (New York: Thunder's Mouth Press, 2006), 47.

11. Kevin Phillips, *American Theocracy: The Peril and Politics of Radical Religion, Oil and Borrowed Money in the 21st Century* (New York: Viking, 2006), xiii. Phillips emphasizes the enormous commercial success of Tim LaHaye,

who coauthored a "series of books on the rapture, the tribulation, and the road to Armageddon that has sold (in various forms) sixty million copies."

12. Rudin, *Baptizing of America*, 195.

13. John K. Roth, "No Crucifixion = No Holocaust: Post-Holocaust Reflections on *The Passion of the Christ*," in J. Shawn Landres and Michael Berenbaum, eds., *After the Passion Is Gone: American Religious Consequences* (Walnut Creek, CA: AltaMira Press, 2004), 249.

14. Ibid.

15. Robert S. Wistrich, *Antisemitism: The Longest Hatred* (New York: Schocken Books, 1993), xix.

16. Ibid.

17. See Jules Isaac, *The Teaching of Contempt: Christian Roots of Antisemitism*, trans. Helen Weaver (New York: Holt, Rinehart and Winston, 1964).

18. Littell, *Crucifixion of the Jews*, 82n.29.

19. Ibid.

20. In the film, for example, the crowd chooses Barabbas after Jesus has been scourged and stands before them beaten and bloodied, whereas in the Gospel they make their choice prior to his scourging (see Matthew 27:20–26). Gibson obviously sets up the scene in such a way as to show that, even when the Roman procurator Pilate is horrified at the sight of "His" suffering, the Jews nonetheless call for more, call for "His" crucifixion, which, though *necessary* to our salvation, is the fault of the Jews. (One wonders: Do the Christians, then, have the Jews to thank for humanity's salvation?)

21. Roth, "No Crucifixion = No Holocaust," 249.

22. On this matter see Alan L. Berger, "Vatican II, *The Passion of the Christ*, and the Future of Catholic-Jewish Dialogue," *Journal of Ecumenical Studies* 43, no. 1 (winter, 2008). Hereafter, this will be cited as "Vatican II."

23. John T. Pawlikowski, "Gibson's *Passion* in the Face of the Shoah's Ethical Considerations," in Philip A. Cunningham, ed., *Pondering the Passion: What's at Stake for Christians and Jews* (Lanham, MD: Rowman & Littlefield, 2004), 160.

24. Quoted in Amy Hollywood, "Kill Jesus," *Harvard Divinity Bulletin* (summer 2004): 34.

25. John Dominic Crossan, "Hymn to a Savage God," in Kathleen E. Corley and Robert L. Webb, eds., *Jesus and Mel Gibson's* The Passion of the Christ: *The Film, The Gospels and the Claims of History* (London: Continuum, 2004), 17.

26. Mary C. Boys, "Seeing Different Movies, Talking Past Each Other," in Paula Fredriksen, ed., *The Passion of the Christ: Exploring the Issues Raised by the Controversial Movie* (Berkeley: University of California Press, 2006), 154–55.

27. Quoted in David Berger, "Jews, Christians, and 'The Passion,' " *Commentary* 117 (May 2004): 30.

28. Richard L. Rubenstein, "The Exposed Fault Line," in Landres and Berenbaum, *After the Passion Is Gone,* 207. For more on this point see Alan L. Berger "Vatican II" (2008).

29. Boys, "Seeing Different Movies," 148.

30. Pawlikowski, "Gibson's *Passion*," 159.

31. John T. Pawlikowski, "L'Affaire Gibson: Has 40 Years of Jewish-Christian Dialogue Run Thin?"; p.6. Paper read at the Western Jewish Studies Association Annual Meeting, Arizona State University, March 13, 2005.

32. See Oren Jacoby, *Sister Rose's Passion* (New Jersey Studios, LLC, 2004).

33. Quoted in Frank Kermode, *The Age of Shakespeare* (New York: Modern Library, 2005), 95.

34. Alan Rosen, *Sounds of Defiance: The Holocaust, Multilingualism & the Problem of English* (Lincoln: University of Nebraska Press, 2005), 74.

35. James Shapiro, in *Shakespeare and the Jews* (New York: Columbia University Press, 1996), discusses the impact on both intellectuals and popular beliefs of British Reformist theology concerning the necessary conversion of the Jews (see chapter 5 of his volume "The Hebrew Will Turn Christian," 131–65). While we do not make a parallel to the contemporary American religious culture, we note that conversion of the Jews remains part of Christian thinking, even if unarticulated, on a popular level among certain evangelicals as well as others. We also wonder about the reason for the promulgation, by the then-cardinal Joseph Ratzinger, now Pope Benedict XVI, of the 2000 document *Dominus Ieus*, which has a clear triumphalistic ring and impacts negatively on constructive post-Holocaust Jewish-Christian dialogue, despite Vatican assertions to the contrary.

36. Riccardo DiSegni, "Steps Taken and Questions Remaining in Jewish-Christian Relations Today," paper read in the series "The Catholic Church and the Jewish People from Vatican II to Today." Pontifical Gregorian University, October 19, 2004: 5. Online at http://www.bc.edu/research/cjl/meta-elments/texts/conferences/Bea_Centre_C-J-Rlatio, November 11, 2004. See the discussion in Alan L. Berger "Vatican II."

37. Jonathan Sacks, *The Dignity of Difference: How to Avoid the Clash of Civilizations* (London: Continuum, 2003), 46.

38. Littell puts it quite bluntly: "The cornerstone of Christian antisemitism is the superseding or displacement myth, which already rings with the genocidal note." See Littell, *Crucifixion of the Jews*, 2.

39. In 1936, Karl Löwith expressed his concern to Heidegger that there was an essential "partnership" between National Socialism and Heidegger's philosophy. "Heidegger agreed with me [about this]," says Löwith, "without reservation and elucidated that his concept of 'historicity' was the basis of his political 'engagement.' He also left no doubt about his belief in Hitler." See Karl Löwith, "Last Meeting with Heidegger," in Guenther Neske and Emil Kettering, eds., *Martin Heidegger and National Socialism*, trans. Lisa Harries (New York: Paragon, 1990), 158.

40. Littel, *Crucifixion of the Jews,* 65.

41. See Emil L. Fackenheim, *To Mend the World: Foundations of Post-Holocaust Jewish Thought* (New York: Schocken Books, 1989), 310.

42. Reported by the International Christian Embassy in Jerusalem News Service, April 29, 2002.

43. See, for example, Eric J. Greenberg, "Open Season on Jews," *Jewish Week* (May 11, 2001).

44. See Umymah Ahmed al-Jalahima, *Al-Riyadh*, Internet edition, May 10, 2002; Dr. Muhammad bin Saad al-Shweyir wrote a similar piece for the September 2002 edition of the Saudi newspaper *Al-Jazirah.*

CHAPTER TWO

1.   Edward H. Flannery, *The Anguish of the Jews: Twenty-Three Centuries of Antisemitism*, revised and updated (New York: Paulist Press, 1985), 39.

2.   Franklin H. Littell, *The Crucifixion of the Jews: The Failure of Christians to Understand the Jewish Experience* (Macon, GA: Mercer University Press, 1986), 79.

3.   These pioneers in the battle to root out the teaching of contempt began their efforts even prior to the Shoah. James Parkes had, for example, long been a voice crying out against Christian antisemitism in the theological wilderness preceding World War II.

4.   Littell, *Crucifixion of the Jews,* 77.

5.   Irving Greenberg, "Cloud of Smoke, Pillar of Fire: Judaism, Christianity, and Modernity after the Holocaust," in Eva Fleischner, ed., *Auschwitz: Beginning of a New Era? Reflections on the Holocaust* (New York: Ktav, 1977), 13.

6.   Michael Phayer, *The Catholic Church and the Holocaust, 1930–1965* (Bloomington: Indiana University Press, 2000), 203.

7.   Jonathan D. Sarna, *American Judaism: A History* (New Haven: Yale University Press, 2004), 312–13.

8.   James Carroll, "Christian-Muslim-Jew: The Necessary Trialogue," Boca Raton, FL: May Smith Lecture on Post-Holocaust Christian/Jewish Dialogue, January 27, 2004, 17–18.

9.   Elie Wiesel, *Against Silence: The Voice and Vision of Elie Wiesel*, vol. 1 (New York: Holocaust Library, 1985), 368.

10. See Edward T. Linenthal, *Preserving Memory: The Struggle to Create America's Holocaust Museum* (New York: Viking, 1995), 260–72.

11. Nachmanides, *Commentary on the Torah*, vol. 1, trans. Charles B. Chavel (New York: Shilo, 1971), 398.

12. See Moshe Weissman ed., *The Midrash Says*, vol. 4 (Brooklyn: Bnay Yakov Publications, 1980), 423.

13. The Baal Shem transmitted this teaching to his disciple Yaakov Yosef of Polnoe, who relates it in the introduction to his *Toledot Yaakov Yosef al HaTorah* (Jerusalem: Agudat Bait Vialipoli, 1944), 19.

14. Yitzhak Katznelson, *Vittel Diary*, trans. Myer Cohn. 2nd ed. (Tel-Aviv: Hakibbutz Hameuchad, 1972), 202–3.

15. Alfred Rosenberg, *Race and Race History and Other Essays*, ed. Robert Pais (New York: Harper & Row, 1974), 131–32.

16. Ibid., 181.

17. See Steven T. Katz, *Post-Holocaust Dialogues: Critical Studies in Modern Jewish Thought* (New York: NYU Press, 1983), 144.

18. Richard L. Rubenstein, *After Auschwitz: Radical Theology and Contemporary Judaism* (Indianapolis: Bobbs-Merrill, 1966), 145.

19. See ibid., 68, 119.

20. See ibid., 135 ff.

21. Ibid., 198.

22. See Richard L. Rubenstein, *After Auschwitz: History, Theology, and Contemporary Judaism*, 2nd ed. (Baltimore: Johns Hopkins University Press, 1992).

23. Greenberg, "Cloud of Smoke," 23.

24. Sara Nomberg-Przytyk, *Auschwitz: True Tales from a Grotesque Land*, trans. Roslyn Hirsch (Chapel Hill: University of North Carolina Press, 1985), 81.

25. Irving Greenberg, "Voluntary Covenant," in *Perspectives* (National Jewish Resource Center, 1982), 17.

26. Irving Greenberg, *The Jewish Way: Living the Holidays* (New York: Simon & Schuster, 1988), 252; emphasis added.

27. Eliezer Berkovits, *Faith after the Holocaust* (New York: Ktav, 1973), 68.

28. In that passage Isaiah cries out, "Truly You are a God that hides Yourself, O God of Israel, the Savior."

29. Berkovits, *Faith After the Holocaust,* 107.

30. Ibid., 69.

31. Emmanuel Lévinas, *Nine Talmudic Readings,* trans. Annette Aronowicz (Bloomington: Indiana University Press, 1990), 41.

32. See Emmanuel Lévinas, *Ethics and Infinity*, trans. Richard A. Cohen (Pittsburgh: Duquesne University Press, 1985), 105.

33. Emmanuel Lévinas, "Useless Suffering," trans. Richard A. Cohen, in Robert Bernasconi and David Wood, eds., *The Provocation of Lévinas: Rethinking the Other* (London: Routledge and Kegan Paul, 1988), 163.

34. See Emil L. Fackenheim, *God's Presence in History: Jewish Affirmations and Philosophical Reflections* (New York: Harper & Row, 1970), 6.

35. See, for example, Emil L. Fackenheim, *The Jewish Return into History* (New York: Schocken Books, 1978), 19–24.

36. Ibid., 246.

37. Emil L. Fackenheim, *To Mend the World: Foundations of Post-Holocaust Jewish Thought* (New York: Schocken Books, 1989), 100.

38. See, for example, Immanuel Kant, T*he Critique of Practical Reason*, trans. Lewis White Beck (New York: Macmillan, 1985), 101.

39. Emil L. Fackenheim, *Encounters between Judaism and Modern Philosophy* (New York: Basic Books, 1993), 191.

40. Quoted in George L. Mosse, *Nazi Culture* (New York: Grosset & Dunlap, 1966), 316.

41. See Jan T. Gross, *Neighbors: The Destruction of the Jewish Community in Jedwabne, Poland* (New York: Penguin Books, 2002).

42. See Ilya Ehrenburg and Vasily Grossman, eds., *The Complete Black Book of Russian Jewry,* trans. and ed. David Patterson (New Brunswick, NJ: Transaction Publishers, 2002), 373.

43. See Dietrich Bonhoeffer, *No Rusty Swords*, ed. Edwin H. Robertson, trans. Edward H. Robertson and John Bowden (New York: Harper & Row, 1965), 226.

44. Littell, *Crucifixion of the Jews,* 3.

45. Harry James Cargas, *Reflections of a Post-Auschwitz Christian* (Detroit: Wayne State University Press, 1989), 15.

46. Rosenberg, *Race and Race History,* 181.

47. Fackenheim, *Jewish Return into History*, 247.

48. See Alice L. Eckardt and A. Roy Eckardt, *Long Night's Journey into Day: A Revised Retrospective on the Holocaust* (Detroit: Wayne State University Press, 1988), 96–97.

49. Ibid., 169.

50. See ibid., 136–43.

51. See, for example, Littell, *Crucifixion of the Jews,* 90–95.

52. See ibid.

53. Leon Klenicki, "Introduction to Main Theme: Overview of Past Ten Years," paper delivered at the seventeenth meeting of the International Catholic-Jewish Liaison Committee (New York City, May 1, 2001), 3.

54. Philip A. Cunningham's paper "Reflecting on the Reflections," which was presented as part of that panel, is a thoughtful attempt to deconstruct, take the theological sting out of, *Reflections on Covenant and Mission*. Cunningham is an insightful scholar, but he fails to convince us that this doctrine is anything other than what David Novak terms "soft supersessionism." In this view, while Jews who reject the Messiahship of Jesus "remain part of the covenant, they are out of step with the fulfillment of the covenant which Jesus began already and which he shall return to totally complete." Cited by Cunningham, 10

55. David Patterson, "Prayers of Victims, Victims of Prayer," in Alan L. Berger, Harry James Cargas, and Susan E. Nowak, eds., *The Continuing Agony: From the Carmelite Convent to the Crosses at Auschwitz* (Baltimore: University Press of America, 2004), 195.

56. On these issues see Berger, Cargas, and Nowak, eds., *Continuing Agony,* see also John K. Roth and Carol Rittner, eds., *Memory Offended: The Auschwitz Convent Controversy* (Westport, CT: Greenwood Publishing Group, 1991).

57. Arthur A. Cohen, *The Myth of the Judeo-Christian Tradition* (New York: Harper & Row, 1969), 217.

58. Patterson, "Prayers of Victims," 199.

59. Quoted by James D. Besser, "Palestinian Nationalists Seen Behind Divestment," citing Dexter Van Zile, *Jewish Week* (July 22, 2005): 26.

60. Ibid.

61. Ibid.

62. Rubenstein, *After Auschwitz: History, Theology, and Contemporary Judaism*, 173.

CHAPTER THREE

1. André Neher, *The Prophetic Existence*, trans. William Wolf (New York: A. S. Barnes, 1969), 277.

2. Ibid., 142.

3. Abraham Joshua Heschel, *Israel: An Echo of Eternity* (New York: Farrar, Straus and Giroux, 1969), 129–30.

4. Our use of the word *myth* in no way implies falsehood or superstition. Just the opposite: In any religious tradition myth is a means of articulating the most profound truths of our spiritual lives. Judaism, like any religious tradition, has its own mythological elements in Scripture, Talmud, Midrash, and Kabbalah.

5. Martin Buber, *Between Man and Man*, trans. Ronald Gregor Smith (New York: Macmillan, 1965), 5.

6. We raise this point hypothetically; as shall be shown in the next chapter, we are not entirely sure that Judaism is, in fact, Christianity's "elder brother," as "elder brother" implies some sort of resemblance, when in this case there is very little resemblance, at least from a theological standpoint. Of course, Christians may have in mind a comparison between Jacob and Esau, the elder brother who was *not* the chosen brother but who, on the contrary, was the "evil" brother.

7. These include Beatrice Brutreau, *Jesus through Jewish Eyes*; Bruce Chilton, *Rabbi Jesus*; John Dominic Crossan, *The Historical Jesus*; Vermes Geza, *Jesus in Historical Jewish Contexts*; Vermes Geza, *The Religion of Jesus the Jew*; Paula Fredriksen, *Jesus of Nazareth, King of the Jews*; E. P. Sanders, *Jesus and Judaism*; and Brad Young, *Jesus the Jewish Theologian*.

8. While, in keeping with Christian teaching, Christians must surely rejoice in having these Jewish converts, it is something heinous to the Jews and must surely be so to post-Holocaust Christians as well. Nevertheless, many Christian churches support Brit Hadashah, especially among the fundamentalist and evangelical denominations.

9. As it is written in the Torah: "Observe and do all the words of this law" (Deuteronomy 31:12).

10. See James D. Tabor, "Josephus on Jesus," http://www.religiousstudies. uncc.edu/jdtabor/josephus-jesus.html.

11. See ibid.

12. See, for example, Plotinus, *Plotinus: The Enneads*, trans. Stephen MacKenna (Burdett, NY: Larson Publications, 2004).

13. See Raul Hilberg, *The Destruction of the European Jews* (Chicago: Quadrangle Books, 1961), 5–6.

14. Quoted in Darrell J. Fasching, *Narrative Theology After Auschwitz: From Alienation to Ethics* (Minneapolis: Fortress, 1992), 21.

15. From the first of eight "Homilies against the Jews," trans. Wayne A. Meeks and Robert L. Wilken, in Wayne A. Meeks and Robert L. Wilken, *Jews and Christians in Antioch in the First Four Centuries of the Common Era* (Ann Arbor, MI: Scholars Press, 1978), 98.

16. Ibid., 171–72.

17. Quoted in Marvin R. Wilson, *Our Father Abraham* (Grand Rapids, MI: Wm. B. Eerdmans, 1989), 93.

18. "Christian Jew Haters," http://www.sullican-county.com/identity/jew_haters.html.

19. Ibid.

20. Ibid.

21. See Cyprian, "Three Books of Testimonies against the Jews," in *The Anti-Nicene Christian Library*, ed. Roberts and Donaldson (Edinburgh: T. & T. Clark, 1869), 78–198; quoted in Franklin H. Littell, *The Crucifixion of the Jews: The Failure of Christians to Understand the Jewish Experience* (Macon, GA: Mercer University Press, 1986), 27–28.

22. Quoted in Mark R. Cohen, *Under Crescent and Cross* (Princeton, NJ: Princeton University Press, 1995), 171.

23. "Christian Jew Haters."

24. "Everlasting Hatred to the Everlasting Nation," http://sami119.tripod.com/shemaisrael/id17.html.

25. Quoted in Robert Wistrich, *Antisemitism: The Longest Hatred* (New York: Schocken Books, 1993), 19.

26. Quoted in Malcolm Hay, *Thy Brother's Blood: The Roots of Christian Antisemitism* (Oxford: Hart Publishing, 1975), 57.

27. "Christian Jew Haters."

28. Quoted in Edward H. Flannery, *The Anguish of the Jews* (New York: Paulist Press, 1985), 95.

29. Quoted in Hilberg, *Destruction of the European Jews*, 9.

30. John Calvin, *Institutes of the Christian Religion*, trans. Henry Beveridge (Grand Rapids, MI: Wm. B. Eerdmans, 1990), 331.

31. See Philip Melanchthon, *Augsburg Confession*, trans. T. G. Tappert (Minneapolis: Augsburg Fortress Publishers, 1980).

CHAPTER FOUR

1.   See, for example, Abraham Joshua Heschel, *Man's Quest for God: Studies in Prayer and Symbolism* (New York: Charles Scribner's Sons, 1954), 69.

2.   See F. M. Dostoyevsky, *The Brothers Karamazov*, trans. Constance Garnett (New York: New American Library, 1957), 588-89.

3.   Such a teaching, admittedly, may have certain theological problems; hence the post-Holocaust Jewish saying that if the soul of Hitler has entered heaven, then the souls of the righteous have left in protest.

4.   Thomas Aquinas, for example, defines faith as the "assent of the understanding to what is believed"; see Thomas Aquinas, *On Faith*, trans. Mark D. Jordan (Notre Dame, IN: University of Notre Dame Press, 1990), 39.

5.   See, for example, Thomas Aquinas, *St. Thomas Aquinas on Politics and Ethics*, trans. and ed. Paul E. Sigmund (New York: W. W. Norton, 1988), 8.

6.   The five levels of the soul, in descending order, are *yechidah*, *chayah*, *neshamah*, *ruach*, and *nefesh*; only *nefesh* is subject to the corruptions of sin. See, for example, Gershom Scholem, *Kabbalah* (New York: New American Library, 1978), 157–58.

7.   Vilna Gaon, *Even Sheleimah*, trans. Yaakov Singer and Chaim Dovid Ackerman (Southfield, MI: Targum Press, 1992), 45.

8.   The single best source for an anthology of Jewish teachings on the Messiah is Raphael Patai's *The Messiah Texts* (New York: Avon, 1979). One place in the Talmud where the Messiah is discussed at length is in *Sanhedrin* 95a–99b.

9.   Among the sages to make this point is the fourteenth-century scholar Hasdai Crescas, who begins his *Refutation of Christian Principles* by listing ten principles crucial to the Christian understanding of the Christ and antithetical to a Jewish understanding of the Messiah: (1) inherited sin, (2) redemption from inherited sin, (3) a triune god, (4) incarnation of the divine in the human, (5) virgin birth, (6) transubstantiation, (7) baptism by the Holy Spirit, (8) the identification of Jesus as Messiah, (9) the giving of a "new Torah," and (10) the casting out of demons; see Hasdai Crescas, *The Refutation of Christian Principles*, trans. Daniel J. Lasker (Albany: SUNY Press, 1992), 2.

10.   For example: Isaiah 11:11–12; Jeremiah 23:3, 29:14, 32:44, 33:7; Ezekiel 39:25; Joel 4:1; Zephaniah 3:20; Zechariah 10:8–10.

11.   See, for example, John Chrysostom, *Discourses against Judaizing Christians* (Washington, DC: Catholic University Press of America, 1979); see also Martin Luther, *Von den Juden und ihren Lügen* (Dresden: Landesverein für Innere Mission, 1931).

12.   Franklin H. Littell, *The Crucifixion of the Jews: The Failure of Christians to Understand the Jewish Experience* (Macon, GA: Mercer University Press, 1986), 2.

13. Darrell J. Fasching, *Narrative Theology after Auschwitz: From Alienation to Ethics* (Minneapolis: Fortress, 1992), 43.

14. In Jeremiah 31:31 it is written, "Behold the days are coming, says the Lord, when I shall make a new covenant with the House of Israel and with the House of Judah."

15. See Karl Rahner, *Foundations of Christian Faith: An Introduction to the Idea of Christianity*, trans. William V. Dych (New York: Crossroad, 1994), 311–21.

16. Emmanuel Lévinas, "Dialogue with Emmanuel Lévinas," in Richard A. Cohen, ed., *Face to Face with Lévinas* (Albany: SUNY Press, 1986), 23.

17. Franz Rosenzweig, *The Star of Redemption*, trans. William W. Hallo (Boston: Beacon Press, 1972), 413.

18. Emmanuel Lévinas, *Difficult Freedom: Essays on Judaism*, trans. Sean Hand (Baltimore: Johns Hopkins University Press, 1990), 90.

19. Ibid., 153.

20. Jean-François Lyotard, *Heidegger and "the jews,"* trans. Andreas Michel and Mark S. Roberts (Minneapolis: University of Minnesota Press, 1990), 22.

21. Ibid., 23.

22. Littell, *Crucifixion of the Jews*, 65.

23. See Max Weinreich, *Hitler's Professors: The Part of Scholarship in Germany's Crimes against the Jewish People* (New Haven: Yale University Press, 1999), 78.

24. The phrase *original sin*, "by which 'in Adam we die,'" first appears in Augustine, *Confessions*, trans. Henry Chadwick (Oxford: Oxford University Press, 1998), 82.

25. Louis Newman, ed., *The Hasidic Anthology* (New York: Schocken Books, 1963), 147.

26. It should be noted that Catholic theologians such as the Belgian Didier Pollefeyt and the German Jürgen Manemann have had the courage to maintain such a position.

27. Michael Phayer, *The Catholic Church and the Holocaust, 1930–1965* (Bloomington: Indiana University Press, 2000), 201.

28. Judith Hershcopf, "The Church and the Jews: The Struggle at Vatican Council II," in *American Jewish Yearbook* (New York: American Jewish Committee, 1965), vol. 66, 107

29. Hans Küng, *Reforming the Church Today: Keeping Hope Alive* (London: T. & T. Clark, 2000), 66–67.

30. Quoted in Thomas F. Stransky, "Holy Diplomacy: Making the Impossible Possible," in Roger Brooks, ed., *Unanswered Questions: Theological Views of Jewish-Christian Relations* (Notre Dame: University of Notre Dame Press, 1995), 53.

31. Quoted in ibid., 53–54.

32. Phayer, *Catholic Church and the Holocaust*, 209.

33. Andrew M. Greeley, *The Catholic Revolution: New Wine, Old Wineskins, and the Second Vatican Council* (Berkeley: University of California Press, 2004), 1.

34. A. James Rudin, "Jump-Starting the conversation between Jews and Catholics," in *National Catholic Reporter (*October 4, 2002): 5.

35. Irving Greenberg, "Antisemitism in 'The Passion,'" in *Commonweal* (May 7, 2004): 12.

36. Ibid.

37. Ibid.

38. Littell, *Crucifixion of the Jews*, 29.

39. Ibid.

40. Gary Wills, *Papal Sin: Structures of Deceit* (New York: Doubleday, 2000), 26.

41. Quoted in A. Roy Eckardt, "Toward an Authentic Jewish-Christian Relationship," in James E. Wood, ed., *Jewish-Christian Relations in Today's World* (Waco: Baylor University Press, 1971), 98.

42. Arthur Gilbert, *The Vatican Council and the Jews* (Cleveland: World Publishing Company, 1968), 179

43. Quoted in ibid., 174.

44. Phayer, *Catholic Church and the Holocaust*, 208.

45. A. James Rudin, Eugene J. Fischer, and Marc H. Tanenbaum, eds., *Twenty Years of Jewish-Catholic Relations* (New York: Paulist Press, 1986), 15.

46. Wills, *Papal Sin*, 26.

47. Mary C. Boys, *Has God Only One Blessing? Judaism As a Source of Christian Self-Understanding*, a Stimulus Book (NY: Paulist Press, 2000), 266. Eric Geller writes of a "yellow caution flag" in the race against time which characterizes the staying power of *Nostra Aetate*. Soon, he observes, "all the witnesses will be dead as will all of the brave and courageous theologians and scholars of the passed decades. Christians of the future will feel no personal guilt or shame, and priorities will lie elsewhere." Eric Geller "A Race Against Time," Opinion Essay, January 2005, 2. Available online at http://www.bc.edu/research.

48. Littell, *Crucifixion of the Jews*, 29.

49. Simon Wiesenthal, *The Sunflower: On the Possibilities and Limits of Forgiveness* (New York: Schocken Books, 1997).

50. David Blumenthal, "Repentance and Forgiveness," *Cross Currents*, (spring, 1998): 81. For a further discussion of this issue specifically with the context of Gibson's Passion film see Alan L. Berger "Vatican II, *The Passion of the Christ*, and the future of Catholic-Jewish Dialogue." Journal of Ecumenical Studies 43 (1) (winter, 2008).

51. Quote in Gilbert, *Vatican Council and the Jews*, 188.

52. Alexander Donat, *The Holocaust Kingdom* (New York: Holocaust Library, 1978), 230.

53. Quoted in Phayer, *Catholic Church and the Holocaust*, 211.

54. See John K. Roth, *Holocaust Politics* (Louisville: Westminster John Knox Press, 2001). Holocaust politics, Roth writes, "refers to the ways—often conflicting—in which the Holocaust informs and affects human belief, organization, and strategy, on the one hand, and in which human belief, organization, and strategy inform and affect the status and understanding of the Holocaust, on the other" (5).

55. George Bull, *Vatican Politics at the Second Vatican Council, 1962–65* (New York: Oxford University Press, 1966), 27.

56. Quoted in Gary Wills, *Why I Am A Catholic* (Boston: Mariner Books, 2003), 230.

57. Stransky, "Holy Diplomacy," 59.

58. Quoted in Wills, *Papal Sin*, 26.

59. James Carroll, *Constantine's Sword: The Church and the Jews* (Boston: Houghton Mifflin, 2001), 554.

CHAPTER FIVE

1. Hubert G. Locke, "The Holocaust, Israel and the Future of Jewish-Christian Relations," in John K. Roth and Leonard Grob, eds., *Holocaust Scholars Respond to the Palestinian-Israeli Conflict*, unpublished.

2. See, for example, Hermann Cohen, *Reason and Hope: Selections from the Jewish Writings of Hermann Cohen*, trans. Eva Jospe (Cincinnati: Hebrew Union College Press, 1993), 122.

3. Emmanuel Lévinas, *Outside the Subject*, trans. Michael B. Smith (Stanford, CA: Stanford University Press, 1994), 30.

4. Franz Rosenzweig, *Franz Rosenzweig's "The New Thinking,"* trans. and ed. Alan Udoff and Barbara Galli (Syracuse: Syracuse University Press, 1999), 96.

5. Cf. the Heideggerian *Sein zum Tod*, or "being toward death," that is an index of "authenticity" in Martin Heidegger, *Sein und Zeit* (Tübingen: Max Niemeyer, 1963), 118.

6. Eliezer Berkovits, *Faith after the Holocaust* (New York: Ktav, 1973), 44–45.

7. Franklin Littell, *The Crucifixion of the Jews: The Failure of Christians to Understand the Jewish Experience* (Macon, GA: Mercer University Press, 1986), 3.

8. For a good discussion of the Presbyterian move, written by a Presbyterian scholar, see John K. Roth, "Duped by Morality? Defusing Minefields in the Israeli-Palestinian Struggle," in John K. Roth and Leonard Grob, eds., *Holocaust Scholars Respond to the Palestinian-Israeli Conflict*, unpublished..

9. Dr. Ely Benaim, a former researcher and physician at St. Jude's Children's Hospital in Memphis, Tennessee, and a close friend of David

Patterson, once consulted with Palestinian physicians about Palestinian children suffering from certain forms of blood cancer. Having worked with Israeli oncologists on the latest treatments for such diseases, he urged the Palestinian doctors to allow him to arrange for the treatment of those children at Israeli facilities. They informed him that such a move would jeopardize the lives of everyone involved, since such contact with the Israelis was forbidden by the Palestinians, *even if it meant saving the lives of their children*.

10.   John K. Roth, "Useless Experience: Its Significance for Reconciliation after Auschwitz," in David Patterson and John K. Roth, eds., *After-Words: Post-Holocaust Struggle with Forgiveness, Reconciliation, Justice* (Seattle: University of Washington Press, 2004), 85.

11.   Harry James Cargas, *Reflections of a Post-Auschwitz Christian* (Detroit: Wayne State University Press, 1989), 99.

12.   Natan Alterman, *Hator Hashevii* (Tel-Aviv: Hakibbutz Hameuchad, 2000), 33; translated by David Patterson.

13.   Ibid.

14.   Emil L. Fackenheim, *Encounters between Judaism and Modern Philosophy* (New York: Basic Books, 1993), 107.

15.   See Nathan of Nemirov, *Rabbi Nachman's Wisdom: Shevachay HaRan and Sichos HaRan*, trans. Aryeh Kaplan, ed. Aryeh Rosenfeld (New York: A. Kaplan, 1973), 147.

16.   Some ideas contained in this section appeared in embryonic form in my essay "Post-Auschwitz Catholic-Jewish Dialogue: Mixed Signals and Missed Opportunities," *Remembering for the Future: The Holocaust in an Age of Genocide*, vol. 2 "Ethics and Religion," edited by John K. Roth and Elisabeth Maxwell. London: Palgrave, 2001, pp. 667–70."

17.   Rabbi Irving Greenberg, discussion with Alan L. Berger, November 27, 1998. The subsequent history of Vatican pronouncements on Catholic-Jewish dialogue continues the practice of sending mixed signals. While it is not our intention to analyze each document, we note two in particular. Shortly after the appearance of *We Remember*, the office of then-cardinal Joseph Ratzinger issued *Dominus Ieus* (September 5, 2000), which asserts the lordship of Jesus and the flawed character of "non-Christian religions." Philip Cunningham notes that this document "points to unresolved questions in the Catholic-Jewish relationships"; see Philip Cunningham, "Implications of Magisterial Catholic Teaching on Jews and Judaism," in Stephen J. Pope and Charles Hefling, eds., *Sic at Non: Encountering Dominus Ieus* (Maryknoll, NY: Orbis Books, 2002), 134. *The Jewish People and the Holy Scriptures in the Christian Bible* (November 2001) appears to be a major point of departure from *Dominus Ieus* in attesting that the Jews' wait for the Messiah is valid. Further, the book rejects and apologizes for the way many Christians have over the course of time misread the Hebrew Scriptures. However, the text does not inquire as to the source of the misreading—which stems from the teachings of Paul and the Church Fathers. Further, the Hebrew Bible is itself referred to by

the supersessionary term *Old Testament*. Moreover, and in contrast to *Dominus Ieus*, which was issued with great fanfare, little publicity accompanied this text, which did not initially appear in English. The official Vatican explanation that the book is a "theological study guide intended for other theologians" may, according to Tullia Zevi—at the time president of the Union of Italian Jewish Communities—disguise the bitter internal Vatican debate over how rapidly and how much the Church needs to change. Tullia Zevi is quoted by Melinda Henneberger, "Vatican Says Jews' Wait for Messiah Is Validated by the Old Testament," *New York Times*, January 18, 2002, A8.

18. Cited by Paul O'Shea, "Confiteor: Eugenio Pacelli, the Catholic Church and the Jews. An Examination of the Responsibility of Pope Pius XII and the Holocaust, 1917–1943." Ph.D. dissertation, Macquarie University, 2004, 32.

19. A. James Rudin, "Reflections on the Vatican's *Reflection on the Shoah*," *Cross Currents* (winter 1998/99): 522.

20. Robert Wistrich, "The Pope, the Church, and the Jews," *Commentary* 107(4) (April 1999): 24.

21. Cited by Anthony Grafton, "Reading Ratzinger: Benedict XVI, the Theologian," *New Yorker* (July 25, 2005): 44.

22. Michael Phayer, *The Catholic Church and the Holocaust, 1930–1965* (Bloomington: Indiana University Press, 2000), 75.

23. Ibid., 4.

24. O'Shea, "Confiteor," 33.

25. Susan Zuccotti, *Under His Very Windows: The Vatican and the Holocaust in Italy* (New Haven, CT: Yale University Press, 2000), 323.

26. Ibid., 324.

27. John T. Pawlikowski, "The Vatican and the Holocaust: Putting *We Remember* in Context," in Judith H. Banki and John T. Pawlikowski, eds., *Ethics in the Shadow of the Holocaust: Christian and Jewish Perspectives* (Chicago: Sheed & Ward, 2001), 225.

28. O'Shea, "Confiteor," 351.

29. Ibid., 352.

30. Cited by David Gordis, "Pope John Paul II and the Jews," in Byron Sherwin and Harold Kasimo, eds., *John Paul II and Interreligious Dialogue* (New York: Orbis Books, 1999), 137.

31. Sergio Minerbi, "Pope John Paul II and the Shoah," in Yehuda Bauer, ed., *Remembering for the Future: Working Papers and Abstracts*, vol. 3 (Oxford: Pergamon Press, 1989), 2978.

32. Gerhart Riegner, "Letter to the Editors," *Service International de Documentation Judéo-Chrétienne*, "Ecclesia and Synagoga: A New Future." vol. XXXIII, no. 3 (2000, English edition), 15.

33. See Harry James Cargas, *Reflections of a Post-Auschwitz Christian* (Detroit: Wayne State University Press, 1989).

34. David Fox Sandmel, "*Dabru Emet* and the Future Direction of

Jewish-Christian Relations," in Edward Kessler, John T. Pawlikowski, and Judith Banki, eds., *Jews and Christians in Conversation: Crossing Cultures and Generations* (Cambridge: Orchard Academic, 2002), 94.

35. Ibid., 97.

36. Edward H. Flannery, *The Anguish of the Jews: Twenty-Three Centuries of Antisemitism*, revised and updated (New York: Paulist Press, 1985), 283.

37. Jon D. Levenson, "How Not to Conduct Jewish-Christian Dialogue," *Commentary* 112(5) (December 2001); 33. My indebtedness to Professor Levenson's argument is apparent. David Novak, in an insightful response to Levenson, acknowledges that *Dabru Emet* "emphasizes what Jews and Christians have in common, while explicitly asserting what does and what should keep the two communities separate and distinct." David Novak, "Instinctive Repugnance," *First Things* 123, (May 2002): 13. It seems to us, however, that *Dabru Emet* runs the risk of succumbing to the temptation Arthur A. Cohen describes as "shallow rhetoric."

38. Ibid.

39. Michael Wyschogrod, "Jon D. Levenson & Critics," *Commentary*, 113(4) (April 2002): 16.

40. Gershom G. Scholem, *On the Kabbalah and Its Symbolism*, trans. by Ralph Manheim (NY: Schoken Books) 1965, 15–16.

41. David Novak, et al., "What of the Future? A Jewish Response," in Tikva Frymer-Kensky, David Novak, Peter Ochs, David Fox Sandmel, and Michael Signer, eds., *Christianity in Jewish Terms* (Boulder: Westview Press, 2000), 368.

42. Peter Ochs, ibid., 371.

43. Cited in Wyschogrod, "Jon D. Levenson & Critics," 17.

44. See Elie Wiesel, *The Gates of the Forest*, trans. Frances Frenaye (New York: Holt, 1966), 32–33.

45. See Augustine, *The City of God (De Civitas Dei)*, trans. Marcus Dods (New York: Modern Library, 2000), 656–57.

46. The reasons why Christians and Nazis view the being of the Jews as "criminal" are, of course, different; one crucial difference is that the Christian believes the Jew is redeemable, whereas the Nazi does not.

47. Quoted in Harry James Cargas, *A Christian Response to the Holocaust* (Denver: Stonehenge Books, 1981), 18–19.

48. Witness the conquering of the Americas: Following the most benign teachings of the Christian tradition, Christians built missions and set up rehabilitation programs designed to "kill the Indian but save the man," a famous slogan coined in 1892 by Capt. Richard C. Pratt, founder of the school for Native Americans in Carlisle Barracks, Pennsylvania. It was as if one could not be a man if one were not a Christian.

49. Henry F. Knight, "The Face of Forgiveness in a Post-Holocaust World," in Patterson and Roth, *After-Words*, 28.

50. Ibid., 29.

Chapter Six

1. Here we would like to express our gratitude to Meghan Julian, who prepared the transcript of this dialogue.

Chapter Seven

1. Emil L. Fackenheim, *To Mend the World: Foundations of Post-Holocaust Jewish Thought* (New York: Schocken Books, 1989), 289 and 291.

2. Ibid., 307

3. Ibid., 306.

4. John T. Pawlilkowski, "The Ever-Deepening Understanding of Jewish-Christian Bonding: *Nostra Aetate* at Forty," in *Chicago*, volume 44: 2, (summer) 205, pp. 139–40.

5. Rabbi Riccardo DiSegni, Chief Rabbi of Rome, commenting on the pope's terminology distinguised two types of response. On the one hand, there was the benign, one might say sociological impact; Italian non-Jews began greeting their Jewish fellow citizens as brothers. On the other hand, and however unintended it might have been, there is a malignant, theological, and unself-conscious impact which reinforces a central tenet of the teaching of contempt, i.e.,the ultimate victory of the younger brother. Rabbi Riccardo DiSegni. Talk given at Florida Atlantic University, Boca Raton, Florida, February 11, 2007.

6. Cited in Moshe Davis, "Jewish Distinctiveness within the American Tradition: The Eretz Yisrael Dimension as Case Illustration," in Alan L. Berger, ed., *Judaism in the Modern World* (New York: New York University Press, 1994), 58.

7. Michael Kotzkin, "Facing the Unresolved Issue in Interfaith Dialogue," *Forward* "Forum" (New York; October 28, 2005): 11.

8. John W. O'Malley, S. J., foreword to Giuseppe Alberigo, *A Brief History of Vatican II* (New York: Orbis Books, 2006), viii.

9. Albert Camus, *The Plague*, trans. Stuart Gilbert (New York: Vintage International, 1975), 308.

10. Emmanuel Lévinas, *Of God Who Comes to Mind*, trans. Bettina Bergo (Stanford, CA: Stanford University Press, 1998), 59.

11. Franz Rosenzweig, *The Star of Redemption*, trans. William W. Hallo (Boston: Beacon Press, 1972), 413.

12. Such as Sheikh Hassan Nasrallah of Hezbollah, Abu Musab al-Zarkawi in Iraq, Sheikh Feik Mohammed of the Global Islamic Youth Center in Sydney, Omar Bakri Mohammed of Britain (currently banned from Britain), Sheikh Mohammed Sayyid Tantawi of al-Azhar University, and, of course, clerics among the Palestinians such as the mufti Sheikh Ikrima Sabri, Sheikh Saad al-Buraik, Sheikh Abd-al-Bari al Thubayti, and Sheikh Omar

Mahmood Abu Omar, known as Osama bin Laden's spiritual ambassador to Europe.

13. Emmanuel Lévinas, *Difficult Freedom: Essays on Judaism*, trans. Sean Hand (Baltimore: Johns Hopkins University Press, 1990), 153.

14. Victor M. Parachin, "Memorial Day: Four Brave Chaplains," *Catholic Order of Foresters Magazine* (June 2002); posted on *Stand Watch* (May 23, 2002).

15. Pierre Sauvage, *Weapons of the Spirit* (1987).

BIBLIOGRAPHY

Alterman, Natan. *Hator Hashevii*. Tel-Aviv: Hakibbutz Hameuchad, 2000.

Aquinas, Thomas. *On Faith*. Trans. Mark D. Jordan. Notre Dame, IN: University of Notre Dame Press, 1990.

_____. *St. Thomas Aquinas on Politics and Ethics*. Trans. and ed. Paul E. Sigmund. New York: W. W. Norton, 1988.

Aristotle. *Eudemian Ethics*. Trans. M. Woods. Oxford: Oxford University Press, 1992.

Augustine. *The City of God (De Civitas Dei)*. Trans. Marcus Dods. New York: Modern Library, 2000.

_____. *Confessions*. Trans. Henry Chadwick. Oxford: Oxford University Press, 1998.

Banki, Judith H. and John T. Pawlikowski, eds. *Ethics in the Shadow of the Holocaust: Christian and Jewish Perspectives*. Chicago: Sheed & Ward, 2001.

Berger, Alan L., ed. "Interview with Elie Wiesel." *Literature and Belief.* 26(1) (March 2007).

_____. *Judaism in the Modern World.* New York: New York University Press, 1994.

_____. "Post-Auschwitz Catholic-Jewish Dialogue: Mixed Signals and Missed Opportunities." In John K. Roth and Elizabeth Maxewell, eds. *Remembering for the Future: The Holocaust in an Age of Genocide.* Vol. 2. London: Palgrave, 2001.

_____. "Vatican II, *The Passion of the Christ*, and the Future of Catholic-Jewish Dialogue." *Journal of Ecumenical Studies* 43 (1) (winter, 2008).

Berger, Alan L., Harry James Cargas, and Susan E. Nowak, eds. *The Continuing Agony: From the Carmelite Convent to the Crosses at Auschwitz*. Baltimore: University Press of America, 2004.

Berger, David. "Jews, Christians, and *The Passion*." *Commentary* 117 (May 2004).

Berkovits, Eliezer. *Faith after the Holocaust*. New York: Ktav, 1973.

Bernasconi, Robert, and David Wood, eds. *The Provocation of Levinas: Rethinking the Other*. London: Routledge and Kegan Paul, 1988.

Besser, James D. "Palestinian Nationalists Seen Behind Divestment." *Jewish Week* (July 22, 2005).

Blumenthal, David. "Repentance and Forgiveness." *Cross Currents* (spring 1998): 81.

Bonhoeffer, Dietrich. *No Rusty Swords*. Ed. Edwin H. Robertson. Trans. Edward H. Robertson and John Bowden. New York: Harper & Row, 1965.

Boys, Mary C. "Seeing Different Movies, Talking Past Each Other." In Paula Fredriksen, ed. *The Passion of the Christ: Exploring the Issues Raised by the Controversial Movie*. Berkeley: University of California Press, 2006.

Brooks, Roger, ed. *Unanswered Questions: Theological Views of Jewish-Christian Relations*. Notre Dame: University of Notre Dame Press, 1995.

Brutreau, Beatrice. *Jesus through Jewish Eyes*. Maryknoll, NY: Orbis Books, 2001.

Buber, Martin. *Between Man and Man*. Trans. Ronald Gregor Smith. New York: Macmillan, 1965.

_____. *Eclipse of God: Studies in the Relation between Religion and Philosophy*. Trans. Maurice Friedman, et al. Atlantic Highlands, NJ: Humanities Press International, 1988.

Bull, George. *Vatican Politics at the Second Vatican Council, 1962–65*. New York: Oxford University Press, 1966.

Calvin, John. *Institutes of the Christian Religion*. Trans. Henry Beveridge. Grand Rapids, MI: Wm. B. Eerdmans, 1990.

Camus, Albert. *The Plague*. Trans. Stuart Gilbert. New York: Vintage International, 1975.

Cargas, Harry James. *A Christian Response to the Holocaust*. Denver: Stonehenge Books, 1981.

_____. *Reflections of a Post-Auschwitz Christian*. Detroit: Wayne State University Press, 1989.

Carmichael, Joel. *The Satanizing of the Jews: Origin and Development of Mystical Antisemitism*. New York: Fromm International, 1993.

Carroll, James. "Christian-Muslim-Jew: The Necessary Trialogue." May Smith Lecture on Post-Holocaust Christian/Jewish Dialogue. Boca Raton, FL, January 27, 2004.

_____. *Constantine's Sword: The Church and the Jews*. Boston: Houghton Mifflin, 2001.

Chilton, Bruce. *Rabbi Jesus*. New York: Doubleday, 2000.

"Christian Jew Haters." http://www.sullican-county.com/identity/jew_haters.html.

Chrysostom, John. *Discourses against Judaizing Christians*. Washington, DC: Catholic University Press of America, 1979.

Cohen, Arthur A. *The Myth of the Judeo-Christian Tradition*. New York: Harper & Row, 1969.

Cohen, Hermann. *Reason and Hope: Selections from the Jewish Writings of Hermann Cohen*. Trans. Eva Jospe. Cincinnati: Hebrew Union College Press, 1993.

Cohen, Mark R. *Under Crescent and Cross*. Princeton, NJ: Princeton University Press, 1995.

Cohen, Richard A., ed. *Face to Face with Levinas*. Albany: SUNY Press, 1986.

Cook, Michael. "An Insider's Account of the Mel Gibson Ordeal." *The Chronicle*. Cincinnati: Hebrew Union College-Jewish Institute of Religion, Issue 63(15) (2004).

Corley, Kathleen E., and Robert L. Webb, eds. *Jesus and Mel Gibson's The Passion of the Christ: The Film, The Gospels and the Claims of History*. London: Continuum, 2004.

Crescas, Hasdai. *The Refutation of Christian Principles.* Trans. Daniel J. Lasker. Albany: SUNY Press, 1992.

Crossan, John Dominic. *The Historical Jesus.* San Francisco: HarperSan-Francisco, 1993.

_____. "Hymn to a Savage God." In Kathleen E. Corley and Robert L. Webb, eds., *Jesus and Mel Gibson's* The Passion of the Christ: *The Film, The Gospels and the Claims of History.* London: Continuum, 2004.

Cunningham, Philip A. "Implications of Magisterial Catholic Teaching on Jews and Judaism." In Stephen J. Pope and Charles Hefling, eds. *Sic at Non: Encountering Dominus Iesus.* Maryknoll, NY: Orbis Books, 2002.

_____, ed. *Pondering the Passion: What's at Stake for Christians and Jews.* Lanham, MD: Rowman & Littlefield, 2004.

_____. "Reflecting on the Reflections." Paper presented at *Reflections on Covenant and Mission.* Boston College's Center for Christian-Jewish Learning and Theology Department, February 9, 2005.

Cyprian. "Three Books of Testimonies against the Jews." In *The Anti-Nicene Christian Library.* Ed. Roberts and Donaldson. Edinburgh: T. & T. Clark, 1869.

Davis, Moshe. "Jewish Distinctiveness within the American Tradition: The Eretz Yisrael Dimension as Case Illustration." In Alan L. Berger, ed. *Judaism in the Modern World.* New York: New York University Press, 1994.

DiSegni, Riccardo. "Steps Taken and Questions Remaining in Jewish-Christian Relations Today." Paper read in the series "The Catholic Church and the Jewish People from Vatican II to Today." Pontifical Gregorian University, October 19, 2004; online at http://www.bc.edu/research/cjl/meta-elments/texts/conferences/Bea_Centre_C-J-Rlatio, November 11, 2004.

Donat, Alexander. *The Holocaust Kingdom.* New York: Holocaust Library, 1978.

Dostoyevsky, F. M. *The Brothers Karamazov.* Trans. Constance Garnett. New York: New American Library, 1957.

Eckardt, Alice L., and A. Roy Eckardt. *Long Night's Journey into Day: A Revised Retrospective on the Holocaust.* Detroit: Wayne State University Press, 1988.

Ehrenburg, Ilya, and Vasily Grossman, eds. *The Complete Black Book of Russian Jewry*. Trans. and ed. David Patterson. New Brunswick, NJ: Transaction Publishers, 2002.

Emmerich, Anne Catherine. *The Dolorous Passion of our Lord Jesus Christ*. El Sobrante, CA: North Bay Books, 2004.

"Everlasting Hatred to the Everlasting Nation." http://sami119.tripod.com/shemaisrael/ id17.html.

Fackenheim, Emil L. *Encounters between Judaism and Modern Philosophy*. New York: Basic Books, 1993.

_____. *God's Presence in History: Jewish Affirmations and Philosophical Reflections*. New York: Harper & Row, 1970.

_____. *The Jewish Return into History*. New York: Schocken Books, 1978.

_____. *To Mend the World: Foundations of Post-Holocaust Jewish Thought*. New York: Schocken Books, 1989.

Fasching, Darrell J. *Narrative Theology after Auschwitz: From Alienation to Ethics*. Minneapolis: Fortress, 1992.

Flannery, Edward H. *The Anguish of the Jews: Twenty-Three Centuries of Antisemitism*. Revised and updated. New York: Paulist Press, 1985.

Fleischner, Eva, ed. *Auschwitz: Beginning of a New Era? Reflections on the Holocaust*. New York: Ktav, 1977.

Fredriksen, Paula. *Jesus of Nazareth: King of the Jews*. New York: Vintage Books, 2000.

_____. The Passion of the Christ: *Exploring the Issues Raised by the Controversial Movie*. Berkeley: University of California Press, 2006.

Frymer-Kensky, Tikva, David Novak, Peter Ochs, David Fox Sandmel, and Michael Signer, eds. *Christianity in Jewish Terms*. Boulder: Westview Press, 2000.

Gilbert, Arthur. *The Vatican Council and the Jews*. Cleveland: World Publishing, 1968.

Ginsburgh, Yitzchak. *The Alef-Beit: Jewish Thought Revealed through the Hebrew Letters*. Northvale, NJ: Jason Aronson, 1991.

Gordis, David. "Pope John Paul II and the Jews." In Byron Sherwin and Harold Kasimo, eds. *John Paul II and Interreligious Dialogue.* New York: Orbis Books, 1999.

Grafton, Anthony. "Reading Ratzinger: Benedict XVI, the Theologian." *New Yorker* (July 25, 2005): 44.

Greeley, Andrew M. *The Catholic Revolution: New Wine, Old Wineskins, and the Second Vatican Council.* Berkeley: University of California Press, 2004.

Greenberg, Irving. "Antisemitism in 'The Passion,'" *Commonweal* (May 7, 2004): 12.

_____. "Clouds of Smoke, Pillar of Fire: Judaism, Christianity, and Modernity after the Holocaust." In Eva Fleischner, ed., *Auschwitz: Beginning of a New Era? Reflections on the Holocaust.* New York: Ktav, 1977, pp. 7–55.

_____. *For the Sake of Heaven and Earth: The New Encounter between Judaism and Christianity.* Philadelphia: Jewish Publication Society, 2004.

_____. *The Jewish Way: Living the Holidays.* New York: Simon & Schuster, 1988.

_____. "Voluntary Covenant." In *Perspectives.* National Jewish Resource Center, 1982.

Gross, Jan T. *Neighbors: The Destruction of the Jewish Community in Jedwabne, Poland.* New York: Penguin Books, 2002.

Gruenagel, Friedrich. *Die Judenfrage: Die geschichtliche Verantwortung der Kirchen und Israel.* Stuttgart: Calwer Verlag, 1970.

Gushee, David P. *Righteous Gentiles of the Holocaust: Genocide and Moral Obligation.* 2nd ed. New York: Paragon, 2003.

Halevi, Judah. *The Kuzari (Kitav al khazari).* Trans. Henry Slonimsky. New York: Schocken Books, 1963.

Hand, Sean, ed. *The Levinas Reader.* Oxford: Basil Blackwell, 1989.

Hay, Malcolm. *Thy Brother's Blood: The Roots of Christian Antisemitism.* Oxford: Hart Publishing, 1975.

Haynes, Stephen R. *Reluctant Witnesses: Jews and the Christian Imagination.* Louisville: Westminster John Knox Press, 1995.

Heidegger, Martin. *Sein und Zeit.* Tübingen: Max Niemeyer, 1963.

Henneberger, Melinda. "Vatican Says Jews' Wait for Messiah Is Validated by the Old Testament." *New York Times* (January 18, 2002): A8.

Hershcopf, Judith. "The Church and the Jews: The Struggle at Vatican Council II." In *American Jewish Yearbook*. New York: American Jewish Committee, 1965. Vol. 66, p. 107.

Heschel, Abraham Joshua. *Israel: An Echo of Eternity*. New York: Farrar, Straus and Giroux, 1969.

_____. *Man's Quest for God: Studies in Prayer and Symbolism*. New York: Charles Scribner's Sons, 1954.

Heschel, Susannah, and Sander Gilman. "Reflections on the Long History of European Antisemitism." In Marianne Hirsch and Irene Kacandes, eds. *Teaching the Representation of the Holocaust*. New York: Modern Language Association of America, 2004.

Hilberg, Raul. *The Destruction of the European Jews*. Chicago: Quadrangle Books, 1961.

Hirsch, Miranne, and Irene Kacandes, eds. *Teaching the Representation of the Holocaust*. New York: Modern Language Association of America, 2004.

Hollywood, Amy. "Kill Jesus." *Harvard Divinity Bulletin* (summer 2004).

Isaac, Jules. *The Teaching of Contempt: Christian Roots of Antisemitism*. Trans. Helen Weaver. New York: Holt, Rinehart and Winston, 1964.

Jonas, Hans. *Mortality and Morality: A Search for the Good after Auschwitz*. Ed. Lawrence Vogel. Evanston, IL: Northwestern University Press, 1996.

Josephus. *Jewish Antiquities: Books XVIII–XIX*. Trans. Louis H. Feldman. Cambridge: Harvard University Press, 1970.

Kant, Immanuel. *The Critique of Practical Reason*. Trans. Lewis White Beck. New York: Macmillan, 1985.

Katz, Steven T. *Post-Holocaust Dialogues: Critical Studies in Modern Jewish Thought*. New York: NYU Press, 1983.

Katznelson, Yitzhak. *Vittel Diary*. Trans. Myer Cohn. 2nd ed. Tel-Aviv: Hakibbutz Hameuchad, 1972.

Kermode, Frank. *The Age of Shakespeare*. New York: Modern Library, 2005.

Kessler, Edward, John T. Pawlikowski, and Judith Banki, eds. *Jews and Christians in Conversation: Crossing Cultures and Generations*. Cambridge: Orchard Academic, 2002.

Keter Shem Tov. Brooklyn: Kehot, 1972.

Klenicki, Leon. "Introduction to Main Theme: Overview of Past Ten Years." Paper delivered at the seventeenth meeting of the International Catholic-Jewish Liaison Committee, New York City (May 1, 2001): 3.

Knight, Henry F. "The Face of Forgiveness in a Post-Holocaust World." In David Patterson and John K. Roth, eds. *After-Words: Post-Holocaust Struggle with Forgiveness, Reconciliation, Justice*. Seattle: University of Washington Press, 2004, pp. 28–54.

Knowles, Melody D., Esther Mann, John T. Pawlikowski, and Timothy J. Sandoval, eds. *Contesting Texts: Jews and Christians in Conversation about the Bible*. Minneapolis: Fortress, 2007.

Kotzkin, Michael. "Facing the Unresolved Issue in Interfaith Dialogue." *Forward* "Forum" (October 28, 2005): 11.

Küng, Hans. *Reforming the Church Today: Keeping Hope Alive*. London: T. & T. Clark, 2000.

Landres, J. Shawn, and Michael Berenbaum, eds. *After the Passion Is Gone: American Religious Consequences*. Walnut Creek, CA: AltaMira Press, 2004.

Levenson, Jon D. "How Not to Conduct Jewish-Christian Dialogue." *Commentary* 112 (December 2001).

_____. *Resurrection and the Restoration of Israel: The Ultimate Victory of the God of Life*. New Haven: Yale University Press, 2006.

Lévinas, Emmanuel. "Dialogue with Emmanuel Lévinas." In Richard A. Cohen, ed., *Face to Face with Lévinas*. Albany: SUNY Press, 1986, pp. 13–33.

_____. *Difficult Freedom: Essays on Judaism*. Trans. Sean Hand. Baltimore: Johns Hopkins University Press, 1990.

_____. *Ethics and Infinity*. Trans. Richard A. Cohen. Pittsburgh: Duquesne University Press, 1985.

_____. *Nine Talmudic Readings*. Trans. Annette Aronowicz. Blooming-
ton: Indiana University Press, 1990.

_____. *Of God Who Comes to Mind*. Trans. Bettina Bergo. Stanford, CA:
Stanford University Press, 1998.

_____. *Outside the Subject*. Trans. Michael B. Smith. Stanford, CA: Stan-
ford University Press, 1994.

_____. "Useless Suffering." Trans. Richard A. Cohen. In Robert Ber-
nasconi and David Wood, eds. *The Provocation of Levinas: Rethinking
the Other*. London: Routledge and Kegan Paul, 1988, pp. 156–67.

Levine, Amy-Jill. *The Misunderstood Jew: The Church and the Scandal of the
Jewish Jesus*. New York: HarperCollins, 2006.

Linenthal, Edward T. *Preserving Memory: The Struggle to Create America's Holocaust Museum*. New York: Viking, 1995.

Littell, Franklin H. *The Crucifixion of the Jews: The Failure of Christians
to Understand the Jewish Experience*. Macon, GA: Mercer University
Press, 1986.

Littell, Franklin, and Hubert G. Locke. *The German Church Struggle and
the Holocaust*. Detroit: Wayne State University, 1974.

Locke, Hubert G. "The Holocaust, Israel and the Future of Jewish-Christian Relations." In John K. Roth and Leonard Grob,
eds. *Holocaust Scholars Respond to the Palestinian-Israeli Conflict*,.
Unpublished.

Löwith, Karl. "Last Meeting with Heidegger." In Guenther Neske and
Emil Kettering, eds. *Martin Heidegger and National Socialism*. Trans.
Lisa Harries. New York: Paragon, 1990, pp. 157–59.

Luther, Martin. *Von den Juden und ihren Lügen*. Dresden: Landesverein
für Innere Mission, 1931.

Lyotard, Jean-François. *Heidegger and "the jews."* Trans. Andreas
Michel and Mark S. Roberts. Minneapolis: University of Minnesota Press, 1990.

Maybaum, Ignaz. *The Face of God after Auschwitz*. Amsterdam: Polak
and Van Genep, 1965.

Maza, Bernard. *With Fury Poured Out: A Torah Perspective on the Holocaust*. Hoboken, NJ: Ktav, 1986.

Meeks, Wayne A., and Robert L. Wilken. *Jews and Christians in Antioch in the First Four Centuries of the Common Era.* Ann Arbor, MI: Scholars Press, 1978.

Mekilta de-Rabbi Ishmael. Trans. Jacob Z. Lauterbach. 3 vols. Philadelphia: Jewish Publication Society, 1961.

Melanchthon, Philip. *Augsburg Confession.* Trans. T. G. Tappert. Minneapolis: Augsburg Fortress Publishers, 1980.

Metz, Johann-Baptist. *The Emergent Church: The Future of Christianity in a Post-Bourgeois World.* New York: Crossroad, 1981.

Midrash Hagadol al Chamishah Chumesh Torah: Sefer Bereshit. Jerusalem: [no publisher given], 1947.

Midrash Rabbah. Ed. and trans. H. Friedman, Maurice Simon, et al. 10 vols. London: Soncino, 1961.

Midrash Tanchuma. 2 vols. Jerusalem: Eshkol, 1935.

Minerbi, Sergio. "Pope John Paul II and the Shoah." In Yehuda Bauer, ed. *Remembering for the Future: Working Papers and Abstracts.* Vol. 3. Oxford: Pergamon Press, 1989.

Moltmann, Jürgen. *The Crucified God.* Trans. Margaret Kohl. New York: Harper & Row, 1975.

Morley, John. *Vatican Diplomacy and the Jews During the Holocaust: 1939–1943.* Hoboken, NJ: Ktav, 1980.

Mosse, George L. *Nazi Culture.* New York: Grosset & Dunlap, 1966.

Nathan of Nemirov. *Rabbi Nachman's Wisdom: Shevachay HaRan and Sichos HaRan.* Trans. Aryeh Kaplan, ed. Aryeh Rosenfeld. New York: A. Kaplan, 1973.

Neher, André. *The Prophetic Existence.* Trans. William Wolf. New York: A. S. Barnes, 1969.

Neske, Guenther, and Emil Kettering, eds. *Martin Heidegger and National Socialism.* Trans. Lisa Harries. New York: Paragon, 1990.

Neusner, Jacob. *Telling Tales: The Urgency and Basis for Judeo-Christian Dialogue.* Louisville: Westminster John Knox Press, 1993.

Newman, Louis I. ed. *The Hasidic Anthology.* New York: Schocken Books, 1963.

Nomberg-Przytyk, Sara. *Auschwitz: True Tales from a Grotesque Land*. Trans. Roslyn Hirsch. Chapel Hill: University of North Carolina Press, 1985.

Novak, David. "Instinctive Repugnance." *First Things* 123 (May, 2002).

O'Malley, John W., S. J. foreword to Giuseppe Alberigo, *A Brief History of Vatican II*. New York: Orbis Books, 2006.

O'Shea, Paul. "Confiteor: Eugenio Pacelli, the Catholic Church and the Jews. An Examination of the Responsibility of Pope Pius XII and the Holocaust, 1917–1943." Ph.D. dissertation. Macquarie University, 2004.

Otzar Midrashim. Ed. Judah David Eisenstein. New York: J. D. Eisenstein, 1915.

Parachin, Victor M. "Memorial Day: Four Brave Chaplains." *Catholic Order of Foresters Magazine* (June 2002); posted on *Stand Watch* (May 23, 2002).

Patai, Raphael. *The Messiah Texts*. New York: Avon, 1979.

Patterson, David. "Prayers of Victims, Victims of Prayer." In Alan L. Berger, Harry James Cargas, and Susan E. Nowak, eds. *The Continuing Agony: From the Carmelite Convent to the Crosses at Auschwitz*. Baltimore: University Press of America, 2004, pp. 187–202.

Patterson, David, and John K. Roth, eds. *After-Words: Post-Holocaust Struggle with Forgiveness, Reconciliation, Justice*. Seattle: University of Washington Press, 2004.

Pawlikowski, John T. *Christ in the Light of the Christian-Jewish Dialogue*. 2nd ed. Eugene, OR: Wipf & Stock, 2001.

_____. "Gibson's *Passion* in the Face of the Shoah's Ethical Considerations." In Philip A. Cunningham, ed. *Pondering the Passion: What's at Stake for Christians and Jews*. Lanham, MD: Rowman & Littlefield, 2004.

_____. "L'Affaire Gibson: Has 40 Years of Jewish-Christian Dialogue Run Thin?" Paper read at the Western Jewish Studies Association Annual Meeting, Arizona State University, March 13, 2005.

_____. "The Papacy of Pius XII: The Known and the Unknown." In Carol Rittner and John K. Roth, eds. *Pius XII and the Holocaust*. London and New York: Leicester University Press, 2002.

_____. "Reflections on Covenant and Mission." In Edward Kessler and Melanie J. Wright, eds. *Theses in Jewish-Christian Relations.* Cambridge: Orchard Academic, 2005.

_____. "The Vatican and the Holocaust: Putting We Remember in Context." In Judith H. Banki and John T. Pawlikowski, eds. *Ethics in the Shadow of the Holocaust: Christian and Jewish Perspectives.* Chicago: Sheed & Ward, 2001.

Pesikta de-Rab Kahana. Trans. William G. Braude and Israel J. Kapstein. Philadelphia: Jewish Publication Society, 1975.

Pesikta Rabbati. Trans. W. G. Braude. 2 vols. New Haven, CT: Yale University Press, 1968.

Phayer, Michael. *The Catholic Church and the Holocaust, 1930–1965.* Bloomington: Indiana University Press, 2000.

Phillips, Kevin. *American Theocracy: The Peril and Politics of Radical Religion, Oil and Borrowed Money in the 21st Century.* New York: Viking, 2006.

Pirke Avos. Brooklyn, NY: Mesorah Publications, 1984.

Pirke de Rabbi Eliezer. Trans. Gerald Friedlander. New York: Hermon Press, 1970.

Plato. *The Collected Dialogues.* Ed. Edith Hamilton and Huntington Cairns. Princeton: Princeton University Press, 1969.

Plotinus. *Plotinus: The Enneads.* Trans. Stephen MacKenna. Burdett, NY: Larson Publications, 2004.

Pollefeyt, Didier. *Jews and Christians: Rivals or Partners for the Kingdom of God?* Leuven: Peeters, 1998.

Pope, Stephen J., and Charles Hefling, eds. *Sic at Non: Encountering Dominus Ieus.* Maryknoll, NY: Orbis Books, 2002.

Rahner, Karl. *Foundations of Christian Faith: An Introduction to the Idea of Christianity.* Trans. William V. Dych. New York: Crossroad, 1994.

Rittner, Carol, and John K. Roth, eds. *Good News after Auschwitz? Christian Faith in a Post-Holocaust World.* Macon, GA: Mercer University Press, 2001.

Rockmore, Tom, and Joseph Margolis, eds. *The Heidegger Case: On Philosophy and Politics.* Philadelphia: Temple University Press, 1992.

Rosen, Alan. *Sounds of Defiance: The Holocaust, Multilingualism & the Problem of English.* Lincoln: University of Nebraska Press, 2005.

Rosenberg, Alfred. *Race and Race History and Other Essays.* Ed. Robert Pais. New York: Harper & Row, 1974.

Rosenzweig, Franz. *Franz Rosenzweig's "The New Thinking."* Trans. and ed. Alan Udoff and Barbara Galli. Syracuse: Syracuse University Press, 1999.

_____. *The Star of Redemption.* Trans. William W. Hallo. Boston: Beacon Press, 1972.

Roth, John K. "Duped by Morality? Defusing Minefields in the Israeli-Palestinian Struggle." In John K. Roth and Leonard Grob, eds. *Holocaust Scholars Respond to the Palestinian-Israeli Conflict.* Unpublished.

_____. *Holocaust Politics.* Louisville: Westminster John Knox Press, 2001.

_____. "No Crucifixion = No Holocaust: Post-Holocaust Reflections on *The Passion of the Christ.*" In J. Shawn Landres and Michael Berenbaum, eds. *After the Passion Is Gone: American Religious Consequences.* Walnut Creek, CA: AltaMira Press, 2004.

_____. "Useless Experience: Its Significance for Reconciliation after Auschwitz." In David Patterson and John K. Roth, eds. *After-Words: Post-Holocaust Struggle with Forgiveness, Reconciliation, Justice.* Seattle: University of Washington Press, 2004, pp. 85–114.

Roth, John K., and Leonard Grob, eds. *Holocaust Scholars Respond to the Palestinian-Israeli Conflict.* Unpublished.

Roth, John K., and Elizabeth Maxwell, eds. *Remembering for the Future: The Holocaust in an Age of Genocide.* Vol. 2. London: Palgrave, 2001.

Roth, John K., and Carol Rittner, eds. *Memory Offended: The Auschwitz Convent Controversy.* Westport, CT: Greenwood Publishing Group, 1991.

Rubenstein, Richard L. *After Auschwitz: History, Theology, and Contemporary Judaism.* 2nd ed. Baltimore: Johns Hopkins University Press, 1992.

_____. *After Auschwitz: Radical Theology and Contemporary Judaism.* Indianapolis: Bobbs-Merrill, 1966.

_____. "The Exposed Fault Line." In J. Shawn Landres and Michael Berenbaum, eds. *After the Passion is Gone: American Religious Consequences*. Walnut Creek, CA: AltaMira Press, 2004.

Rubenstein, Richard, and John K. Roth. *Approaches to Auschwitz: The Holocaust and Its Legacy*. Rev. ed. Louisville: Westminster John Knox Press, 2003.

Rudin, A. James. *The Baptizing of America: The Religious Right's Plans for the Rest of Us*. New York: Thunder's Mouth Press, 2006, p. 47.

_____. "Jump-Starting the Conversation between Jews and Catholics." *National Catholic Reporter* (October 4, 2002): 5.

_____. "Reflections on the Vatican's *Reflection on the Shoah*." *Cross Currents* (winter 1998/99): 522.

Rudin, A. James, Eugene J. Fischer, and Marc H. Tanenbaum, eds. *Twenty Years of Jewish-Catholic Relations*. New York: Paulist Press, 1986.

Ruether, Rosemary Radford. *Faith and Fratricide*. Eugene, OR: Wipf & Stock, 1996.

Sacks, Jonathan. *The Dignity of Difference: How to Avoid the Clash of Civilizations*. London: Continuum, 2003.

Sanders, E. P. *Jesus and Judaism*. Minneapolis: Augsburg Fortress Publishers, 1987.

Sarna, Jonathan D. *American Judaism: A History*. New Haven: Yale University Press, 2004.

Scholem, Gershom. *Kabbalah*. New York: New American Library, 1978.

Sefer Yetzirah: The Book of Creation. Trans. with commentary by Aryeh Kaplan. York Beach, ME: Samuel Weiser, 1990.

Shapiro, James. *Shakespeare and the Jews*. New York: Columbia University Press, 1996.

Sherwin Byron and Harold Kasimo, eds. *John Paul II and Interreligious Dialogue*. New York: Orbis Books, 1999.

Sifre on Deuteronomy. New York: Jewish Theological Seminary, 1993.

Stassen, Glen H., and David P. Gushee. *Kingdom Ethics: Following Jesus in Contemporary Context*. Downers Grove, IL: InterVarsity Press, 2003.

Tabor, James D. "Josephus on Jesus." At http://www.religiousstudies.uncc.edu/jdtabor/josephus-jesus.html.

Tanna debe Eliyyahu: The Lore of the School of Elijah. Trans. William G. Braude and Israel J. Kapstein. Philadelphia: Jewish Publication Society, 1981.

Vermes, Geza. *Jesus in Historical Jewish Contexts.* Minneapolis: Augsburg Fortress Publishers, 2003.

_____. *The Religion of Jesus the Jew.* Minneapolis: Augsburg Fortress Publishers, 1993.

Vilna Gaon. *Even Sheleimah.* Trans. Yaakov Singer and Chaim Dovid Ackerman. Southfield, MI: Targum Press, 1992.

Weinreich, Max. *Hitler's Professors: The Part of Scholarship in Germany's Crimes against the Jewish People.* New Haven: Yale University Press, 1999.

Weissman, Moshe, ed. *The Midrash Says.* 5 vols. Brooklyn: Bnay Yakov Publications, 1980.

Wiesel, Elie. *Against Silence: The Voice and Vision of Elie Wiesel.* 3 vols. New York: Holocaust Library, 1985.

_____. *A Beggar in Jerusalem.* Trans. Elie Wiesel and Lily Edelman. New York: Random House, 1970.

_____. *The Gates of the Forest.* Trans. Frances Frenaye. New York: Holt, 1966.

_____. *One Generation After.* Trans. Lily Edelman and Elie Wiesel. New York: Pocket Books, 1970.

Wiesenthal, Simon. *The Sunflower: On the Possibilities and Limits of Forgiveness.* New York: Schocken Books, 1997.

Wills, Gary. *Papal Sin: Structures of Deceit.* New York: Doubleday, 2000.

_____. *Why I Am a Catholic.* Boston: Mariner Books, 2003.

Wilson, Marvin R. *Our Father Abraham.* Grand Rapids, MI: Wm. B. Eerdmans, 1989.

Wistrich, Robert. *Antisemitism: The Longest Hatred.* New York: Schocken Books, 1993.

_____. "The Pope, the Church, and the Jews." *Commentary* 107 (April 1999): 24.

Wood, James E., ed. *Jewish-Christian Relations in Today's World*. Waco: Baylor University Press, 1971.

Wyschogrod, Michael. "Jon D. Levenson & Critics." *Commentary* 113 (April 2002): 16.

Yaakov Yosef of Polnoe. *Toledot Yaakov Yosef al HaTorah*. Jerusalem: Agudat Beit Vialipoli, 1944.

Young, Brad. *Jesus the Jewish Theologian*. Peabody, MA: Hendrickson Publishers, 1995.

Zuccotti, Susan. *Under His Very Windows: The Vatican and the Holocaust in Italy*. New Haven, CT: Yale University Press, 2000.

About the Authors and Contributors

$\equiv$

The Authors

ALAN L. BERGER holds the Raddock Family Eminent Scholar Chair for Holocaust Studies and directs the Center for the Study of Values and Violence after Auschwitz at Florida Atlantic University. He has also taught in the Department of Religion at Syracuse University and been the Gumenick Visiting Professor of Religion at the College of William and Mary. Berger has written more than ninety articles, essays, and book chapters. He has lectured on the Holocaust, Jewish literature, and Christian/Jewish relations throughout America, Europe, Australia, South Africa, and Israel. He is on the planning committee of Lessons and Legacies of the Holocaust. Among the books he has authored, edited, or coedited are the following: *Crisis and Covenant: The Holocaust in American Jewish Fiction* (1985), *Children of Job: Second-Generation Witnesses to the Holocaust* (1997, cited in *New York Times* article about the second generation), *Judaism in the Modern World* (editor, 1994), *Second-Generation Voices: Reflections by Children of Holocaust Survivors and Perpetrators* (coeditor with his wife Naomi, 2001, winner of B'nai Zion Media Award, 2002), *Encyclopedia of Holocaust Literature* (coeditor with David Patterson, 2002, Booklist Best Reference Book of 2002, and Outstanding Reference Source 2003–RUSA), *The Continuing Agony: From the Carmelite Convent to the Crosses at Auschwitz* (coeditor, 2003, nominated for the American Catholic Historical Association's John Gilmary Shea Prize), and *Jewish-American and Holocaust Literature: Representation in the Postmodern World* (coeditor, 2004). He edits the series "Studies in Genocide: Religion, History and Human Rights" for Rowman & Littlefield. Moreover, he is on the editorial boards of *Studies in American Jewish Literature* and *Literature and Belief*. He is a member of the Commissioner's Task Force on Holocaust Education in the state of Florida. Berger was awarded the Doctor of Letters, *Honoris Causa*, by Luther College, 1999.

David Patterson holds the Bornblum Chair of Excellence in Judaic Studies at the University of Memphis and is director of the university's Bornblum Judaic Studies Program. He is coeditor, with John K. Roth, of the Weinstein Series in Post-Holocaust Studies, a participant in the Weinstein Symposium on the Holocaust, and a member of the Scholars' Platform for the Beth Shalom Holocaust Centre, Cambridge, England. Having published more than one hundred articles and chapters in journals and books, his books include *Open Wounds: The Crisis of Jewish Thought in the Aftermath of Auschwitz* (2006); *Wrestling with the Angel: Toward a Jewish Understanding of the Nazi Assault on the Name* (2006); *Hebrew Language and Jewish Thought* (2005); *Along the Edge of Annihilation: The Collapse and Recovery of Life in the Holocaust Diary* (1999, winner of the Koret Jewish Book Award); *Sun Turned to Darkness: Memory and Recovery in the Holocaust Memoir* (1998); *The Greatest Jewish Stories Ever Told* (1997); *When Learned Men Murder* (1996); *Pilgrimage of a Proselyte: From Auschwitz to Jerusalem* (1993); *The Shriek of Silence: A Phenomenology of the Holocaust Novel* (1992); *In Dialogue and Dilemma with Elie Wiesel* (1991); and others. He is coeditor, with John K. Roth, of *Fire in the Ashes: God, Evil, and the Holocaust* (2006) and *After-Words: Post-Holocaust Struggles with Forgiveness, Reconciliation, Justice* (2004); he is the editor and translator of the English edition of *The Complete Black Book of Russian Jewry* (2002) and coeditor, with Alan L. Berger, of the *Encyclopedia of Holocaust Literature* (2002).

THE CONTRIBUTORS

DAVID P. GUSHEE is University Fellow & Graves Professor of Moral Philosophy at Union University. He has served for eleven years at Union, a Tennessee Baptist college, after three years on the faculty of Southern Baptist Theological Seminary and three years on the staff of Evangelicals for Social Action. Besides serving as a professor, Dr. Gushee preaches, lectures, counsels, and writes. His writing includes several dozen syndicated columns each year for Associated Baptist Press and Religion News Service and regular articles for *Christianity Today*, *Books and Culture*, and other magazines and journals. He is the author or editor of nine books, including the coauthored *Kingdom Ethics: Following Jesus in Contemporary Context* (IVP, 2003), which was named best theology/ethics book of the year by *Christianity Today* in 2004. His most recent books are *Getting Marriage Right: Realistic Counsel for Saving and Strengthening Relationships* (Baker, 2004), and *Only Human: Christian Reflections on the Journey Toward Wholeness* (Jossey-Bass, 2005). He has taken a leadership role in the evangelical community to address issues such as climate change and torture. Dr. Gushee and his wife Jeanie have been married twenty-two years and have four children. They live in the west Tennessee town of Jackson.

JOHN T. PAWLIKOWSKI is a priest of the Servite Order and Professor of Social Ethics at the Catholic Theological Union in Chicago, where he also directs the school's Catholic-Jewish Studies Program. He has authored or edited some fifteen books, including *Christ in the Light of the Christian-Jewish Dialogue* and *Ethics in the Shadow of the Holocaust*. He has contributed numerous articles both to scholarly and to popular journals, including *America*, *Commonweal*, *Holocaust and Genocide Studies*, and the *Journal of Ecumenical Studies*. He has served for five years as president of the International Council of Christians and Jews. For many years he has also served on the Advisory Committee on Catholic-Jewish Relations of the United States Conference of Catholic Bishops and for a time on the National Council of Churches' Christian-Jewish Relations Commission. He served four terms by presidential appointment on the United States

Holocaust Memorial Council. There he was involved with the key committees that worked on the basic building design of the United States Holocaust Memorial Museum and its permanent exhibition. He continues as a member of the museum's Academic Committee and its Committee on Conscience and chairs its Church Relations Committee.

JOHN K. ROTH is the Edward J. Sexton Professor Emeritus of Philosophy and the founding director of the Center for the Study of the Holocaust, Genocide, and Human Rights at Claremont McKenna College, where he taught from 1966 through 2006. In addition to service on the United States Holocaust Memorial Council and on the editorial board for *Holocaust and Genocide Studies*, he has published hundreds of articles and reviews and authored, coauthored, or edited more than forty books, including, most recently, *Genocide and Human Rights: A Philosophical Guide*; *Gray Zones: Ambiguity and Compromise in the Holocaust and Its Aftermath*; and *Ethics during and after the Holocaust: In the Shadow of Birkenau*. Roth has been Visiting Professor of Holocaust studies at the University of Haifa, Israel, and his Holocaust-related research appointments have included a 2001 Koerner Visiting Fellowship at the Oxford Centre for Hebrew and Jewish Studies in England as well as a 2004–5 appointment as the Ina Levine Invitational Scholar at the Center for Advanced Holocaust Studies, United States Holocaust Memorial Museum, Washington, DC. In 1988, Roth was named U.S. National Professor of the Year by the Council for Advancement and Support of Education and the Carnegie Foundation for the Advancement of Teaching. During the 2007–8 academic year, he will be the Robert and Carolyn Frederick Distinguished Visiting Professor of Ethics at DePauw University in Greencastle, Indiana.

INDEX